FAR PASTURES

*Other books in the R.M. Patterson Collection
from Horsdal & Schubart*

FINLAY'S RIVER

THE BUFFALO HEAD

TRAIL TO THE INTERIOR

FAR PASTURES

by R.M. Patterson

Horsdal & Schubart

Horsdal & Schubart Ltd.
4252 Commerce Circle
Victoria, B.C., V8Z 4M2

Cover photograph by R.M. Patterson.
Text and photographs are reproduced from the first edition, published
in 1963 by Gray's Publishing, Sidney, B.C..

Printed and bound by Best Gagne Book Manufacturers,
Toronto, Ontario.

Dedication: To the memory of a great Canadian, Sir Edward Peabody,
G.C.V.O., the man who pronounced a blessing on this Odyssey, many
years ago, with the words: "I think that it will be a great adventure."

Canadian Cataloguing in Publication Data

Patterson, R.M. (Raymond Murray), 1898-1984.
  Far Pastures

ISBN 0-920663-17-6

1. Patterson, R.M. (Raymond Murray), 1898-1984 2. Frontier and
pioneer life—Northwest, Canadian. 3. Northwest Canadian—Biography.
4. Northwest, Canadian—Description and travel—1867-1950. 5.
Northwest, Canadian—History—1870-1905.* 6. Canada, Northern—
History. 7. Canada, Western—History. I. Title.
FC3693.3P37A3 1993   971.2'02;092   C93-091356-6
F1079.P3P38 1993

CONTENTS

FOREWORD

He came to our untamed frontier wilderness as a pioneer, took his lumps and bruises, became a skilled northern traveller and left a literary heritage. Those who delight in Canadian outdoor adventure will be pleased to learn that R. M. Patterson's finely crafted tales will be available to future generations, for as an author he was unique on several counts. His qualifications were remarkable. He had the advantage of an academic background, a great eye for country and a keen ear for dialogue. Through this he developed a writing style described by Bruce Hutchison as a "mixture of Thoreau and Jack London."

Born in the north of England on May 13, 1898, he was just old enough to serve as a gunner in World War I, 1917-18. Nine months of this was spent in Silesia as a guest of the Germans. Patterson recalled his prisoner-of-war experiences as simply another adventure. Following this, he took a degree in modern history at Oxford and tried to settle down to a career at the Bank of England. He suffered an attack of what he termed "claustrophobia" and "itchy foot" which brought him to Canada in the early 1920s.

Working his way west through jobs on farm and ranch, he discovered the prairies and mountains. In 1924 he decided to take the homesteader's gamble of a five-dollar filing fee with a vow to stick it out for three years, and struck out for the Peace River country to locate and stake out 320 acres that he could develop.

As one adventure led to another he wrote home regularly, and fortunately, his mother and a friend preserved every letter. He began describing the characters whose trails crossed his, and picked up the accents of natives, half-breeds, Scandinavians and Orientals who were struggling for a place in the vast sweep of country.

Until Patterson came along, Canadian history books highlighting adventure had been appearing and disappearing in three categories. There had been a succession of regional histories, in limited editions, culled from letters, diaries and photographs of pioneer families. University and trade presses had published important histories by academics, researched in the archives of governments and corporations. Then there was the professional adventurer, from "away", who sweeps through the country, often raising an expedition to power through dangerous waterways, or to challenge by ski or snowmobile perhaps, with radio and back-up. Following in the tracks of the early explorers, equipped as they never were, in six weeks or so they have enough material for a book. This was not the Patterson modus operandi.

Before putting pen to paper Patterson paid his dues. He learned how to fork a bronc, throw a diamond hitch, drive a dog team and read a river before running fast water. Then he wrote about these things, and his companions, with humour, style and remarkable dialogue.

He honed his writing style, patiently and laboriously, it seems, in this impatient age of computers and electronics. Writing in school copy-books in pencil, he scratched out many words. He was fussy about finding the right term, and strove to be literate but lucid, striking out a long word when a short one would do. He had tremendous admiration for the English author, Norman Douglas (1868-1952), and his style.

When his adventurous life began to seem noteworthy, he turned his longhand into typewritten manuscripts through the help of friends. His articles were published in *The Beaver* in Canada and *Blackwoods* in the United Kingdom. One of his exploits in the Northwest Territories brought him two letters from London publishers and he was on his way. His first book, *The Dangerous River* (1954), was published in London, New

York and Canada with translations in Spanish and Dutch, which brought him a world-wide readership. A lively correspondence built up with loyal fans and the result was a string of popular titles. Forty years in the western mountains led to *The Buffalo Head* (1961), *Far Pastures* (1963), *Trail To The Interior* (1966) and *Finlay's River* (1968). One reviewer commenting on *The Buffalo Head* wrote "... once again we accompany the author in his flight from the twentieth century." Patterson's reply is worth quoting: "But if the old times and the old ways are not worth keeping, they still may be worth recording for the benefit of the mechanized, enlightened posterity to whom a horse will have become a snob symbol and a canoe nothing but an unsafe craft...."

The pleasing thing about his life-style and narrative is the faithful way he kept in touch with, and maintained the friendship of, the rugged individuals he wrote about. From Gordon Matthews, his Nahanni partner, and Albert Faille, the prospector, to Paul Amos, the Stoney hunter, he managed to keep in lively contact. When Patterson ran the Buffalo Head ranch in the Alberta foothills, Paul would ride with him, checking the fences and cattle. From Paul he picked up native mountain lore and customs, and they became close, firm friends. In the evening of his life on Vancouver Island he enjoyed visits from a string of old-timers like Bert Sheppard, cattleman from High River, the McDougalls from Finlay Forks, and F. C. Swannell, the pioneer surveyor whose career had started in 1898.

His books are Patterson's living testimony and undying record of many known and unknown achievers who challenged an untamed frontier, helping to develop two western provinces and the Northwest Territories. "And so," he wrote, "in my character of unrepentant old-timer, I have arranged these word-pictures of the West."

Canada is enriched by keeping the memory green.

Gray Campbell, Deep Cove, 1993

INTRODUCTION

Some reviewers may say that this book should never have been written. To them I can truthfully reply that I never intended to write it. It was an accident, and nothing but.

Perhaps I should explain—and in doing so I can point to well-known precedents. Two of my favourite authors, Norman Douglas and Joseph Conrad, have written articles and, in the case of the former, a whole book, discussing the sources of their various works and their reasons for writing them. Following humbly in the footsteps of these giants, I propose to write something here and now about the origins of this simple record, *FAR PASTURES*. I do this in the hope that it may be of interest to some reader, just as the explanations of those great writers have been to me. It may also serve as a warning to other would-be authors—just how Something can, unless you keep a careful eye on it, build up out of practically Nothing. Especially, of course, if you have a slave-driver of a publisher like Gray Campbell, only twenty miles away and hounding you from dawn to dewy eve.

The thing began with an interchange of letters between Gray and myself when I was living in Spain. I had the idea of gathering together, in book form, some stories and articles of mine that had already appeared in *Blackwood's Magazine* and *The Beaver*. These stories were purely of western Canadian interest—or so I thought—and here was a western Canadian publisher who might be interested.

Gray was cautious and non-committal. Faced eventually, on my return to Canada, with seven or eight *Blackwood's* stories, he became a little more enthusiastic. "Even so," he said, "we ought to throw out two of them. That one on the Pribylov Islands stands apart from all the rest, and the one about Calgary is becoming dated."

"All right," I said. "But if we don't want the one about Calgary, then we ought to throw the one on the Macleod Trail out, too. They make a pair."

So that was decided upon. Then Gray said to me (and here you have the wisdom of the serpent and the thin end of the wedge and all that sort of thing) "Do you think you could write a few words just to put these stories in their proper setting? I mean, make them into a proper sequence, in chronological order?"

I fell for that one. "You mean," I said, "a few odds and ends about homesteading in the Peace River country, or something—to lead up to them?"

"Yes," he replied. "Just something to make a frame for these stories—nothing more."

I bought it—it sounded so simple. Then my pen took charge and the summer of 1963 became a wreck . . . . .

The various *Beaver* and *Blackwood's* stories have all been carefully checked, smoothed out, and, in some cases, turned inside out—I hope, to their improvement. But in fact and in spirit they remain unaltered. One *Blackwood's* story, Chapter Eight of this book, *Fort Simpson, McKenzie's River* defied all efforts at re-alignment. If you did anything at all to it, it fell apart. So I was forced to let it alone. It is partly historical—and for that very reason it is not without topical interest in this year of ice-jams and floods at Fort Simpson, 1963. It contains an account, written in 1844, of what might well have been the identical flood. But the chapter must remain a thing apart—a lone wolf among the rest, if we are to include it at all. Wing Commander G. D. Blackwood, writing about it to me in 1954, said that he hardly knew in what category to place it, "but it is such a man's story that I should like to accept it for my magazine." Furthermore, it clears up a point about which many readers of my *Dangerous River* have written. "How," they say, "did that trip of yours really end?" Well now, if they read Chapter Eight, they will know the answer: it ended as it began—with a dog fight.

All the events described in this book took place as related. No fictional characters appear in it, and, except in very few instances, people appear under their own names. Conversations are not made up. In many cases I remember them clearly. But, to supplement memory, it so happens that two people in England preserved every letter that I ever wrote to them from Canada; and these letters have now all been returned to me. Together with diaries and old accounts they form a complete record of things seen through the intensely interested eyes of a green-horn newcomer—things which might now seem, to those same eyes, routine and comparatively uninteresting. They record the inner life of a small corner of this vast country; the things that make (or, till recently, made) it unique; the things the tourist never sees.

In a smoking-room of a transatlantic liner, back in the Thirties, I was talking with a Harvard professor and a Canadian mining man about the Mackenzie Mountains in the North-West Territories. A fourth man horned his way into the party. He listened for a while, and then, not being of the listening sort, he took a hand. "Oh, yes," he said. "The mountains. I know them well. Seen 'em all several times: Banff, Lake Louise, and all that. Let me tell you a story . . . . ."

Even to intimate knowledge of that description, this book will, I hope, be a useful supplement.

R. M. Patterson,

Victoria,

British Columbia.

September, 1963

ACKNOWLEDGMENTS

It would have been impossible to write this book in its present form without the kind permission of Wing Commander G. D. Blackwood of *Blackwood's Magazine*, and of Miss Malvina Bolus, the editor of *The Beaver*, to use again material which had already appeared in one or other of those two periodicals. Chapters Seven, Eight, Eleven and Twelve, and part of Chapter Ten, were originally published in *Blackwood's*; Chapter Fifteen first saw the light of day in *The Beaver*. They have been variously shortened, lengthened and otherwise trimmed, but in essence they remain the same and I am grateful for the use of them.

I have to thank Mr. George W. Pocaterra of Calgary, Alberta, for his kindness in allowing me to use his photograph of the Stoney Indian, Paul Amos, the old hunter; and also Mr. Cecil Clark of Victoria, B.C., who has most kindly contributed the photograph of "the author" used on the back cover.

I wish to thank the publishers, and also Messrs. Hope Leresche and Steele, the agents of the late Crosbie Garstin Esq., for permission to use the verses at the head of Part One and Part Two. These verses are taken from Mr. Garstin's book *The Ballad of the Royal Ann*, published in London by William Heinemann in 1922.

The letters of the fur-traders, and Chief Trader McLean's description of the break-up at Fort Simpson, are taken, with the kind permission of the Champlain Society (Toronto), from their Volumes XXIV and XIX respectively —*The Hargrave Correspondence* and *John McLean's Notes of a Twenty-five Years' Service in the Hudson's Bay Territory*.

There remains the poem, *Mirage*, quoted in full at the head of Part Four. This appeared in *Country Life* (London) some ten years ago. A year or two after its appearance I wrote to the editor of *Country Life* for permission to use it in a book that I was writing. I was informed that copyright rested with the author, Mr. Geoffrey Holdsworth, and for him *Country Life* gave me an address in Spain. I wrote to that address and, after a long time, my letter was returned, unopened, to me by the Spanish postal authorities: Mr. Holdsworth had died in a Spanish hospital.

I have used this poem therefore, not knowing whom now I can ask for permission, yet feeling that it should not remain buried indefinitely in the files of a weekly paper. It expresses so beautifully what so many of us must feel when we look back on the things that have vanished and the days that are gone.

Part One

PEACE RIVER

1924 - 1927

My mare splashed deep in crocuses,
She flung her head and tossed her mane,
Jingled her bit and sniffed the breeze.
I touched her flank and gave her rein.

And now she flings the miles behind
And hurtles at the miles before,
Crazed by the bugles of the wind,
Trembling and thrilling to the core.

She spurns the pools to splintered glass,
Blurred landmarks rise, are past and gone,
And still across the sunlit grass
I see my shadow hurrying on.

"Prairie Song (Alberta)" *by* CROSBIE GARSTIN

CHAPTER I

Homesteading

The flood of homesteaders which, for some twenty hectic years around the turn of the century, submerged the old West, has now abated; in fact, except as regards a few isolated pockets of good land, it has dried up and vanished. In its day, and in the right districts, it laid the foundations for many a successful farm.

On the debit side, it did a vast deal of harm: in its unplanned onrush it broke up many a good ranch and turned wrongside-up hundreds of thousands of acres of the finest grassland, the selection of a thousand years of Nature's testing. Greedy and ignorant politicians turned the homesteader loose in the semi-arid lands of the western prairies, counting only human heads and taking no account of human misery. But a rainy season might come—perhaps even two running—heartening the newly-arrived "nester" in the squat, sod-walled hovel which sat so forlornly on the bald-headed prairie, dwarfed by the optimistic, mortgaged barn. Good June rains, twice running, and then a phenomenal crop off the virgin land—a very miracle, and one that confounded all the prophets of gloom!

That was when the mischief was done. Of course, reasoned the delighted homesteader, these old-timers, these ranchers with their warnings of dry seasons and long years of drought, are liars one and all, thinking only of hanging on to their grazing leases, worried for their creeks and springs. And home from the little sod-houses would go

3

ecstatic letters—to cramped valleys at the head of Norwegian fiords, to bleak villages on the Baltic, to crowded
Holland, to some labourer's cottage deep in the Sussex
Weald. And out would come a fresh spate of homesteaders,
single men and families—out to this amazing Eldorado
where every man could pick and choose for himself 160
fertile acres. Inevitably they saw themselves as landed pro-
prietors, for 160 acres was an estate back home in Western
Europe.

But the prairies were not Western Europe. Nor, in
southern Alberta, was a quarter-section an estate: it was
just another peasant holding, only on a larger scale. And
the dry years would come back, and the sun would blaze
down, and the great white summer clouds would swing on
eastwards, never unloading one decent shower of rain. The
arid, hopeless summers would go by—and, sooner or later,
one more bust homesteader would say for the last time,
"To hell with it—I'm through!"

Westward the course of empire would take its way—and
some foothill ranch would gain a choreman, or a lumber-
camp a teamster; or a cabin might spring up by some lonely
mountain lake in British Columbia where there would be
water and wood without end, and fish and game for the
taking—paradise after that sun-blasted, man-made desert of
dust and weeds. And the mortgage company would own
the vast, useless barn with the red paint now sanded off its
south and west sides by the drifting soil; the lifeless, unwanted house; the acres of stinkweed and pigweed and
tumbleweed, and the sagging fences. And a fat lot of good
the outfit would be to the mortgage company (there was
some consolation in that) for the rancher, too, by this time
would be gone—chased out by the nesters into the hills,
into his last stronghold of the mountains. Not that he
would have had the land back anyway, for as a grazing
proposition it was ruined, a liability in place of an asset.
That was the real futile tragedy of it—the destruction of
that wonderful sod of grass, the drying up of the sloughs,

the useless cutting of the trees that shaded the prairie creeks and rivers, the lowering of the water-table. Man, the desert-maker, at work.

That was homesteading on much of the bald-headed prairie of the south and west. But further north, in the parklands and the brush country, it was different. There might be more snow in wintertime, and some of the land might have to be cleared of trees—but there were, as will be seen, so many advantages that a man stood a very good chance of winning his bet with the government: 160 acres (or, in the case of an ex-soldier, 320 acres) to a filing fee of $5 that he couldn't stay the course and fulfill the simple conditions: six months residence in each of three consecutive years, so many acres broken to crop, so many head of cattle.....

While the main flood of homesteaders was over by the early Twenties, there still remained room in the West for late-comers. However, to find anything good you had to go further afield—perhaps into the Peace River country. There again, of course, the more accessible districts were settled pretty closely, at least as regards naturally open land. But if you went far enough—northwards, say, from Peace River town to Battle River on the Fort Vermilion trail— you could still find open prairie just as the Lord made it, with the black furrows of the buffalo trails cutting across it, threading between the poplar bluffs, running purpose-fully over the grassy uplands. There, if you were lucky, you could have the best of both worlds; for though the Battle lay a good five hundred miles to the northward of the Old Man River in south-western Alberta, and though you were, literally, away back in the sticks, yet the Chinook, the warm south-west wind, would blow there for days on end in a good winter—just as it did on the Old Man—lick-ing up the snow, laying the grass bare, making life sweet and easy for man and beast.

It was there that I came to anchor—on the prairies of the Battle River. Settling there was the result of a chance meeting, for I had planned to go on north to Fort Vermilion. But that chance meeting was a piece of luck for me, for this bit of country had everything that the northern parklands had to offer to the earlier homesteaders, plus a few extra blessings of its own to boot.

There were open prairies with scattered woods and bluffs for shelter; there was timber on the low, fringing hills, and a good river with slow-flowing tributary creeks that could be dammed to make watering places the year round. There was plenty of game—deer, moose, bear and prairie chicken —and a certain amount of fur. And the Peace River, turning north at Peace River town, came within eight miles or so of the settlement. That made it possible to ship heavy goods (wire, lumber, nails, groceries etc.) downstream on board the old sternwheeler *D. A. Thomas* to our landing during the summer months when the muskegs to the south of the Battle River country were impassable. It then only remained to lug the stuff off the beach, haul it by wagon up the almost vertical trail to the plateau, and crash on home with it over the stumps—a proceeding that never failed to draw winged words from our storekeeper, Joe Bissett, who felt very strongly that, while we were about it, we might at least have cut the trees off reasonably flush with the ground.

There was no village either north or south of the Battle River. Here and there lay a homestead, sometimes a group of homesteads as on Little Prairie—but otherwise a scattering of rampant individualists, men who needed room around them. They were men like Kipling's "Voortrekker", of whom he wrote: "His neighbours' smoke shall vex his eyes, their voices break his rest."

And the Battle River prairies were the right place for them. For there was a time-lag there, due to the fact that these fertile grasslands formed, as it were, an island in a sea of bush, muskeg and gravelly hills. In the rest of the West it might have been 1924 when I first saw the Battle: here I had stepped back into 1900—even into Biblical times in some ways, for grain was threshed with a flail on Little Prairie, and winnowed by tossing it with a scoop-shovel in a high wind. Seed-grain was cleaned by putting it through a hand-turned fanning mill. Fields were seeded, more often than not, by means of a hand-operated broad-caster—which meant that the owner tramped up and down his ploughing with the contraption slung around his neck, churning away at the handle much after the fashion of the old-time hurdy-gurdy operator, grain flying right and left; more or less, one hoped, in the right place.

Much of the ploughing was done with the walking plough —though the lighter horse-drawn farm implements could be, and were, hauled in over the winter trails on sleighs. But there was no power-driven machinery of any kind on the Battle. No car had ever penetrated into that oasis of Time. No radio screeched and ranted. There was not even so much as the poot-poot of an electric light plant engine. No farm produce was shipped out, for there was no way of shipping it. So no wheat was grown, except a few garden patches of it by those who kept chickens. Oats were the crop: oats that could be fed to cattle and horses: oats that could be sold to incoming homesteaders, to pack outfits headed north to Keg River, Hay River or the Fontas—to all travellers on the trail. Now and then out would go a bunch of cattle over the long, frozen trail to the railroad, or to fatten up on some quarter-section of oats in the Bear Lake country — driven by frozen horsemen, trailing behind sleighs loaded with oat bundles. But that was all.

All, that is, except the fur. There was a comical misconception prevailing in the Provincial Department of Lands to the effect that a homestead was a farm and a home-steader a farmer. That may have been the case elsewhere, but not on Battle River in the early Twenties. There home-steads were in the nature of investments—land that would increase in value as time went on. In the meantime they provided hay and oats and pasture for the saddle- and pack-horses that would take their owners back, in the fall, to their far-off traplines; they were the summer homes of men who worked in the woods in wintertime — of those who liked the free and easy life and who raised a few head of cattle on the open range—of newcomers like myself who were learning the ways of a new and strange country. One way and another—with the possible exception of the Scandinavians on that geological miracle, Little Prairie (of which more later)—the settlers of the Battle were a collection of happy-go-lucky sportsmen who worked "outside" when they needed cash, and who lived off the country and enjoyed life when they were at home. The homestead, at some future date a saleable asset, was in the nature of a by-product. Close settlement, when it came, would drive many of these earlier settlers on: they were men to whom far pastures would look always green.

The taxes on my homestead and soldier grant (320 acres in all) amounted to $4.50 a year. And there was no income tax—or, if there was, none of us ever dreamed of paying it. Some of the fellows had war disability pensions. With a pension, and with that sort of taxation—or lack of it—and with a home and a garden, and a moose or two, and hay and oats and horses; and no money tied up in land, and a good trapline and a pack of fur to go out in the spring— well, damn it, what more could a carefree bachelor ask?

And there was another thing, important in a community of young men with roving instincts: you could go away (as I did to the Nahanni River) for a year on end, leaving a cabin full of quite valuable things, unwatched and in the middle of nowhere, and locked with only a flimsy padlock that a single blow from an axe-head could smash. And not a thing would be touched. Indian, half-breed and white man—you could trust the lot. That alone is enough to show that the whole setup was an anachronism, backward and primitive.

Wives were few and far between (two, to be exact, among all the whites) so there were few rows and no social climbing. Mail, and newspapers well past their prime, found their way out from Peace River at rare intervals. But mostly the outside world could go to the devil its own way, with our Fortunate Island of about thirty-five miles by ten paying little heed, sunk in "the deep backward and abysm of time" (Shakespeare). No real estate man, thank God, had ever heard of the Battle, so one prime element of discord and unrest was lacking. But, hicks though we certainly were, we were not without means of passing the time agreeably: somebody would distill a scalp-raising crock of home-brew —a partnership, all complete with prospectus, being set up for the purpose, each member contributing a 25 lb. box of dried fruit and his quota of sugar. Or there would be a moochigan (in English, a dance), in the course of which a magnificent supper, together with home-brew and also less lethal and more legal drinks, imported with tremendous personal restraint over the trail from Peace River, would be consumed. Or somebody would promote a horse race. Or July would draw near and Sports Day with it, making necessary a settlers' meeting at Joe Bissett's store . . . . And, if at any time we needed further rousing out of our pathetic contentment, there was always the trail to town. A trip to Peace River acted as a safety valve and rarely failed to produce something unexpected.

CHAPTER II

Summer Days of a Homesteader

First causes have always interested me—the first spark that touches off a train of events leading up to some completely unforeseen action. In this particular case the first link in the chain that ended in my wild midnight ride with Jean Arnault was the fact that George Robertson attended the basket social at Judah. On the face of it, that sounds a bit far-fetched; for the community hall at Judah and the Little Prairie of the Battle, over which Johnny and I raced our horses by the faint light of the stars, lie a full hundred miles apart. Yet it was so—and now let me explain.

George Robertson and I had made a trip in to Peace River town from the Battle. Each of us had some business to see to—but the main reason was that we had stayed put long enough and it was high time to make a move before the moss began to grow. What George had been up to I don't know, but I had been living alone and working on my barn, slowly and awkwardly, adding round after round of logs to the walls, learning the hard way—and I was only too pleased to hear the thud of hoofs on the grass and to see George down below there, talking about going places. Magic words!

The trail to town, we figured, was a bit over eighty miles —and by "trail" I mean just that; not "road". Between

Little Prairie and the Clear Hills Trading Post there was a two-rutted track that took in everything: gravelly hills, rocks and beaver meadows; old beaver dams so high and steep that a horse-drawn wagon strained up them at a snail's pace, teetered over the top and then slammed forward and down till you wondered if pole, neck-yoke and breeching could possibly take it; muskeg through which the horses floundered up to their bellies and the wagon up to the reach, and which in the rains could be quite impassable. Thirty miles and only one cabin—and it deserted. Then came the Whitemud Bush: stumps and water-filled potholes; then more trail and more beaver meadows.

George took a light team, Trix and Midge, and a light wagon—a democrat. I slung a few things into the democrat and rode my strawberry-roan mare, The Urchin. It was mid-July; the days were long and we slept the first night at Steve Gjerstad's farm, sixty miles south, in the Bear Lake country. From there we made the twenty-odd miles in to town the following morning, on dirt roads mostly, sun-scorched and dusty.

Down the tumbled hills with their thickets of wild roses the road snaked and twisted, down off the plateau into the deep trench of the Peace River. The steelwork of the long bridge shimmered in the midday heat, and the long hot street down from the station into town was empty of life. The cool, shadowy cavern of the Hart River Livery Barn was like an oasis; soon we had the horses watered and fed; soon we were out into the sunlight again, and headed for Macnamara's Hotel. The father and mother of all thirsts was on us: we were so hot and dry that the first beer hissed as we sluiced it down our parched throats. Others followed it. Then we crossed the road to lunch at Nagle's Grill; and by that time we were feeling so bright and gay that we soon had Chris Iverson, the chef, and his helper, the lovely Mabel, the belle of Peace River, in a state of helpless laughter. For a while nobody could get served, and the business of the place slid to a breathless, exhausted stand-still.

Then we set about our own affairs and our various com-missions for friends on the Battle; but every now and then we came back to Macnamara's for more beer; the idea being to drink Mac's outfit dry—a hopeless proposition, I now realise, like breaking the bank at Monte Carlo. Still, we tried—and one result was that George got himself into the frame of mind where he'd gladly have gone fifty miles to get to a dance, and fifty more to hear himself call the square-dances.

But he didn't have to go that far—and, when we met in Mac's tavern at 5:30 p.m. for a really serious onslaught on the beer, George said to me: "Pat, how about we go up the hill tonight to Judah, to the basket social?"

Judah was a station and settlement on the railway line to Edmonton. I knew that. And George seemed to have figured out ways of getting there and back. But what exactly were we getting into?

"Basket social?" I said. "What the devil's that?"

"Well, it's a dance they're having. And every girl brings a supper basket complete. And before the supper dance the girls are put up to auction. Naturally the pretty girls com-mand quite a price; but then they know they'll fetch it any-way, whatever they've got in their baskets, so they're not always just as particular as they should be. So, ten to one, if you want a really good supper, Pat, the thing to do is to run your eye over the culls and buy yourself an ugly girl . . . . . What's that you say? Well, no—you don't *have* to buy one with a face like a boot; but you know what I mean —something that's not too fancy. You can bet your last dollar her basket'll have everything in it: a roast chicken, salads, creamy cakes—and you know you *like* creamy cakes: look at what you did to that one my sister made a week ago! We won't stay too long, and we'll buy a couple of nice medium-priced girls, and you just see what their baskets'll hold. Trust me. Everything you've ever dreamed of. Those homely wenches don't intend to be left on the shelf, and that's their way of getting off it. You share her supper with the girl you buy, dance the supper dance with her—and as many more as you can talk her into giving you. And the money goes to some project they're busy with at Judah. What about it?"

George had a way with him: he could smile his way into anything and be welcome. He'd be right in his element; and, if they ever asked him to call the square-dances for them, he'd stay till the sun was high. But I knew nobody at Judah and I have always been a bit shy with strangers. It sounded like a night's pure hell to me, and I said so. Besides I had mentally devoted the night to beer, and then more beer; and supper would be served by the lovely Mabel.

In the end we decided to go our separate ways and meet again in the morning. We went down to the livery barn and saw to the horses, and I got my pack and walked up towards the station. The Old Colony Rooms lay up that way, run by Miss Helps—a white building, clean and comfortable. Macnamara's was all right if you got one of his better rooms; but it could be noisy, and the Old Colony was quiet. Helping to make the noise yourself—there's nothing wrong with that. Rather the reverse, in fact. But having to listen to somebody else's uproar is a pain in the neck, and I wanted nothing of that.

George left his bedroll and stuff at the barn. From now on, he said, he was going to drift with the tide, and whatever beach he ended up on would be all right with him. As for me, Macnamara and Mabel passed the happy hours. But a day (and a homesteader) can hold only just so much —and, what with the beer and the good food and the morning's ride and the laughter, the end came well before midnight; and I made my way up the hill to the Old Colony, found my room, and flopped gratefully into bed and so to sleep . . . . .

The summer nights are short in the North, and the sun had already risen when I was roused from a cool slumber

by my door opening softly. Then it closed again very gently
—and then, from the corner of the room towards the river,
there came a sort of muted scuffling. Being now more than
half awake, I turned over to see George arranging his bedroll on the floor, presumably with a view to sleeping in it.

"Hullo," I said. "When I last saw you, you were drifting
pretty happily with the tide. Did you end up on a reef or
something?"

"No," he replied. "Everything's as right as rain. Except
that I'm just about bust flat—this has been quite a night—
so if it's all right with you I'm bunking in here till we con-
nect with that road cheque that's coming to us. It'll be in
on train day, and I'll pay my whack then."

"O.K. with me, and I'll fix Miss Helps. But there won't
be any whack for you to pay: I've got this room anyway.
I'll tell you what you can do: I'm leaving town on train
day. You're staying. You can buy me a bottle of Scotch—
Peter Dawson. That'll be your whack of the room. Fetch
it out in the democrat—I might smash it if I tie it on my
saddle—and when you get back I'll ride down to the Battle,
and together, we'll slaughter Peter Dawson. Now tell me
what happened. How did it go?"

"Well, Pat, it was a dandy evening. You should have
changed your mind and come. They put on a good dance;
there was nothing a man could kick at except their square-
dance caller—more like an old raven croaking than a man.
I called one just to spell him off; after that they kept me
at it and I couldn't quit. Boy, was he mad! I soon had them
stepping lively . . . . ."

Just as I had thought: George had found himself a
square-dance caller's heaven!

"From the financial angle," he went on, "there were
incidental expenses like a bottle of rye and my share of
the car gas—but the thing that bust me was, I bought
myself a lovely blonde. Pat, she was a real beauty, the
belle of the ball, and I just *had* to buy her for the honour
of the Battle. I couldn't do less, could I? Her basket, too—

what a supper! I had to go to $23.50 for her—and do you know, there wasn't a solitary one of those Judah pikers would raise me to $25? Not a one!"

Times were not too good, and $23.50 in those far-off days had the purchasing power of about $70 today—a fairish price for five dances and a supper. But George didn't grudge a penny of it, and when I dropped off to sleep he was still raving on about this wonderful girl— and when I slipped quietly out that morning to water and feed the horses, he was still dancing with her in his dreams . . . . .

I rode out of town the evening of train day with my share of the road cheque in my pocket. George was in funds again and all was well. I rode to Gjerstad's that night, and to my homestead the next day. I had got town out of my system and it felt like coming home to ride down the last ridges of the hills and out of the trees into that wind-rippled lake of green, that old lake bottom that was Little Prairie. There it lay under the evening sun, ten feet of black prairie soil with never a stone, never even a pebble, in the whole six square miles of it. There was no store, no post office nor village—only the small homesteads of the Scandinavians and our one tame Russian, Sepailov. It was suppertime when I rode through: nobody was about, but you could tell the time of day by the blue curls of wood-smoke drifting away from the scattered farmsteads on the south-west wind. The grey-green of the swaying, rustling oats, bleaching a little here and there, made the surface of this lake of grain—broken in places by small golden islets that were stacks of hay. Two trees—two tall white poplars far apart—flung their lengthening shadows east-ward. They were sacred trees: they, and no other trees, had been growing there when the Scandinavians first set eyes on this small but perfect prairie. They had preserved them; and it was a Norwegian who once had said to me: "By golly, Petersen, what would I be cutting my tree for? Because it is a trouble to plough around it? Surely, no!

Dot was my only tree—all the tree I got. A brave tree to wenture so far alone into the grass—no, by Yesus, I never cut dot tree!"

Through this well-ordered peace I rode, observed no doubt, but seeing nobody. Then on into my own wilderness between Little Prairie and the Battle. Being their northern outpost, as it were—three miles north of Little Prairie, and still four miles south of the river, and no other man to east or west of me at all—I was accepted by the Scandinavians as friend and ally. To them I ranked as an honorary Swede, and my name was Petersen . . . . .

Living up to my role of Swede, I got to work again on my barn next morning. The last round of logs was up; and the next job seemed to be to saw out a doorway so that, even though there was no roof on the building, I could at least tie The Urchin inside in the shade and be sure of having her when I needed her, instead of loping all round the horse pasture after her on foot, rattling a pan of oats. After a frantic struggle with a crosscut which I would now immediately condemn as blunt and needing setting, a doorway appeared. Triumphantly I spiked the logs in place, butting up to the door-frame. Then I went and caught The Urchin and tied her inside to get her used to the new setup: the sooner she connected the barn with the idea of oats, the better. Not only that, but she was a temperamental beast: anything strange upset her; and then, if no other horses were about, she would buck and rear up and fling herself over backwards. Several times I only escaped by inches from having the saddle horn rammed through me—once on frozen ground.

Next I set to work on the rafters, cutting and hewing tall, thin, fire-killed jackpine into size and shape. I fixed up a tripod to hold the jackpine sticks upright, and a block to butt them on. I set this arrangement just outside the north door of the cabin: that way the chips and slivers would be right handy for the cookstove; and also from there, from the gentle rise on which the cabin stood, I could get a long view to the westward. There was nothing man-made in that view to break the great sweep of parkland, rising in the far distance to a line of low hills—nothing, that is, except the old log buildings of a long-deserted homestead, McCracken's. Their dark, squat shapes protruded from the willow brush two miles west of my cabin—and right in front of them ran the Peace River-Fort Vermilion trail. From the cabin you could spot anything moving along that trail, especially in summertime and after midday. Then a string of packhorses, a hurrying democrat (there were no cars: the muskegs and the beaver dams saw to that), even a single rider—all would trail behind them a cloud of sunlit dust. As the sun worked round into the west, even the humblest rider on the humblest nag rode "trailing clouds of glory."

Hewing at my pine-trees, I kept my field glasses handy, dangling from a peg on the shady north wall of the cabin —and the particular cloud of glory I was interested in was the one that would accompany George Robertson and Peter Dawson. And on the afternoon of the third day, sure enough it came—the only moving thing on the trail since early morning.

Down went the axe and I grabbed the field glasses. The democrat dipped into the dry stream bed that ran past McCracken's. Then it appeared again, and for a fraction of time I caught sight, against the dark log buildings, of a pinto that had to be Trix running alongside a bay. George's super-sombrero, tall-crowned and floppy-brimmed, settled it beyond all doubt—and I downed tools and headed for my creek, carrying soap, towel and clean clothes . . . . .

CHAPTER III

The Night Riders

Something over an hour later I rode away from the
cabin, down the grass slope and then north-westward
across the fireweed prairie, making for the Fort Vermilion
trail where it dipped down into the trees and down bench
after bench to the Battle River Crossing.

Things were moving ahead of me, perhaps two miles
away. The sun was into the north-west now, and the late
afternoon light, glinting on a thousand acres of purple
fireweed, made it hard to see what or why. But as I rode
closer, the circling, wheeling objects took shape clearly:
a man alone on horseback trying to drive south three loose
horses that were set on heading north, and which wouldn't
stay bunched—a tough proposition in any man's language.
The man was Jean Arnault, a French-Cree halfbreed,
descendant of some French-Canadian voyageur of the fur-
trade days, and known on the Battle as Johnny Arnold.

"Lend me a hand," he shouted to me as he rode to and
fro behind the unwilling horses. "Lend me a hand with
these cayuses. I want to corral them down at my place
and they don't want to go. I got a bottle of rum there—
we'll make ourselves a few egg-nogs before we have supper. Will you come?"

On many an evening this might have been a sound
idea. But not on this one.

"Leave your cayuses," I said, "and come down with me
to the Crossing, to the Robertsons'. Did you see George

18

go by an hour or two ago? Well, he has a bottle of Scotch
for me. We'll take a drink or two out of that and see the
boys. Then we'll come back up here in good daylight
and pick up your horses, and you'll see—they'll practically fly the seven miles from here to your corrals. Then
we can complete the rest of the programme the way you
said. How would that be?"

A look of pleasurable anticipation took possession of
Johnny's dark, lean countenance. "That'll be better yet,"
he said. "Drinks to the north and drinks to the south of
us: the Battle's surely getting civilised."

All this time his eyes had been running over The
Urchin. "That's the mare you bought from Mike Miller,"
he went on. "I'd like to trade you out of her. Now here's
a good horse—quiet and fast. Suppose we swap our saddles
over and you can try him?"

So we did that and I swung up on to Johnny's bay. I had
no intention of trading off The Urchin, but a change
was pleasant and that was no dream of Johnny's about
the bay being fast. Holding the eager horses down to a
lope, we rode once more northwestward towards the edge
of the trees . . . . .

That was quite an evening down at the Crossing. I soon
found that I was not the only one for whom George had
brought out a drop of something-or-other. There was Ole
Olstad, a lively, alert Norwegian trapper and homesteader
from nearby. Mike Miller had brought his smiling face
and gay, high-pitched voice to the party—he was a Russian and his true name, they said, was Mikhail Milroff.
Bob Henderson and Ring Reid were there, partners from
Big Prairie to the north of the Battle. To a man they were
trappers and hunters, using their homesteads as bases and
to live on in summertime. They were men who needed
elbow-room: many of them would move on northwards
when close settlement came to the Battle River prairies.

One by one the vultures gathered also—and by vultures
I mean those gifted with noses that can sniff a drink

from afar. But no man grudged them a snort. It was a
dry summer: the river hills were yellow and the humans
were a bit dessicated, too. In fact it was difficult for anyone
present to avoid partaking of about half a dozen variegated
brands of firewater; hospitality was rampant and the din
of voices grew. I could hear Ring's voice raised as he
shouted at Ole about a moose that had smashed his fences
and walked up to him as he was ploughing. There was an
old game trail through Ring's place and the game per-
sisted in using it. Three taut barbed wires would snap
like cotton threads as the huge deer swung through them:
the moose would never even falter in their stride. Ring
said he always worked with one eye on the trail and a rifle
handy when he needed meat. No need for him to go
hunting . . . . . Mike's high-pitched roar came to me. He
was telling tales of Ed de Meldt—a legendary character
and the strongest man in northern Alberta. Amongst other
feats, de Meldt had been known to pick up a 45-gallon
drum of gasoline and lower it gently into a floating canoe,
without dropping it in or damaging anything. And in the
words of the old song:
     "If you don't think that's clever,
     Just try it for yourself."
     Mrs. Robertson, George's mother, saved all our lives—
as she always did—by suddenly producing unlimited coffee,
together with cakes and scones and pies, and home-made
bread with jam made from the wild fruit that grew along
the Battle.
     A couple of fiddlers were imported. They sawed and
scraped away in a corner till one's feet itched—in fact
there would have been a dance only nobody was going to
saddle up and leave the party to ride half the night, alert-
ing the half-breed families. We already had the only white
girl in the whole country, George's sister, Ethel. She did
her best for us—she danced with everybody till she was
pretty well played out. Some of the men, the better dancers,
tied handkerchiefs on their left arms, thus becoming

"ladies". I found myself dancing soulfully with Ring Reid; he was just the right height for me and it was like dancing with a feather.

The fiddlers were not overlooked. We kept them fed and just nicely primed. They surpassed themselves, and their wild music (and perhaps the Scotch and the rye as well) went to the feet of our best halfbreed dancer. He stepped forward, tossed back his raven hair and spoke to the fiddlers in Cree. They broke into the Red River Jig and the moccasined feet of the dancer began to thud on the cleared floor.

But something was wrong: the music sagged and then trailed off into silence. It was the leading fiddler who was in trouble. "Hey, Louis!" he shouted to a friend. "Fetch me my rubbers, quick! How the hell can I play a jig in my moccasins only?" The rubbers were brought; Jerome Bonaparte was now able to get a grip on the floor and ply his heel-and-toe as a fiddler should; the music started up again; the dancer's feet flew . . . . .

Outside, darkness had long since fallen, but the buildings and the trees and the river crossing were lit by the streaming fires of a magnificent aurora. Around midnight Johnny Arnold's husky voice sounded in my ear: "I guess our daylight's somehow got away from us," it was saying. "But the Lights are out pretty strong. We could see to pick my horses up if we go now. I'll go and saddle up."

Well, there was always hope. And Peter Dawson had died some time ago, and most of the Big Prairie fellows were leaving, anyhow. So we said our thanks and good-byes, and practically everybody piled out of the house into the wavering half-light of the aurora.

Johnny appeared out of the black darkness of the Robertsons' barn, leading the roan and the bay. The horses were edgy and excited, and the little knot of men, all talking and laughing by the garden gate, was doing nothing to calm them. I took The Urchin from Johnny, cheek-strapped her, turned her head away from home, got my foot

in the stirrup and my right hand on the horn—and was
spun into the saddle as she whirled and reared. I thought
she was going to come back over, but she didn't—she leapt
straight into action and swept round the corner of the
garden fence, almost jamming my knee.

A fraction of a second later and a roar of cheering greeted
Johnny's safe arrival in the saddle after a fight with his
horse, who wanted to follow The Urchin. I let fly with
an answering yell, "Yee-a-a-upp!", and I could feel the
muscles tense under me as The Urchin gathered speed.
I was about a length ahead of Johnny, and I turned in my
saddle to see if he had cleared that fence corner. My hat
blew off as I did so, and Johnny leaned out and caught
it before it could fall to the ground. He came up on my
left and passed the hat to me—which again made the
horses leap forward into a gallop. As we wrestled them
back into a lope I could hear Johnny's voice, a bit breathless: "Pretty good, I think, that Cossack stuff of mine?"

The trees, big beautiful white poplars in full leaf, rushed
past on either side. They arched over the old wagon trail,
shutting out the faint light, and all we could see for certain was the dim white ghosts of the reeling tree-trunks
as they whirled by. Not a breath of air was moving and
we felt only the wind of our own speed in our faces.

And now the river flat lay behind; suddenly the ground
upheaved in front of us and we swept up the forty-foot
step on to the first bench. There were several of these
steps and benches; the horses wished to gallop up the
steps—and after the second step we let them go on galloping. They were excited and so were we—and while the
rush of the night air might be cooling our faces and clearing our heads after that frantic evening, it was doing
nothing to cool down our abundant store of literally ardent
spirits. Rather did it bring with it a feeling of wild and
reckless exhilaration. So we galloped on in the summer
darkness, sitting low in our saddles and leaning forward

on the horses' manes as a concession to the overhanging branches that we couldn't see.

"I think the horses want to race." Johnny's voice came huskily out of the darkness, above the pounding of the hoofs on the black soil. "This bay I'm riding is fast," he added. "You'll see."

Oh, I'll see, will I? Of course, what he's still aiming to do is to trade me out of The Urchin: that's the idea of this evening and obviously it's taken root, Well, just wait till we get out of the bush and on to the open prairie. Then we'll see who's going to show who what!

So my thoughts ran—if you can call them thoughts—but I made no reply. And at that moment the last mad rush up the last bench came. It was like flying—it was like being swept up on a rising cloud. A magnificent feeling. The fact that there was a horse underneath me had somehow ceased to have any meaning: I was alone, hurtling through the night air in some godlike fashion—and sometimes there was a voice on my left, in the other rut of the trail, and sometimes there wasn't. Who cared? This lunatic rush was all that mattered now in the whole wide world, and it was going on for ever and ever. In aeternum, Domine. In saecula saeculorum. Amen.

The trees ended suddenly as we topped that last crest and shot out on to the prairie. The aurora had faded and dawn was still only a dim greyness in the north-east. We rode now by the faint glimmer of the stars.

"So they want to race, you think?" I said to the dark shadow on my left. "Well then, what about just—damn —well—LETTING THEM?!" And I fetched The Urchin a crack with my quirt and let a yell out of me that put the first one deep in the shade. Johnny came back with a selection from the war-whoops of North America—and the rush of the wind in our faces increased and the drumming of the hoofs quickened. Somewhere off to the left, on the fireweed prairie, Johnny's three horses may have heard the din and wondered. But nobody gave a thought to them: we had forgotten that they ever existed.

Heading due south, we smoked along the prairie trail in silence. Now at last this was speed—we were going all out with nothing in reserve. And yet the horses were still just level in the trail. Could it be that, over a distance, they were evenly matched?

Minutes went by—and then, suddenly, I felt my weight in the saddle grow less and The Urchin faded away from beneath me. A snatch of fear made me catch my breath —and then dark shapes loomed faintly on my right and I knew: we had reached McCracken's and the horses had dipped down into the dry stream bed that we couldn't see. I heard Johnny give a yell as his horse plunged down the slope—but I was handling things differently: I was flying across the narrow depression on my own. I still held the lines in my bridle hand and the quirt still dangled from my right wrist, but The Urchin was galloping across away down below there, all by herself. She was keeping level with me, thank God, and soon—ah, here she came! And I felt myself settle gently into the saddle once more, safely across, the first man on earth to fly a creek bed without wings! I tried to tell Johnny of the wonder that had befallen me, but he was living in a world of his own and calling a square-dance. Useless! I have told many a man since then, and not one has believed me. But I was there on that night, and I *know!*

"Places all! You know where; I don't care!" So the square-dance had come to an end—that was something! And we galloped on without speaking, the horses neck and neck.

It would be Little Prairie next and the trail, still due south, would run in between the orderly fences of the Scandinavians. But that was miles ahead: time had no meaning on this night of nights, and distance was no longer our master but our slave. Why, there was nothing that was beyond our reach—and I laughed aloud as I thought of all the things I could do to improve the Battle River prairies! I'd make a real country out of this. A good job nobody had thought of doing it before—but then, obviously, you had to ride like a madman to climb far enough above the everyday world to see the Way clearly.

And I had. I'd ridden into some Fifth Dimension where demigods could fly and horses went on forever. Now that the Power was on me I'd fix things. First of all I would— but at that moment a thundering roar came from beneath the pounding hoofs, and the Vision left me and I came back to earth again. The miles had flown, just in those few moments when I had ridden amongst the wheeling stars and held the Secret of Life within my grasp. And a damn shame it was, to lose all that—the chance might never come again. For now we were on Little Prairie and nearing journey's end.

That roar was the level-hewed logs of Oscar Nord's bridge beneath our horses' feet. It put new life into all concerned. The Urchin leapt into the air as her feet hit the timber. From the two humans came a burst of laughter and wild yells, and the maddened horses increased their speed. You wouldn't have thought they had it in them— but they had. We treated Nord's buildings to a serenade of song, whoops and square-dance calls and fled on . . . . . Those dimly seen lumps coming up on the right were old man Erikson's house and barn. We gave him a song, too —that old song of the North that has for its chorus, twice repeated:

"When the ice-worms breed again!"

As we passed Erikson's it seemed to me that suddenly there was a light there—and then it was gone again. Without any warning Johnny's horse shot ahead just as if he'd been stung. As I drew level again Johnny called to me. "Did you hear anything?" he asked.

"I might have heard a door bang shut. And there was a light. We must have roused old Erikson. That song, the way we were singing it, would waken the dead."

"We must have roused the old man. Steady on now—here's Sepailov's gate. God, what a ride! Ten miles from the Crossing—how long did we take?"

I peered at the luminous dial on my wrist. That was odd: there were two dials now where only one had been before. With a tremendous effort I got them into focus.

"Twenty-three minutes. But mind you—we didn't really start to travel till we hit the prairie. Say seven miles of it at the full gallop."

"I guess so. We surely came fast. Now we'll go at a walk across the oats and calm the horses down a bit. I want some eggs from Sepailov—we've earned that egg-nog."

Had we? Oh well—on this night anything went. Like George in Peace River, I was swimming with the tide.

We rode the heaving horses quietly along the wagon trail through the oats to Sepailov's house. Then we gently roused Sepailov by shouting through an open window and by hammering on his door with the loaded quirt. A wrathful shout came from within, and a lamp was lighted. Then, suddenly the door flew open and the Russian stood there, tense and facing us, a savage-looking double-bitted axe in his hands. Johnny's plea for eggs seemed to soothe him.

"Oh my, oh my, oh my! Such a commotions iss, such a goings on! Shall be wild men on quiet Battle now where all was peace. Eggs? At such a times of night? Who laughing iss in darkness? New homesteader Patterson? Iss learning wild ways and shall surely go to devil, but shall have eggs to go with. Yess. Eggs shall have if devil needs." And Sepailov disappeared, chuckling, pleased with his wit and pleased with his mastery over the English language—which, if English is to a Russian as Russian is to an Englishman, was pretty good.

Sepailov brought us a dozen eggs in a small cotton sugar-bag. We paid for them and mounted. Johnny took the eggs from Sepailov, holding them high in front of him: had he held them out to one side his horse would have seen them and taken them as the signal to break into another gallop, whereas what Johnny wanted was to go quietly and get home with the full dozen.

I settled that idea for him. I didn't want to go anywhere quietly; this was no night to waste, ambling along like a couple of old squaws. I was in good voice and I let out a yell that might have been heard at the Crossing. The Urchin needed no second yell—we were off!

The bay, it later transpired, reacted instantaneously, and with such force that the egg-bag swung back and smashed two eggs on Johnny's nose. Flying along in the lead, I could hear curses from my companion and pleas to go easy for God's sake; and, at the same time, Sepailov's roars of laughter dying away in the distance. Egg yoke, by this time was dripping into the bay's mane. Johnny thought that was a pity—he didn't want an ants' nest on his horse's neck—so he held the eggs as far out to the side as he could reach. This lent wings to the bay's feet, this sight of a bagful of eggs inexplicably pursuing him; and soon we were tearing along level again, with Johnny trying to explain to me about egg yolk and how it would attract ants —he had ants on the brain now in place of square-dances —and how, if we didn't ease up within half a mile, we'd kill ourselves against his corrals.

I thought that, too—but, what with listening to Arnold on Ants, and the memory of Sepailov's laughter, I was helpless. I was rocking in my saddle and the tears coursed down my cheeks. In broken accents I managed to convey to Johnny that, if he didn't get that bag of eggs out of his horse's sight, we'd not only hit his corrals—we'd go clean on through them and wind up in kingdom come. That penetrated; and from there on the eggs travelled in front of his nose again and we regained control. Gently we slowed down to a lope and then to a walk.

We offsaddled and turned the horses loose to roll—and roll and roll. I've never seen horses roll like that: in the greying light they showed black from head to foot with sweat, and they rolled and grunted and shook themselves and snorted—and they got down and did it all over again, wriggling their backbones in the dust, rubbing their cheeks on the black soil till they were plastered solid. Then, after one last shake, they stood side by side, motionless. In their own good time they would drink at the creek, and hay was down for them when they needed it.

I watched them for a while, then I walked up to the house, up the yellow pathway of lamplight that streamed from the open door, and into the kitchen where Johnny had been boiling a kettle. Two steaming mugs sat on the well-scrubbed table and a large cake sat between them. Johnny pushed one of the mugs towards me. "Here," he said, "drink that and help yourself to cake. They can't say it's a long time between drinks on the Battle." And he set to work with guile and blandishment to separate me from The Urchin.

For ages, it seemed, we led each other up and down the garden path. Then, at the third egg-nog Johnny's whole outlook changed. He got on to ants again—and then decided that nobody was going to fool him into parting with a valuable horse like that bay just because it had egg-nog and ants in its mane. Naturally, I agreed with him—the sequence of reasoning being perfectly clear to me at the time, though I would have to think for a bit before I could set it down now.

No, Johnny went on, it wasn't every horse in the country that got an egg-nog shampoo as a regular thing. But there was the sorrel in that bunch of three on the fireweed prairie that we'd forgotten about. Now there was a *real* horse! We'd better ride back and pick up the bunch as soon as we'd finished the rum . . . . .

At the fourth drink, dimly persisting towards the North, I got Johnny weaned from the sorrel and well on the trail to Hay River. By the fifth we were on the Great Slave itself and searching for the outlet to the Mackenzie. Time passed unheeded and, with fingers dipped in egg-nog, we drew maps on the wooden surface of the table . . . . .

Ten eggs had made five rounds of egg-nog. And now the rum was gone and the cake was a ruin. We blew the lamps out and walked out into bright sunshine and the cool freshness of the morning. I went down to the creek and bathed my face and hands. That was good but sleep would be better—I had been on the go now for over a full day. The morning breeze rustled the dry grass on the bank, and the soft bed of needles beneath the shadowy spruce looked inviting. I took my jacket off and folded it into a pillow . . . . .

I had the impression, half-dreaming and half-waking, of riding through a forest of green, rustling trees. It was cool in their shade but the swaying branches kept getting in my way . . . . . I opened my eyes to find a willow branch waving just above them—and that was a queer thing to see, under an overhanging spruce. But at the other end of the green spray of willow was a small brown hand. Following up from the hand one came to a small brown face with a lovely bloom on it, as of ripe plums, dark brown eyes and a head of raven hair—Johnny's small girl. She had been sitting there, gently waving the willow branch over me, to keep away the mosquitoes. There was hospitality for you!

The child watched me for a minute to make sure that I was really awake. Then she jumped up and ran through the trees to the house, shouting out something in Cree. After a wash in the creek I followed her; good smells of cooking were drifting on the breeze; breakfast would be welcome. Then it dawned on me that it was blazing hot, and I looked at my watch: I had slept for seven hours and this was Sunday dinner . . . . .

I rode away from Johnny's place in the evening, full of tea and more cake. The Urchin was subdued and I felt a bit that way, too. We went quietly past Sepailov's and turned north up the Little Prairie road. The heat of the day was over but no one seemed to be moving. Then, as I drew near, old Erikson came out from his house and down to his gate. He waited for me there, leaning on the top rail, puffing away at his pipe.

"Good evening, Mr. Petersen."

"Good evening, Mr. Erikson."

"Do you come from Peace River?"

"No—I was down to see Johnny Arnold."

"Ah—I did not see you go down. I t'ought may be you come from Peace River. Dere was a *wild* bunch went down south last night—I hope maybe you meet them on the trail and tell me who. Dere was maybe six or seven— and up to no good, you bet, because they ride yust like the devil is after them. And they kick up one hell of a row! My stomach troubles me and I am sleeping badly, and I hear the whole damn crazy bunch come over Nord's bridge—whoop, yell, sing by Yesus; and one man is laughing like a mads—yust like a mads! Wild men from the Battle! I do not know what the hell they ride away *from*, but I yump out of bed and I give them both barrels of my old shotgun—she is my twelve-gauge, you know—yust to help them on their way . . . . ."

So *that* was what had sent Johnny Arnold's bay forging ahead of The Urchin just at this point. Just as well I hadn't touched that trade. I'd have been no further ahead, next Battle River Sports Day, with a horse that had to be shot in the rump before he could outrun The Urchin. And sounding like six or seven "mads"! Well—that just showed what a man could do when he gave his mind to it. Thoughtfully I rode on, over Oscar Nord's bridge and then northeastward, picking my way across the open country towards my cabin on the ridge . . . . .

Next morning I got to work again on my barn rafters —though not failing to keep an eye on the distant line of the trail. It was twelve days now since George Robertson had ridden up, talking about a trip to Peace River. A

pleasant interlude—in fact there was nothing wrong, that
I could see, with a homesteader's life so long as a man
was careful not to get himself into a rut, doing nothing
but work his fool head off around the cabin till the moss
grew on him.

CHAPTER IV

The Trail to Peace River

I have always been susceptible to the lure of roads. They beckon to me, promising always something new hidden beyond the horizon. They do not beckon in vain, and I want to follow them all to see where they go—every one of them, whether it be some old Roman road marching straight as an arrow over hill and dale, or a faintly marked Indian trail snaking tortuously into some remote valley of the mountains. And now into my life had come this road from Peace River town to the Battle—my first experience of a wilderness trail. To be sure, it started out as a graded road, ungravelled. But that didn't last long: soon it was just two ruts winding along in the green grass between fences. Then the fences faded out, but the two ruts still kept on, through wild country, fanning out in swampy places, climbing over old beaver dams, till you found yourself once more following a winding wagon-track in the green grass between fences. After eighty miles or so you had reached the promised land, the prairies of the Battle River.

One source of income to the established settlers of the Battle was the hauling in, by wagon or sleigh, of materials and effects for the incoming homesteader. This was done at so much per pound, plus stopping expenses along the trail for horse and man. In addition, you went along yourself more often than not, and helped with the loading and unloading and in all the various jackpots into which the unmade road and the weather could land the outfit. These were many, and one ended by knowing the man who was doing the hauling—George Robertson, it might be, from the Battle River Crossing, or old Duncan McTavish; or perhaps Bill Asmussen from Big Prairie, beyond the river —very well indeed. They became friends, and with them I met the people who lived along the trail. These last were a new world to me and I observed them with interest and curiosity, being quite unaware in my early days that this curiosity was mutual and, on the part of those observing me, intense. Here let me step aside and explain.

Men of many races can come to the Canadian prairies and be absorbed into the general scene without exciting any special attention. But just let an educated Englishman turn up—one who has been forcibly educated, I mean, with the stick at an English public school, and preferably one with an Oxford degree as well—and then see how tongues will get busy! The same thing applies to an educated Frenchman. They also do not leave their lovely home-land too easily, and so are equally rare birds on the prairie. A reason has to be found for the presence of these exotics.

That doesn't take long. As I made firm friends, one by one they would smilingly reveal to me the secrets of my own past—beginning usually with "I bet you've never heard what they say about you down around Bear Lake?" Or some such remark.

No—I never had. And it was always worth hearing, and never anything malicious in it. The most popular story was that I was heir to a title and estate in Scotland, and one of the conditions of the will was that I had to prove up a homestead in western Canada before inheriting. That was the one I liked best myself: there was a castle in it and plenty of money; nobody had thought of putting in a grouse moor, but I'd have seen to that myself. A thoroughly *nice* idea and God bless the kind soul who thought that one up!

Then there was the tale that had me one of London's

leading barristers—on a par, at least, with the then recently
created Earl of Birkenhead; and now, after a nervous breakdown, proving up a homestead in search of new health
and strength. That yarn left me completely cold: I quite
frankly preferred Battle River to the London bar—at least,
as I imagined it. I had never wished to have anything to
do with the law—not, that is, until my arrival on the
Battle, when I soon discovered within myself a fine capacity
for breaking it, just as good as anybody else's in those parts.
London barrister—heaven forbid!

And there was that one, that legend, I mean, that
honoured me with a double first at Oxford—it didn't say
in what—and that now had me proving up a very isolated
homestead so as to have a quiet place in which to write
my masterpiece. I bet it was Jack Blackgrave that started
that off, and out of pure hellery. He and I, comparing
notes one day on Big Prairie, had found that we had caught
the same train for the City every morning from Lancaster
Gate for a spell of months in our London days . . . . . Yes,
that would be Jack Blackgrave all right—he had been
through the same mill himself, and nobody else knew what
a double first meant, anyway. But they surely respected it
—and my forensic capabilities—and gradually it began to
dawn on me why I was so often chairman at a settlers'
meeting or secretary to the Sports Committee: I had a
reputation and the Battle was all there to profit by it.

There were other stories; and they got mixed, producing
curious hybrid varieties. Then, after a spell I put in in a
lumber-camp, a rather sinister note crept in, enhancing,
if anything, the esteem in which I was held.

It came about like this. At this camp of George McRae's
near Driftpile the motive power was the horse. The logs
were skidded in from the bush to the mill, hitched up at
the fore end on small horse-drawn sleds known as "go-
devils". They swung into line and then came up on to a
ramp of sawdust from which a long skidway (heavy logs
topped with railroad metals) ran at a gentle slope down to

the saw. I was in charge of that skidway and it was up to me, armed with a canthook, to keep the logs straightened out and rolled right up to the sawyers. It was a good job, there in that sunny clearing that was sheltered by the tall timber, and through the quiet autumn days. I liked it. There were moments, of course—times when the saw broke down and the skidway plugged up three logs deep, or when all the teamsters came in from the bush at once after some traffic jam in the trail. And there were awkward teamsters to contend with—and a few that were awkward on purpose . . . . .

I told one of these, the French-Canadian foreman's son, exactly what I thought of him, and I left nothing out. That evening my friend, Roy Scott, also from the Battle, met the foreman, a blustering, bullying character, with an axe in his hand, looking for me.

"Patterson?" said Scott. "I don't know where he's got to. What do you want with him?"

"I show him!" the foreman shouted furiously. "By God, I feex him!"

"I wouldn't, if I were you," Scott said in a voice that was full of meaning.

"And why not?"

"You know why he's here, don't you?"

"No, I do not. Why?"

"Well, a guy somewhere down east got mad with him —just the same as you—and he went for him. And Patterson killed him. That's why he's here. This is a nice quiet place . . . . ."

At this shocking intelligence the gunpowder all ran out at the foreman's heels—and shortly afterwards he removed himself and his family from McRae's Camp. Scott took over his job. A most satisfactory bit of work, from every angle.

Scott never returned to the Battle, but that story got there somehow—on its own feet and still further embellished. It became blended with the others, and together they begat some truly nightmarish offspring—which, I now realise, did me no harm at all. On the contrary, they provided me with an acceptable social background to this new life that I had chosen in the West. As for the dweller on the trail to Peace River, what he might see approaching his house would not necessarily be the straightforward, commonplace "me", riding a little strawberry roan or sitting in a sleigh. He could not be blamed if he saw approaching a madly eccentric barrister, with homicidal tendencies and a wholly human fondness for beer and whisky, heir to a castle in Scotland and engaged, in the loneliness of his homestead, on an earth-shaking work of the most scholarly erudition.

Well, all I can say is—it must have brightened his day for him. I only wish those madmen on the Battle had let me in on the fun a bit earlier . . . . . And now it's time we saddled our horses and got going on the trail; and, as we ride, I'll tell you how a few of the denizens looked to me.

The first place one hit, after thirty miles of nothing at all, was the Clear Hills Post, an isolated country store and farm with a bit of fur coming in on the side. This outfit belonged to old man Stonehewer and his family, and one could ride in there at any time of day and be sure of a good meal. And not only that. During my first year or two there resided with the Stonehewers a very pretty schoolmarm, in from Calgary to teach the little halfbreeds their ABC. She was a drawing card if ever there was one: young and ardent bachelors would ride forty miles and more, from the Big Prairie of the Battle, simply to try and get that girl to see reason—reason in this instance being marriage and the delights of a homestead on Big Prairie. Not a hope—they were butting their heads against a brick wall; and it was a nasty shock to the most optimistic of the Battle River suitors when he rode in one golden September evening around the opening of term, dressed to kill and even carrying a guitar on which he had been practising all summer, to find that the lovely girl had not returned. The new teacher's name was Gustavus Gundmundson, a very pleasant young man of Icelandic descent, but no real substitute. They say that guitar never twanged again, and I shouldn't wonder a bit—a man doesn't get over a jolt like that in a hurry. Old man Stonehewer was rather put out, too: the girl from Calgary had brought quite a lot of trade to the place, he told me, and it needed all it could get.

"Not doing so well?" I asked, in between bites. I had stopped to take on board food for man and beast, and the old man was talking to me as I ate.

"Well, I guess as well as it kin," he said "but that ain't no Eldorado. If I'd ever set eyes on the doggoned place I'd surely never have taken it on. Mebbe they've told you we got it on a trade? Well—the guy that owned it had it advertised in the *Portland Oregonian* like it was another Klondike—furs and gold dust and a farm thrown in. Wild and wonderful. And I up and offered him a fruit farm for it—and he bit. So we traded, sight unseen."

"A *fruit farm?*" I said. "For *this?*" And I had a sudden vision of rows of perfectly pruned trees, just like a booster folder from the Kelowna Chamber of Commerce, available on request.

"Ye-es," said old man Stonehewer. "Oh well, hell! I guess we got stung all right. Still, I'd 'a given something to see that guy's face when he seen what *he* got!"

The next schoolhouse south along the trail was Three Lakes School—and remember this: the trail itself was only a thread of sparse settlement, with nothing but unbroken wilderness to the east and west of it for hundreds of empty miles. The teacher at Three Lakes was a retiring sort of a man: I would see him sometimes as I rode by—busy around a small garden, but he never looked up or waved. Then he departed, and Three Lakes sent in a petition to Edmonton asking that they might be assigned a girl in his place. They got one—and Mike Miller rode all the way from Big Prairie (we figured it out at sixty-three miles, one way) to see what she was like. He found a soured and elderly spinster with enormous spectacles. He was so upset about this that he turned right round and rode all the way back to the Battle, only stopping to graze his horse. Even so, he got there too late: the humorist who had brought the news that the new schoolmarm was beautiful as the day had already ridden on, towards Keg River.

Clear Hills and Three Lakes school districts then decided to lay their cards on the table. Once again they petitioned Edmonton. How, they demanded, could they be expected to go ahead and prosper if they were not supplied with marriageable schoolmarms who could give the settlement a run for its money? The government, in its turn, wanted to know why it should be expected to educate and train a never-ending string of girls just to stock up the wilder parts of the Peace River country. It's the gist of the argument I'm giving you—not verbatim, but within a word or two.

The upshot of all this was that the cause of education rather hit the skids in the Clear Hills-Three Lakes country—and there the matter rested for a while. Stalemate.

Battle River fared no better. We had a very attractive little schoolmarm somewhere out in the wilds of Big Prairie, but she met her destiny in the person of Jack Maule (English—ex-R.A.F.) and the Battle acquired a third white wife. Exactly what the government was complaining about.

Her dark-eyed, nut-brown ex-pupils bore their loss bravely: they took to trapping in the vicinity of their homes, in place of school—and not without incident. Young Agnes Bonaparte caught a coyote, but it got away with her trap on its foot. She gave chase and followed the confused trail in the snow till her child's strength gave out and she collapsed—being found later, and quite by accident, by Ring Reid, almost frozen. Raymond Ghostkeeper was crossing the Battle River, in a Chinook and near some fast water, to look at one of his traps, when he went through the ice. Luckily he was in shallow water, but even so he could not get out again on to the river ice. He too was found in time, also by pure chance, and was taken home to be warmed and revived, and spanked later for not knowing rotten ice from good. Pauline Bonaparte found a coyote working loose from a trap she had set. She fetched it such a clip with a hatchet that the animal succumbed—but not before it had bitten her in the arm. As might be supposed, the various parents were by now decidedly in favour of school, and the more school the better. Soon one more petition was wending its way to Edmonton—and soon after that was granted Cupid was setting one more arrow on the string . . . . .

Riding on south from Three Lakes School you soon saw, on your left hand, two small log houses set within a yard of each other. The log buildings and corrals of a pioneer farm completed the picture. The two houses belonged, one each, to Tom Ryan and to Mrs. Beatty, better known as Aunt Belle. There again a man could stop overnight or at noonday and feed himself and his horse. If he stopped overnight he could sleep in Tom Ryan's cabin. But one ate always in Aunt Belle's—and how! Even now the memory of Aunt Belle's creamy cakes and desserts makes my mouth water. Stopping there, one hot summer's day, for the noonday meal and watching the magnificent preparations for it, I made some remark about how good cream *not* out of a can was going to taste for a change. I had ridden forty miles that morning and I was twenty-six years old and ravenous.

Aunt Belle looked at me. "What you need," she said, "is a snack while I'm fixing things. Here's a dipper and here's a mug. Go down to the spring-box and take the lid off and you'll see the cream-can set in the water. Dip yourself out a mug of ice-cold cream and enjoy it and I'll be ready with your dinner when you get back." I needed no second telling—and always afterwards, when I stopped there, Aunt Belle would greet me with a laugh and hand me the mug and the dipper, saying, "You know what that's for. Get going!"

You have to be living an active life, of course, to be able to handle a diet of straight cream. And I was.

I don't know what the history of that pair had been. I know only one thing from their past: they had been to the Klondike. The famous Trail of '98 lay only twenty-six years back when I drank that first mug of cream. And these two had made it! All through my life I have admired most in men the simple things: courage, persistence, endurance, loyalty to a friend and hardihood. Not every man who made it from Skagway to Dawson had all these qualities, by any means. Some of the most accomplished twisters in western America somehow managed to get there. But no man could reach the golden river by the Chilkoot Pass route without some of them—persistence and endurance at the very least. Ever since I was able to read I had known the names of the famous creeks—Dominion, Gold Bottom, Bonanza, Eldorado, Sulphur—names to conjure with. And now, here were two people, not old, who had actually seen it go $100 to the pan—who had lived through all the frozen, back-breaking hell of the trail, and the tossing, foam-crested rapids of the river; all the golden glory and the riot and the bitter tragedy of it. Dead, indeed, to all romance must the traveller be, I thought, who would not try to make Tom Ryan's by nightfall. I rarely failed.

Part of their income was the weekly cream cheque from that cream which Aunt Belle so lightly gave away. Once a week she would hitch up a team to sleighs or democrat and drive the thirty miles in to the comic old Edmonton, Dunvegan and B.C. Railroad—to the creamery. Sometimes the team would come tearing home that same evening as if on winged feet—sixty long miles. Sometimes it might not be till noon the following day if she had stopped overnight with a friend.

For the rest, it was cattle, fur, and the stopping business
—helped out by the moose and the deer, and by a garden
from which came those delicious salads. It seemed to be
a happy place—"port after stormie seas."

They—or one of them—had adopted a small girl from
the Mission, Frances, eight years old when I first saw her,
mostly Indian. From time to time Tom Ryan would give
Frances a calf from the bunch that ranged and grew fat
outside their fences in summertime, coming in, in winter,
to be put on feed—oat bundles and hay. She had, Frances
confided in me, six head of cattle and a saddle-horse.
"Them cattle of mine is just eatin' fools," she told me,
that first hard winter. "I figured twenty ton of hay should
see me through, but I'll have to borrow from Uncle Tom
if a Chinook don't happen along soon . . . . ."

Hot days and the warm smell of the grass and the poplar
trees; cold days of winter and the snuffle of the black north
wind and the hiss of dry, drifting snow—those twin homesteads were always welcoming. And, in any case, what
could I do but turn in? My mare, her mind all set on
oats, refused to pass that gate!

Not many miles from Tom Ryan's there dwelt a curious,
hermit-like character—I never knew his real name—
known as Tarnation Pard. I owed my introduction to him
to the thoughtfulness of old Duncan McTavish who, as
we were driving out with a load of my stuff at around
ten below, said to me, "There's a guy here, Pat, that'll
be something new to you. He has about the same standard
of living as a gypsy tinker. He's always chasing himself
with his work, about a season behind; he's crazy on religion,
and he can't open his mouth without saying: 'Tarnation
pard.' That's the guy—up there on the knoll. No—you're
damn right we won't go in. Not on your life. We'll just
pass the time of day."

We drove up to where a wild, ragamuffin figure was
frantically trying, in forty-two degrees of frost, to mud-up
the chinks in the walls of a dilapidated log cabin—a job

that he might have done with ease in September. He and
Duncan exchanged greetings and I was introduced.

"Well," said Duncan. "Getting nicely fixed for the winter?"

"Tarnation, pard, I'll say I am. Yis—God and I is get-
tin' things kinder fixed between us."

This was more than Duncan had bargained for, and
involuntarily he cast a wild glance around. Then he
turned again to the scarecrow who had never stopped slab-
bing away like a beaver.

"But yous is doin' most of the work?" he queried anxiously.

"Well, tarnation, pard, you might put it so. But if God
didn't give me strength, then where'd I be? So I reckon
he's doin' his bit at the shack, too!"

Further south on the trail from Tom Ryan's there were
other stopping places: there was Herbert's—or one could
put up with Clarke and Murphy, two energetic and well-
organised bachelors who seemed to take it in turn, by
weeks or months, whatever the system was—one doing
the cooking and the other all the rest of the housework.
Or there was Steve Gjerstad's well-ordered farm—and
Steve shouting "Emma! Emm-ma! Here comes Mr. Petersen from Battle River and his roan mare. Make ready
the room and hurry with supper!" And Emma going on,
as always, about "that nasty old hawk that's been at my
poor little chickens again . . . . ." She was Pennsylvania
Dutch, and it sounded to me just like "my po' lil churns."
But the little room was white and spotless, and always the
sun seemed to be shining into it.

And there was Peter Rackham—something of a newcomer himself who, after a season or two, made an expedition out to Seattle and returned with a brand-new wife,
dark-haired, flashing and buxom. Peter had a comfortable
enough farm all right, but Lord knows what sort of a picture he had painted in order to coax this large and hearty
young woman out of her city home and up to the Peace

River. Now she was lonely and felt herself wasted in this wilderness of white where few things moved, where coyotes sang at evensong, and where the great white snowy owls scratched and sidled along the roof-peak on moonlight nights, sounding from within like queer, uncanny climbing things with claws.

She was explaining all this to George Robertson and me one grey winter noonday when the mercury outside was hanging around thirty below zero. We were headed north. Our horses were in the barn, watered and fed and warm, and we were thawing out in the warm kitchen watching the preparations for our dinner. Mrs. Rackham was telling us all about city life—things we wouldn't hardly believe, she said, like elevators and moving stairways and all manner of wonders—why, they even had a heated towel rail in her home, and each member of the family a towel of a different colour—this last being directly *at* George and me who had used, each of us, the same clean towel that was hanging from a nail by the wash-bowl. Evidently we had done something wrong there—neither of us knew what. Well, someday, Mrs. Rackham went on, we'd just have to comb the hay out of our hair and go see for ourselves. Then we'd *know* something . . . . .

George grinned and asked me, in a stage whisper, if old, out-of-date London was not a back number compared with Seattle. Not wishing to stop the flow, I reached out under the table and kicked him on the shin.

"And now all I ever see is a bunch of breeds and Indians, and you hicks and hayseeds from the Battle whizzing up and down the trail in sleighs. And, Lord, I just don't like those breeds at all. Why, their faces ——." But we never heard just how horrible the breeds' faces were to Mrs. Rackham, for at that moment the door flew open, a cold grey mist swirled over the floor, and in came Peter Rackham, ushering in Sepailov, our one and only Russian from Little Prairie of Battle River, now headed south and, like us, needing a hot meal.

Sepailov was introduced; then he took a seat. The flood
of words went on and Sepailov listened intently, fixing a
basilisk, unblinking stare on Mrs. Rackham, who hardly
noticed him. Sepailov knew a lot of English in a haphazard
sort of way. Also he was a student of the dictionary and
loved long words, using them frequently and, as often as
not, getting the accent in the wrong place.

Suddenly he clapped his hands and burst into a roar of
laughter. "Ah—ha! ha! Oh-h-ho! ho! ho! So new homesteader's wife iss! You are very corpulent! Yess, indeed!"

With that, he relapsed into silence, and so did everybody
else. Dinner was served and eaten in a strained, crimson-
faced hush—like trying not to laugh in church—and as
soon as possible George and I said good-bye politely and
got going, sitting together on the driving seat, banging each
other on the back and shouting delightedly above the
jingling of the sleigh bells. Sepailov we left at the Rackhams', still staring fixedly and quite unaware that he had
said anything out of the ordinary. Very likely that, or some
similar remark, may have been the recognised compliment
to a new bride in that old, traditional Russia from which
he had come.

You could always count on Sepailov to come up with
something fantastic in the way of language. The July following that episode at the Rackhams' I found myself chairman of a settlers' meeting at the store. I forget the precise
object of the meeting, but that doesn't matter; we soon got
sidetracked, anyway. I called on Slim Jackson to read the
minutes of the last meeting—which he did. After the usual
amount of backchat we got them passed, and also a surplus
of seven dollars from the sports fund disposed of—to Pat
Macaulay who was fortunate enough to draw the king of
clubs. The cards were the happy suggestion of the chairman, who wished to avoid an uproar, and who also hoped
that he might himself prove to be the winner.

At this point the strains of the Red River jig, played
softly on a fiddle, like angel music, began to be heard. We

hardly noticed the playing at first, and yet, like bagpipes in the distance, it made itself felt. Moccasined feet began to keep time on the rough plank floor . . . . .

Our secretary was the first to wake up: he made a dive over the counter and grabbed something and lifted. Up into view came a diminutive half-breed, Louis Savoy, known as "the Bishop", clutching a brand-new fiddle, part of Joe Bissett's stock-in-trade, which he had been quietly playing out of sight there on the floor. Slim took the fiddle and bow from the Bishop's grasp and laid them on the counter. Then, down the dark, cool alleyway between the saddles and the coils of rope and the kegs of nails and staples, he administered to the Bishop the bum's rush, landing him outside on the sunlit prairie with these parting words: "This ain't a swarry, Bishop. This is politics, and you'll mind that another time."

As the laughter subsided I became aware that somebody was orating: Sepailov, of course, the man with the single-track mind—he had seized the golden moment while everybody was laughing at Slim and the Bishop. And now there was no holding him.

What was he after this time?

Everything, it seemed, and all at once. He was urging us all to join the new political party, the United Farmers of Alberta, now in power at Edmonton; to fix up a cemetery; and to build a community hall.

"Joining U.F.A. so shall get in ground floor and share in all patronage and dirty work to benefit of all, and so get road to outside and bridge over Battle, no more to upset wagon in river when navigation shall be in tumult and maybe daredevil homesteader drowned. All voting in same direction, so shall be listened to at Edmonton, and no longer stupid nonentities stampeding to every point of compass like pack of fools lost in bush . . . . . And cemetery necessary iss, for shall die and be buried in ground unconsecrate or shall go bad in hot weather on Peace River trail ——"

Here Bob Henderson broke in. He opposed this cemetery business on the grounds that Sepailov was away ahead of development, and we'd far better wait till somebody died and not meet trouble half-way. "And if Sepailov objects to becoming offensive, he'd better die in a cold snap so that we can get him out frozen."

But Sepailov was like an eel—he was off on the community hall trail now, leaving Bob high and dry in the cemetery.

"Community hall for civilisation iss, for so shall have place where all may meet, from oldest of feeblest old men to youngest of young flappers and all be blessed amity. And shall have concerts and debates instead of only wild dances with floods of hooch and 'alaman a bootjack, promenade a horseback', and 'swing old squaw in a four hands half', and have another drink and ride home and say you have had fine moochigan with pack of breeds who are scum of earth and ——"

At this point Sepailov was interrupted by shouts of "Order! Order!" and "Sit down!" Bedlam supervened, and I tried to bring Sepailov to earth by hammering on the counter—and finally succeeded in so doing by bellowing "Hey!!" The feeling of the meeting was with me when I pointed out that the speaker's last remark was both irrelevant and in bad taste.

"Well, I have been well dressed up by Mr. Chairman, and my tongue ran away with me so I taste bad to all now. I had finished, anyway, so shall sit down." Which he did, with a bow, only to rise again hastily. While he had been speaking, his closest neighbours had managed to substitute two spools of barbed wire for the keg that Sepailov had originally adopted as his seat for the meeting.

But it was when we dealt with the thorny subject of the road that we really raised the roof. There we were—an island, cut off from the outside world, and with all the drawbacks of an island as well as its advantages. Something, it was vaguely felt, ought to be done about this, but beyond that there was no agreement. Big Prairie wanted the road, when it should reach out to us from the south, to run north along the section line that crossed the Battle at Joe Bissett's crossing. Little Prairie, and all those who lived south of the river with the exception of Sepailov, wanted the road to run a mile or so further east, through their lovely green lake of grass and grain, and then over Nord's bridge and straight on northwards to hit the Battle at the old crossing—just the way Johnny Arnold and I had galloped through the summer darkness in quest of the rum.

Feelings ran high. Sepailov was in league with Joe Bissett and with those of Big Prairie who were road-minded. This to the Scandinavians of Little Prairie was rank treason, and for it they would gladly have shoved Sepailov under the river ice. Then there were those on both sides of the river who were doing very nicely as things were and who didn't particularly care if a road never came. They had what they wanted, the things they had come so far to seek: freedom from interference, the sense of achievement and adventure, the pleasure of building a new outpost on the edge of the unknown. And there was the game, the trapline, the free range, the building logs and the corral rails for the taking—where else could men live like this in this cramped century? Why kill it all just for the sake of some vague "progress", which might prove to be only change?

These were the men always to be found on the frontier, swept forward on the first lapping of the first wave of a rising tide. They knew what lay behind them and they could see what a road would bring: schools, a bridge over the Battle that would be a major job of construction and so a tax burden, a post office, perhaps a police post and, with it, regulations and restrictions where now there were none. And for all these things which they did not want they would be made to pay. And the game would be gone, and every sod-busting farmer who had mined out his arid acres in southern Saskatchewan would be up on the Battle, turning good grazing upside-down, starting up another mess of weeds and dust.

Could we have gazed into some crystal ball we should have seen also the Mackenzie Highway running through our quiet prairies, and a railroad following it, feeling its way north towards the ores of Pine Point. The thunderous din of enormous trailer-trucks, freighting drilling and mining equipment to Hay River for the Lower Mackenzie, for Yellowknife, for any place where anything might be needed all the way from Fort Reliance to Aklavik—all this was to come. Fortunately, perhaps, for our peace of mind, this knowledge was hidden from us then.

And now we, the restless ones, the nomads and the hunters of that pioneer settlement, have gone, taking our way of life with us. But the grey-faced, dusty truck-driver of today—does he ever catch a glimpse down below the roaring highway, in the grass-grown ruts of the old trail near McCracken's, of a ghostly, speeding democrat, drawn by a pinto and a bay, driven by a laughing young man in an enormous sombrero? Or does he ever hear, in the darkness, shouts and laughter and the frenzied pounding of hoofs—some phantom party riding homewards hell for leather, well primed with "floods of hooch", from some wild moochigan?

But in those far-off days a road to Great Slave Lake was nothing but a silly, impossible dream. All we thought of then was a road to Peace River town; and periodically we would get at this problem, hammer and tongs, in Joe Bissett's store, with the opposing factions pulling hard in opposite directions, and the contented hunters and trappers doing their utmost to muddy the troubled waters. I find some account of one of these meetings in an old letter of mine, written from my homestead to a friend:

"We had a settlers' meeting at the store the other day on the subject of roads. Slim Jackson was chairman and I was elected secretary for the occasion. The Vikings, the Scandinavians from Little Prairie, turned up in force

dressed in stout mackinaw and in their best fur hats—
beaver, muskrat, mink, and two with wolves' heads. With
their yellow beards and long moustaches and with the up-
turned ear-flaps standing out from their heads, they looked,
for all the world, like Kipling's Vikings in *Puck of Pook's
Hill*—the Winged Hats. Our Slav, Sepailov, was the main
cause of the trouble. He orated like Cicero and set forth
with many flourishes the Big Prairie view as to the proper
location of the northbound road (*when* it reaches us, which,
I imagine, will be in the pretty dim future), winding up
with: 'And now shall sit down, but first shall say, God help
the King—for, in law, road of King iss, so thanks must be
to Caesar for Caesar's road!'

"Seizing on this muddled peroration, Ole Olstad rose to
ask Sepailov if he'd remembered to write to King George
to thank him for that moose he'd shot, a couple of weeks
back, in the bush near Bozeman's cabin—all game being,
like the roads, the King's. (Laughter and uproar.)

"Then Slim (who was definitely a south-of-the-river
man) in a weak moment allowed himself to be drawn into
an argument with Sepailov;—and in less than five minutes
everybody was bellowing at his neighbour—for the simple
reason that if you bellowed at anybody further away he
couldn't hear you. This continued—and if there was ever a
lull the Winged Hats, with their deep, booming voices,
broke in and shattered it. They alone knew what they
wanted—Sepailov's blood—but they were in a Berserk rage
and words were almost beyond their compass. Old John
Petersen, a man slow to speech, was only heard once, but
he was one of the few who gained a hearing. His voice
would quell Babel itself. 'Your damned trail, Sepailov,' he
roared, 'is that crooked it would break a snake's back to
follow it.' After which profound observation, made with a
quid of chewing tobacco in his mouth, he sat down and
glowered."

There the letter passed to other things. But with the
odd lull, and with oil deftly thrown on to the flames by

the hunter-trapper fraternity, we kept up this outrageous din throughout the winter afternoon until twilight laid its dusky shadows on the wind-wrinkled snow. Then teams were hitched to sleighs, and cinches were tightened on saddles, and we drove and rode away with a sense of duty done. What sort of a record I, as secretary, kept of the proceedings I do not recollect and cannot imagine. One thing, however, is certain: there can have been forwarded to Edmonton no coherent, unanimous request for a road. Our oasis of Time was safe, at least for a while longer.

CHAPTER V

Itching Foot

It's all very well for me to sit here at my desk and try to write objectively about "the restless ones, the nomads"; but, to be quite honest, I was one of them myself; and for me, after three years on the homestead, the signposts pointed north.

Not that there was anything wrong with the Battle— far from it. But I had camped by the Peace River and watched it flowing on into the North,* seen the riverboats go by, asked a thousand questions and listened to men talking of far northern places. And I had got from Ottawa the maps of the big rivers—Athabasca, Slave, Mackenzie, Liard. On winter nights I would spend hours with these maps spread out on the big table in the cabin—completely absorbed and far away from Battle River.

Two coal-oil lamps, burning clearly and steadily, would hold down two corners of the map in use. The nearer corners would be weighted down with books—Sir William Butler's "*The Wild North Land*" perhaps; or Warburton Pike's "*The Barren Grounds of Northern Canada*". And, if either of those two classics was needed for reference, its place would be taken by Pirsson's "*Rocks and Rock Minerals*", or Norman Douglas' "*South Wind*"—or anything else out of a small but variegated library. At strategic points on the map there would stand, flickering a little as

* "The Buffalo Head," pp. 70-72.

I moved, a couple of candles in their home-made wooden holders.

All would be brightly lit and snug—and no sound except the cheerful woofle of the fire in the box-heater; the pong of a log drawing away from a spiked window-frame as it shrank beneath the dead cold of forty or fifty below zero; or, if it was warmer and the wind was blowing, the hiss of crystallized, drifting snow, scratching past the door like blown sand.

The names on those maps fascinated me and I followed them downstream, northwards, picturing to myself every feature. There was the Chenal des Quatre Fourches—I could almost see my canoe following that channel in the marshland, nosing its tortuous way through the mazes of the Athabasca Delta towards Fort Chipewyan. Wildfowl without end, de Meldt had told me, summered down in those winding waterways.

And the Slave Rapids—there, between the two candlesticks—one of them bore the name of Pelican Rapid. That would be a sight to see: a colony of those nightmarish birds nesting in the northern wilderness!

"A very queer bird is the pelican.
Its beak can hold more than its belly can."

Well, could it? Was that sound natural history? Anyway, the Slave River dropped twenty-seven feet at the Pelican Rapid, and the Slave was *twice* as big as the Peace—a thunderous roar of creaming waters!

And there was Lobstick Island at the outlet of Great Slave Lake into the Mackenzie. I knew what a lobstick was: a spruce with a tuft of green branches at the top, stripped of all its lower branches—a landmark. But what in the world was a demi-charge? Some sort of a rapid, but what?

Away down the Mackenzie, beyond Providence, beyond the fast stretch that was called the Line, the left bank ended abruptly in Gros Cap—the great cape that stands above the meeting of two great rivers, the Mackenzie and the Liard. It was the Liard that caught and held my imagination: the River of the Mountain the old fur-traders had called it long ago—the river that reached far back into the West, beyond the Rockies, right to the Coast Range. Some of the fellows from the Battle trapped on rivers that flowed into the Liard. They went away back, northwestward, in the fall with packhorses, and when they reached their traplines, that was home for the winter—though precisely *where* "home" was, in Alberta or British Columbia, they did not know. And they certainly did not care.

Far up the Liard there was a stretch of canyon country where the fur-traders had travelled once upon a time, but where men no longer went. Surely a trapline in that forbidden fastness would be the trapline of a dream? And surely a canoe, handled with care, could find its way into those distant mountains? One would have to find out a few things about canoes, of course . . . And I pushed the two candlesticks westwards, up the Liard, into the foothills. Obviously the going was tough in those parts: the candlelight shone now on names like Hell Gate, Devil's Portage and Whirlpool Canyon. And Rapid of the Drowned . . . . .

The years on the homestead had been spent mainly alone, learning how to do things without help, devising ways and means of shifting heavy weights, and of raising into position logs that were beyond any human strength. They had also been spent in learning *not* to do fat-headed things—a knowledge that is more valuable in the North than any other. Two examples of that sort of lesson will suffice. Each was learnt the hard way—and here follows lesson number one.

When cutting the logs for my barn I camped right on the job—in the bush about seven miles from home, coming home once or twice to clean up, bake more bread, and so forth. Camp was in the midst of a dead forest—beautiful fire-killed jackpine with the blackened bark now shed away from it, of all sizes up to two feet in diameter, sound as a bell. It was wintertime; the snow was knee-deep in the

bush and the weather was clear, cold and still—hanging
around zero to twenty below. I made my usual type of
camp: a lean-to tarpaulin shelter with a long fire of this
splendid wood in front of it. There I was most comfortable,
cutting my logs and skidding trails by day, lying reading
by my fire in the evenings until bedtime.

One day the weather warmed up till it got above freezing. I sweated quarts, and by quitting time the Chinook
had begun to blow. It increased in fury, howling mournfully through the lifeless forest. Dead trees, leaning against
each other, sawed up and down in the wind till the quiet
hillside resounded to the squalling of these giant fiddles.
Now and then one heard in the distance the crash of a
falling tree. But it was too late to do anything about that
now: it was just as unsafe to move in the dark as to stay put.

The near miss came just as I was dropping off to sleep—
lying in my eiderdown, drowsily watching the glow of the
embers and listening to the wind. There was a splintering
crash from behind the lean-to. Then a thud that shook the
ground, together with minor smashes. Several things hummed through the air like bullets, and a twelve-foot length of
a six-inch pine whirled into sight over the top of the lean-to
and landed in the snow beyond the fire. Then silence once
more except for the wind.

That was a two-foot pine, about sixty-feet long, falling.
It had missed the lean-to by seven paces. Camp was moved
next morning into the green timber. The demonstration
had been a great success and the lesson had been absorbed:
Never make Camp in an Old Burn.

The second lesson was taught to me by The Urchin. I
had lent my big wood auger to my Norwegian friend,
Andrew Clauson—and now I needed it. So I saddled The
Urchin and rode down to Andrew's place (he was the
owner of one of the two trees) on Little Prairie. I was out
of eggs, and so I took with me an empty sugar sack.

The wood auger was about two feet long, a formidable
piece of metal with its sharp corkscrew point and shaft.

I got it from Andrew and I tied it solidly behind my saddle, point to the off side in case I should catch my leg on it when mounting. I also got a dozen eggs from Andrew and he handed me the bag with the eggs in it after I was in the saddle. Then he opened his gate and I rode quietly away. We had been talking and Andrew had failed to notice anything dangerous in the way I had tied the auger.

By that time my homestead was fenced, and there was a gate in the south-west corner. On top of the heavy tamarack gatepost I had nailed a short piece of board. This made a sort of shelf on which I could deposit any parcel I was carrying before dismounting from The Urchin—with special reference to eggs. Usually this worked well enough, but not on this morning. For some reason The Urchin was all up in the air, and every time she saw my hand reach stealthily out with the egg-sack she would break into a mad gallop, and away we would career over the prairie—only to return after a fight and a lot of bad language, and start all over again. Three times round at that game was enough, and I decided to calm the horse down as far as possible and then jump lightly off, holding the eggs.

So I rode The Urchin round a bit, halting her now and then. Then I stopped her near the gate and, holding the eggs close to me with my right hand, put my left hand on the horn and swung out of the saddle. It was a good swing and it would have worked like a charm, only I had forgotten the wood auger. I drove the point of that clean through the leg of my old khaki drill trousers—and there I was, fixed: left foot still in the stirrup, right leg impaled and stuck behind the saddle, and a dozen new-laid eggs clutched to my chest. I should have dropped the eggs and tried to get back into the saddle, but I was so mad that I just hung on.

It took about one fiftieth of a second for The Urchin to realise that something was not as it should have been. She gave one magnificent buck. By the grace of God my trouser leg tore and set me free. I executed an involuntary sideways

somersault in mid-air and fell flat, face downwards, on to
a large and very active ant-heap, still clutching the eggs
as a drowning man clutches at a straw. The ant-heap
softened my fall—but what a mess! Lying there, winded
and gasping, on top of what had been a dozen eggs—and
on about a million ants, each one of which was now firmly
convinced that there really *was* Pie in the Sky! Egg-yolk
and ants again! And a fool of a horse bucking about the
landscape, trying to kick the saddle off . . . . .

Still, that was a fortunate escape. With a pair of stout
new pants on, I could have hung there and been smashed
and kicked to pieces. Or the wood auger could have driven
into my leg and torn a large-size hole in it—and perhaps a
leg broken as well. But, no. Once again lucky. And once
again the lesson had got home. This time it ran as follows:
*Think, especially when you are Alone, what the Conse-
quences may be of any Action, however Simple.*

I carried that lesson with me into the Nahanni country;
and believe me, it's one that it pays to remember!

One evening of my last September on the homestead I
saw a rider coming up the slope from my south-west gate.
I was busy fixing things for supper. It had been the day in
the week that I devoted to the chores: cutting wood, clean-
ing the cabin, trimming lamps, baking bread, making
raisin-and-apple pies, washing a shirt or two, sharpening
tools, doing anything else that lay around clamouring to
be done—a devil of a day, the price that a bachelor pays
for his freedom. A twelve-hour day, and now I was ready
for my supper and who was this who was coming, riding
slowly out of the trees by the gate and across the tawny
autumn grass?

It proved to be John Petersen from Little Prairie on his
horse, Peanut. We tied Peanut in the barn and old John
came in and sat down in the big armchair and looked
around.

"By golly, Petersen," he said to me, "you have it all so
well fixed you are surely comfortable here. And the smell

of new bread—that is yust like home. You have a fine homestead here, now you have found water on this hill. Many
a man would have taken this land but all were scared of
the water." And with that he lapsed into silence, while I
went ahead laying out supper for two. The crisp, golden
loaves were just out of the oven and I wiped them lightly
over with melted butter. The smell became even more
delicious and John and I sniffed it again, looked at each
other, and nodded approvingly. Then I went down into the
cellar for eggs, and when I came up John was deep in a
stray copy of *The Morning Post,* a conservative London
newspaper, now defunct . . . . .

His rumbling voice, with a note of anxiety in it, broke
in on the sizzling of the ham and eggs. He had been reading about the new proposals of Lloyd George's government
regarding the simplification of land tenures and transfers
in Britain; and old John was not by any means one who
thought much of change just for change's sake. If things
suited him he liked them to stay the way they were. Now
he wanted to know whether these Lloyd Georgian land
proposals, if they should ever become law, would have
effect in Canada. I told him, no.

"Well", he said, "I am a citizen not only of Canada but
of the whole Empire now, and I am not so certain. But,
by Yesus, I will *make* certain! I will draw out my title deeds
from the bank, and then, if any doggoned son of a bachelor
comes to tell me that my land is not mine, I will shoot him
dead . . . . . Thank you. You are very kind and I am hungry
and your bread smells yust as good as any wooman's bread.
I will be glad to eat." And with Lloyd George and his
shady schemes thus provided for, we sat down to a tremendous supper.

On the edge of the wilderness it was always considered
bad manners to ask a man the reason for his journey; so
naturally I treated this evening visit as a matter of course,
though inwardly I was wondering. But over coffee, and
through a haze of tobacco smoke, John came out into the

open. It seemed that word had got around that I was thinking of throwing a canoe into the Peace River and taking a
trip north. This had been discussed on Little Prairie, and
now John Peterson had come as an ambassador from the
Winged Hats: they wished me not to go.

"Petersen, I tell you—it is foolish to go into such a wild
places. You do not know what you meet with there—rapids,
storms, a damn bear clean your camp out and smash your
canoe—and then where are you? You think you know this
country, and indeed you have learnt much, but you do not
yet know how bad she can be. No—you stay here. We need
you. Many will be coming here—you will see all settled,
away beyond McCracken's, right to those hills where now
you see nothing. And we need you because you are south-
of-the-river and you think as we do—but you speak better
English, and when we want a thing said you will be our
man, you will speak for us."

"It's about all I can do to speak for myself, John. How
about Slim Jackson? He's south-of-the-river and a lot
handier with his tongue."

"No. You are near us and we will have you. Now, I tell
you what we will do. You have a fine homestead, all fixed
up. You take a trip outside and you find yourself a woomans
and you marry her and bring her back—English, Canadian, maybe you find a Swede, what does it matter? We
look after your place for you and it shall be yust as good
when you come back as if you are here."

"Pretty lonely for a woman, John?"

"No. You will see: settlement will come. And besides,
we have thought of that. *We will see that you get the post
office!* There now! Always, with the post office, there is
something for the woomans to do—keep track of the stamps,
read the postcards, talk to the mans when they come riding
for their mail. That, and a few schickens to mind—that is
not loneliness. She will be happy . . . . ."

God's truth, but I felt honoured that I had been asked
to stay: I, a greenhorn newcomer, helped, taught—and now

wanted. And not only honoured but deeply touched. It was hard to have to tell old John that the thing—I mean the lure of the North—had made a lodgment in my head and that I had to go. "But I'll be back," I said, after we had talked the matter up and down and inside out for an hour or so.

"Maybe you will be back, but I do not think it will be for long. In English you say, 'Far pastures look green.' Some see it that way, and maybe you are one of them. But I tell you now, Petersen—in all the North you will never find any pasture so green as is our Little Prairie. Yet you will always think there is yust one more Little Prairie, further on some place, maybe yust over the next hill. So you had better go. But we will look after your place for you till you come again—as I have said."

And so they did, while I went away to the South Nahanni River.

Part Two

NORTHWARD HO!

1927 - 1929

Birch canoes travelling on rippling keels,
Paddles a-flash in arms that never fail
The long day through. The echoing canyon peals
With river songs. Comes evening primrose pale;
The North-Lights weave on night's star-dusted veil
Patterns of fire, flame-pennons finely spun.
Now camps are made and wood-smoke rises frail.
Upon these roads are high adventures won.

"A Ballad of Roads" *by* CROSBIE GARSTIN

CHAPTER VI

Life with a Dog Team

Dogs pervaded the atmosphere in those March days— dogs and a variegated outfit that cluttered every room of the little house in Edmonton, Alberta. We were going north over the old trail to the Sikanni Chief River—the trail that, sixteen years later, was to become the first leg of the Alaska Highway, but which, in '28, was still the happy-go-lucky, half-forgotten back door to the Liard and Lower Mackenzie Rivers. We were going that way, over the "Long Portage" from the Peace to the Sikanni Chief, so as to reach Liard River waters in May and to avoid the ice which would block the Great Slave Lake, on the main Mackenzie waterway, till July. We were going up into the Mackenzie Mountains, through the canyons of the South Nahanni, to hunt, trap, and look for a deposit of placer gold, found about 1905 and then lost again, and subsequently adorned with a tangled story of murder and sudden death till it had become a legend.

Above all we were going efficiently. I had just put in a season alone on the Nahanni, and Gordon Matthews had hunted, traded and driven dogs for several years in the cold eastern country on the shores of Hudson's Bay. With these things behind us we rather harped on the efficiency factor: no haywire, shaganappi outfit for this trip, we told each other: if anybody knew how to profit from previous experience of the North and from past mistakes, it was us—and this time we were going to show the world!

Well, well, well! Live and learn!

And so, day by day, the outfit grew. Canoes, and heavier stores lay at the wholesalers; weapons, ammunition and personal gear were added to the chaos in the house. Two years supply of tooth paste for two men is no mean item, even cutting it fine. Then came a first aid kit and elements of a medicine chest; the druggist was impressed, but not half so much as we were—one twenty-foot Freight canoe and one sixteen-foot Prospector could not be stretched indefinitely.

The dogs, five of them, big strong Alsatians, lived in the yard. They were one family: father, mother and three sons, and savagely inclined to all but us. In the afternoons we would hitch them up to the long oak sled and run through the quiet streets, down the hill by the Parliament Buildings and on to the frozen Saskatchewan River. Then hard up the river for half an hour, back again in the red light of the sunset, and home to Mamselle who would be howling her head off in the yard. She was about to present us with a litter of pups and so was out of these afternoon jaunts, much to her disgust.

That was the trouble with those dogs—their excitable temperament and the awful row they kicked up—and our main worry was to get them out of Edmonton before some infuriated neighbour should poison them. In the meantime they sang to their hearts content—and then came the memorable day when we came home to lunch and found the gate open and the dogs gone. Out we tore, blasting on dog whistles, searching the frozen streets, falling foul of the city police—no luck.

I came back and found Gordon gloomily at the lunchtime bread and cheese. "Have some beer," he said. "I've phoned the pound and the police. They've probably pulled down a couple of children somewhere—better drink all the beer up before we're arrested. And have a look under my bed— Mamselle always meant to have them there if she could. Not that I care, now."

I looked. Mamselle seemed very pleased with herself, but it was difficult to see just how large her family was. Just as I was looking, a crash of sound—melody, it seemed, for once—heralded the return of the truant pack. Hastily we slammed gates and doors and hitched them up for their run on the river.

Train day was March 8th and zero hour found us at the station with the five Alsatians, the two best pups in an old lunch basket, and a beautiful Husky, a child's pet, who had taken second prize in the Edmonton show. I had added him to the zoo and he followed me quietly, almost timidly. Not so the wolf pack which strained from Gordon's hands like a five pointed star, hoarse and dribbling with excitement.

The Edmonton Dunvegan and British Columbia Railway was to carry us to the end of steel at Spirit River, Alberta, and it didn't seem to appreciate the honour we were doing it. The conductor—a caricature of a Toby Jug—and the baggage man, were both hostile. "You can't put them dogs in here," was their refrain. "We got no place for them." It was no time for discussion; "Is that so?" said Gordon. "You watch!" I jumped into the baggage car and Gordon thrust the chains into the hands of one of Edmonton's leading citizens, a kindly and an upright man, who had come to see us off and was now probably regretting it. The dogs swirled round him and there he stood, tall and dignified and unprotesting, chained hand and foot upon the snow.

Up came the pups. "Not in here you can't ——" began the baggage man, but his oration ended as Mamselle was boosted up to me, and he climbed with agility on to a stack of crates. "Keep that bitch off for the love of Mike," he pleaded; and then, "Oh, God, here they come!"

The dog team took possession of the car, and we threw their tickets and our own on to the snow for the benefit of the Toby Jug, and waved goodbye to Mr. Evans. Simultaneously, the engineer, who must have been getting impatient, started the train with a shattering jerk that threw the baggage man off his perch. He lit, shouting for help, between Mamselle and Poilu,—a poor place even for an emergency landing; so we boosted him up onto his crates again and told him to stay there till we got things fixed up a bit. The Jug's face appeared through a sliding door and was understood to be bawling something about "sleeping car tickets." "Go and chase yourself," Gordon told him; and he went, just in time as Sammy and Yukon fetched up against the steel door with a frustrated slap. Spud, the Husky, was curled up quietly in a corner, his tail swept over his nose, watching quietly. The remaining Alsatian, a lightly built, coyote type and a strong thief, was trying to work his way into a box of New Brunswick kippers. A fight was going on in the pup basket, which was upside down.

"Take your time, fellers," said the baggage man from his perch. "I ain't worryin' about my job—I got my wife and family to consider, and I never had no alibi like this before. Let that coyote dog have all the kippers he can hold; let's have one sweet tempered hound in the bunch just to remind us of home: the railroad'll call it civil commotion or maybe an act of God." And he went on to tell us just how far removed this "animal act" that we had staged in his baggage car was from being either of these things.

That day and night to Spirit River will never be forgotten by either of us. Nor will it ever be clearly remembered. On egg shaped wheels and over a springy and uneven track the old E. D. and B. C. lurched its way northwestward towards the Peace River. Somehow we fed, at stopping places along the line, and somehow we slept—one of us always with the dogs to prevent some swaying pile of crates from collapsing on them, and to give the baggage man a hand. He had been properly introduced to each dog after we had chained them up, and was now bearing his lot with patience and amiability. Not so the Jug. He had lost face, and he knew it, and it rankled.

Train day (there were two trains a week) had brought

its usual quota of the idle and the curious to Spirit River station. Train days as a rule ran pretty much to pattern, but this one was different—our dumb friends took care of that. Securely laced into the canvas carry-all of the dog sled, and with the pups raising Cain beneath her, Mamselle screamed monotonously. Sammy got loose and raced up the tracks after a toboggan containing a small boy who began to yell, and drawn by two nondescript collies who bolted. The toboggan upset, the small boy was flung out into the snow, and the collies started a private war on their own. Then Sammy arrived and took a hand—all of which did us no good socially. The Husky sat quietly, shifting his feet a little on the ice—missing nothing, saying nothing. The rest wrapped themselves and their chains around me, and a little, insignificant sort of a man standing beside me kept repeating in a gabbling monotone the words: "It's a doggone scandal, that's what it is—a doggone scandal." One way and another, the general atmosphere was becoming hostile.

A young provincial policeman came to the rescue and got the key of a disused grist mill by the station. Into this he helped us to move the outfit and the dogs. "They look like a nice team," he said, "But I'd get them out of town first thing tomorrow. They need work, and if they kick up a row like that *all* the time, people'll start to get sore. And you couldn't blame them."

You certainly couldn't. The people of Spirit River never forgot that visitation. Indeed, the whole of the Fort St. John country remembered it for years to come. Twenty-five years afterwards I fell into conversation with a man who was selling Indian sweaters by the Cowichan River on Vancouver Island. He had come from the Peace River country, he told me. Did I know it? I did—and, what was more, I had gone through the western part of it once with a dog team. His face lit up. "You don't mean to tell me you were one of those two guys—say, I'll just have to hear about this, here and now! To think that I missed seeing it! But I didn't get to those parts till two years after you went through. I heard about it, of course, but . . . . ."

What it is, to be a part of history!

Night fell on Spirit River. An uneasy peace reigned so long as we were with the dogs, and all was silent as we walked up the street to the Chinaman's to get some supper. Half way through we noticed him standing outside, listening. He came in shaking his head, "I tinkee damn dog he gettee loose he kill section man's kid—eatum. Maybe kill eat all Spillit Liver—lestaurlant finish, I go bloke." Hurriedly we choked down our coffee, grabbed a slice of pie apiece and fled back to the frozen darkness of the grist mill.

We breakfasted in relays in the morning and hitched up in the first light. The pups had to be inside the carry-all, and Mamselle had to be inside with them to keep them fed and warm. Her head was thrust, serpent like, through the lacings and dangled, mournful and uncomplaining, over the side. The rim of the sun heaved itself over the horizon and turned the grey silence of the frozen fields into a blaze of diamonds. The toboggan pointed west, and the team lay quietly in its harness.

The young policeman came to see us off and we stood talking for a little while. "The Nahanni," said the policeman, enviously. "I'd give something to be coming with you." Far down the white line of the road, as he was talking, a dark shape hove into view, followed by a second and then a third. Suddenly, as if jerked to their feet by an invisible string, the team leaped into action. They hit the trail with the pent-up energy of two idle days, and Gordon, who had been leaning on the handles of the sled, was yanked off his feet and taken from us like a marionette being dragged from the stage. Ceremony was at an end, and I gave the policeman a parting wave and tore after my struggling partner, who had regained his feet and was now riding on the flying sled, and cursing the dogs with imagination and vigour. Had he seen the disaster that was in the making he might have done something about it, upset the toboggan or something—but he was still concerned merely with bolting dogs. I tried to shout a warning, but the uproar of the pups, excited by the squeal of the snow beneath the runners, and the screams that came from Mamselle's dangling, seemingly dismembered head, defeated me, and the ghastly outfit swept on.

The grain tanks were each drawn by four horses and the teamsters sat high, rimed and frosted, and muffled to the eyes against the thin east wind and the cold of 20 degrees below zero. Faced with the horrid zoo that rushed towards them the leading horses were plainly becoming anxious. Tails in the air and crab-stepping sideways, they sidled towards the bank on their right and began to climb, in spite of their teamster's frantic efforts to balance the load, and unmoved by his muffled cries and threats. And, with the tipping of the sleighs, a golden fan of grain flooded across the road, just in time to receive the impact of the dog sled and bring it to a standstill. The bitch's screams ceased abruptly, the dogs sat down and wagged their tails in a pleased sort of way, the pups were silent, and several people said "My God!"

Starting on a conciliatory note, the conference between Gordon and the teamster—who continued to sit like some strange god of the harvest, half submerged in a mound of wheat—quickly took a belligerent turn. "Hauled it all the way from Fort St. John, and what do I have to meet but a goddam menagerie, and over goes the whole flaming works, right in sight of the elevators!" Gordon was sensitive about his dogs. "And driving those old crowbaits of yours the way you do," he countered, "you're damn lucky to have got this far without upsetting . . . . ." Our efforts to repair the damage were in vain and the war clouds were darkening, when suddenly intervention came from the dogs. Unnoticed, and clawing their way slowly forward through the barrier of wheat, they came out onto firm snow like a cork out of a champagne bottle. Away they went! Yipe,

Yipe, Yipe went the pups! Mamselle got her head inside the lashings and the uproar of a family fight inside the toboggan faded away into the distance. All in all, it seemed to be time for us to be getting after them.

We were never popular along the road through that pioneer farming country to Fort St. John, and usually we were in trouble. Unbidden, we attended for one brief moment a pig-killing, and things were looking black when some angel sent across Poilu's nose a piebald cat which had the grace to flee towards the open gate, and we found ourselves again upon our road—in, out, just like the clowns in a pantomime. At nights we slept in vast, cavernous stopping places among the whiskered teamsters of the grain haul, cooking on the red hot stove, eating on our bunks back in the shadows, and listening to our pack of unloved reprobates raising Cain in some loose box or outbuilding. Everybody was glad to see the last of us in those early days —everybody except one golden Scandinavian girl in the little hamlet of Rolla. "Oh, the lovely dogs!" she cried. "Yust make them stop till I get my camera." But Poilu had spotted a collie up the trail, and we were far away before our corn-haired Freya could return.

This sort of Flying Dutchman existence obviously could not last for ever. The dogs had calmed down and were working well in harness by the time we overtook our outfit, which had preceded us loaded on two returning freighters' sleighs. For a change we hitched the toboggan to one of the sleighs, chained the two most unruly dogs to the other sleigh and turned Spud, Poilu and Sammy loose to follow as they pleased. There and then, on the steep descent to the Kiskatinaw River, the fights began.

It may have been that Spud walked a shade too close to the toboggan—too close to Mamselle. That could have been the trouble—but Poilu had evidently had his eye on Spud for some time, and his onslaught was one of appalling savagery, only equalled by the ferocity with which the children's pet countered. Locked together they rolled across

the road, and over the edge on to the steep snow slope that
ran down to the river. Sammy joined in for the honour of
the family and Gordon and I followed, Gordon brandishing
a long dog driver's whip. The first swipe landed fair and
square on Sammy, the only innocent member of the party,
and precisely at that moment I caught my moccasin on a
snag and fell heavily on the victim of the whip, knocking
the wind out of him and getting a stranglehold. That settled
Sammy. The fracas was travelling rapidly down hill and
the footing was bad, and with his second effort Gordon just
missed cutting his own throat. Winding up for a prodigious
third, he tripped over a stunted willow, passed at a staggering run clean through the battle and measured his length,
face downwards in the snow, which began instantly to melt
around him in a thin, blue haze of profanity. Before he
could get up the fight rolled over him, leaving a trail of
blood in the snow, and fell the last five feet onto the river
ice where it continued unabated. Up above, on the grade,
the two McLeod brothers, the freighters, had stopped the
sleighs. They had a grandstand seat for the show, and,
judging by their cheers and laughter, they were enjoying
it to the full.

That was the first of many times that we had to tear the
contestants apart, chain them to trees or to moving sleighs,
and lick our own wounds afterwards. The place names of
those gory skirmishes echo down the years like the honours
on some war-torn battle flag—Taylor Flats, Charlie Lake,
Nig Creek, Blueberry River . . . . . Each fight had some
distinctive feature, but all took place in some maddeningly
inaccessible spot—under a sleigh, in down timber, or in
thick willow brush, where the whip lash could not come.
Usually there was nothing for it but to wade in and drag
the warriors apart, and that frequently involved the two of
us pulling on opposite ends of a living chain of dog, hoisted
waist high off the ground and holding only by two sets of
teeth. Finally something would have to give: a state of
armed truce would prevail again, and the two grisly appari-

tions would hobble onwards, as close to one another as they dared, with torn cheeks and ears, slashed legs and eyes almost closed—each with a chip on his shoulder.

We crossed the frozen Peace River and came to Fort St. John where, at Finch's store, we trans-shipped our load onto Clay Martin's sleighs. Clay was to freight the outfit over the Long Portage to the Sikanni Chief River, and this he did, capably and well, and without incident apart from the usual run of trail and camp life. The last outpost homestead lay behind us, so that from here on we were free of man-made hazards in the shape of grain tanks and pig stickings, and we lay in peace at nights round the camp fire, under sheltering spruce and close to some icebound stream.

Our mode of travel was simple. Clay started with two sleighs, each drawn by two horses—one sleigh carrying nothing but horse feed in the shape of oats and oat sheaves, and the other loaded with our outfit, more horse feed, and finally the two canoes, nested one inside the other and lashed upside down on top of the load. The dog toboggan would normally have been lashed on top of the first sleigh, had we not had to provide some sort of safe accommodation for the puppies. The toboggan was made of oak and had oak handles, much like those of a walking plough. It was about eight feet long and eighteen inches wide, and a full size canvas "carry-all" was laced on to it, having vertical canvas walls and, to cover the load on top, folding flaps which could be laced together down the centre. Into this carry-all we put the pup basket, and into it we also laced Mamselle, to her intense disgust, to care for her offspring and keep them warm. She could get her head through the lacings, but no more; when we moved it dangled mournfully over the side—and, when we travelled at speed, it screamed monotonously from its queer, upside-down position. The five working dogs were hitched strung-out in single file, Poilu in the lead. The harness was simple —each dog had a collar, much after the fashion of a horse-

collar, and a backstrap and bellyband, while the traces
ran from the collar of the lead dog via the various back-
straps and collars of the others to the toboggan.

In this way we started from Fort St. John, following the
sleighs. Almost immediately the zero weather faded out
and a Chinook—the warm, south-west wind—hit us, lick-
ing up the snow which we so much needed. By March
19th we were at the Blueberry River, and I see in my diary
of that date: "at six p.m. on this March evening lying on
the oat bundles, barefooted in a blaze of sunshine. Suggested scouring out the copper tea pail with wood ashes,
but Gordon said it was an antique, made at York Factory
in the eighteenth century and had never yet been cleaned.
Thought of all the bearded voyageurs who had drunk tea
from it and decided that to scour it would be sacrilege."

This warm weather was followed again by zero tem-
peratures and grey days of driving snow; but while it
lasted the sleighs dragged heavily and the dogs were
scarcely able to pull their sled. We turned them loose and
hitched the sled to a runner of the rear sleigh—and so
the little outfit plodded forward over open prairie, through
poplar bush and shadowy spruce, Clay sitting on the forward sleigh and prodding his team gently over some twenty-
odd miles a day, using a long willow as a goad. Across the
river and creek valleys, cut deep into the plateau, we took
one sleigh at a time, using four horses—and later, towards
the Sikanni, one sleigh was left "cached", laden with feed
for the return journey and guarded against moose and
deer by a line of fluttering scraps of gay-coloured blanket.
Camps were made, wherever possible, in the green timber.
A fire was lit immediately, and tea made, while feed, sleeping bags and grub boxes were being unloaded. The horses
were turned loose to roll in the snow and to pick up any
grazing that might be going; water was fetched from a
spring or from a hole chopped through the ice of a stream,
and wood was cut. Then, while Clay tied and fed his
horses outside the circle of the firelight, we cooked supper

and fed and bedded down the dogs. A time of contentment
followed: full fed and warm, men, dogs and horses took
their ease around the fire. Conversation flared up and died
away again—the price of fur was discussed; the qualities
of Hereford cattle or the misdeeds of the wolverine. One
by one the eiderdowns were unrolled and flung down upon
the mats of spruce boughs. For a little while one lay and
watched the sudden flaring of the embers or the winking
of the stars through the tree branches. But not for long—
soon there was no sound in camp save that of a gentle
snoring, or the small yelping of some dog pursuing his
dream rabbit.

At regular intervals, governed by their co-efficient of
recuperation, the two bloody-minded gladiators, Spud and
Poilu, would take to each other again—and devilish was
the din when at last they overplayed their act and upset
the pup basket in the course of a sanguinary scrap. Like
a streak Mamselle was into it, not caring whom or what
she bit; and simultaneously, Clay Martin charged in, eager
to help but blinded by the firelight. He fetched Gordon a
resounding, two handed crack on the behind with the
bendy willow switch that he used to prod the horses along
with, seven foot long and the thickness of a man's thumb.
It must have reminded Gordon of his schooldays in
England, at Wellington. A shocking outcry from man and
beast profaned the frosty air . . . . . but when we had
tidied up the pieces, and when all was still again and
Gordon had got over being mistaken for a dog, something
told us that this would be the grand finale—for a long
time to come, anyway. We were right. We were making
camp in the warm, soft afternoons, and breaking camp in
the small hours, after the frost had had time to tighten
up the trail again and make the pools iron hard and
the sleighing good. The next morning we hit the trail
about three a.m. Reluctantly, from their spruce lined nests
in the snow hobbled two bloodstained grotesques, throwing
queer, misshapen shadows under the pale light of the

moon. They no longer took any interest in each other, and what with the touches Mamselle had added, only with difficulty would a stranger have recognised them as dogs.

And in this way, and with such simple diversions, two hundred miles slipped by.

CHAPTER VII

The Sikanni Chief River

The Alaska Highway will bring you to Fort Nelson now, and the Sikanni Chief, after its century and a quarter as an avenue of the fur trade, is silent again except for the noise of its own rapids or the passing of some trapper's canoe. But in 1928 it was very much alive; and when, at the end of the long trail from Fort St. John, we dropped down off the plateau into the river valley, we came upon a scene of bustle and activity. Here, at the confluence of Conroy Creek and the Sikanni, lay the encampment of the fur traders: men were whip-sawing lumber and building boats and scows; woodsmoke was rising heavily into the frosty air from a dozen tents and cabins. Clay halted the horses, and our dogs lay down in their harness to chew the ice from between their toes—weary, and for once disregarding the uproar of the strange dogs of the encampment. A black-robed figure broke from a little group of men and shouted a welcome—it was Father Gouet of the Oblate Fathers hastening towards us (and towards the pup-basket) with outstretched hand, a gesture that was mistaken by Mamselle, who was unfortunately running loose. There was no time for long-winded explanations: Father Gouet clutched his black robes around him and streaked for safety, while we swiftly kicked over the pup-basket. For, by chance, we had discovered that Mamselle could be diverted from any purpose, however fell, by the uproar of her puppies fighting. As usual, this worked; and so Father Gouet's cloth and a little of his dignity were saved. But it was evident that there could be no peace here for us, so we drove on down the river ice to Kenai Creek, and on the whole, and as usual, everybody was quite glad to see us go.

There, on that sunlit point between Kenai Creek and the Sikanni, a happy month went by. The canoes were unpacked and overhauled and a cache was built for the outfit and the grub. A comfortable camp was made for ourselves and warm, sheltered lairs for the dogs; much sorting and bagging was done, and the cook-stove was set up to vary our fare with roast duck, pies, and questionable cakes. For, by now, the northern spring had come; there was open water on a nearby horseshoe slough, an old bed of the Sikanni, and the ducks were returning from the south. Fat and well-fed they came, mallard, widgeon, teal and butterball; they were wary too, but the long crawl through the reeds to the blind, and the cautious pot-shot, seldom failed to produce something for the larder. The days were growing warmer—and then winter would turn in his tracks and lash a parting storm at us with its bite of zero weather; and, after one of these spells, Gordon would drive the dog-team up-river to the Conroy or down-stream to Natla Creek, or both of us would range the country in search of deer or moose. On one such expedition I snowshoed all day through the bush, westwards towards an isolated, flat-topped remnant of an older, vanished plateau. I reached its eastern base in the late afternoon and climbed the steep slope in an incredible depth of snow and alder tangle. The western side was sheer, and there I camped on the very edge, between two pines. Some far-off Sikanni hunter may have seen and been puzzled by that lonely fire; for below, and stretching far into the west, lay a vast, empty, purple country, broken here and there by other flat-topped mesas, fading away into the golden sunset, across which ran the line of the Rockies, black and sharp-fanged like some gigantic saw.

Who was there, then, to prophesy that war with Japan would so soon bring the rumble of trucks and the glare of head-lights into that lovely scene, like a jagged tear across a perfect canvas?

Back at camp all was peace. Spud and Poilu, recovering fast from their latest battle and active once more in their hatred, had been carefully kept apart. And then, returning one gay morning of early May from the duck-blind, I met Kenai Creek, its ice covered with muddy water and odd flotsam, flowing upstream against itself, and in the distance there was a muttering as of thunder—the Sikanni Chief had "gone out." For almost two days that old and ever new spectacle of the North swept past our point. Great trees upheaved themselves from the flood, stood poised for an instant, fell, and were drawn back under to be ground between huge blocks of ice; and these in turn would be up-ended, only to fall again with a shattering crash, grinding and smashing against each other till the point shook and its occupants trembled with it. Ice jams formed below us, backing up the Sikanni until its waters lipped at the little flat—and these would give way again with a roar and a rush, each flood leaving its quota of six-foot floes upon our grassy slopes. Then at last the ice came no more, and a free and very shallow Sikanni remained, chattering over the stones. It was time to make a way through the ice-blocks and the silt to the river, to load the canoes and to follow the ice out; a time for haste, since the water would drop still lower before it could rise again; and it was in the ensuing scurry and bustle that Poilu got loose, walked straight over to Spud and practically spat in his eye, and so inaugurated the last Homeric scrap. Within the range of Spud's chain was an old hay-rake—we had often wondered how it came to be on that lonely point—and naturally the fight took place in perfect safety, from the dogs' point of view, under the long corridor of the rake's teeth.

With a groan of disgust we started to crawl in after

them when, suddenly, we remembered the pepper. Twenty
years previously a fond great-aunt had brought for me,
from Ottawa, a dog story then much in vogue—'Beautiful
Joe.' In this book, a fight between two big Newfoundlands
was stopped by the leading human character, Miss Laura,
in what seemed to my small-boy mind, a neat and work-
manlike manner—she stepped daintily up to the com-
batants and sprinkled pepper on their noses. This bit of
animal lore must have made a deep impression, since I
had remembered it in Edmonton and, anticipating trouble,
had laid in pepper enough for ourselves and sufficient for
a prolonged dog-war besides—and this was now unpacked
and available.

Now was the time—and we ran over to the cache where,
after a frenzied sixty seconds, the pepper came to light,
conveniently located, of course, at the bottom of the outfit.
Armed with a fistful of the stuff we tripped daintily—just
like Miss Laura—back to the hay-rake, and while one
optimist pronounced a blessing with the words, "This'll
teach them some sense," the other leaned over and
sprinkled the dogs' noses with pepper, and said "Amen."
With a sense of duty humanely done, we awaited events.

For perhaps a second there was a dreadful, stunned
hiatus. And then we realised that either these were super-
dogs or the authoress of 'Beautiful Joe' was talking through
her hat. The fracas that broke out now was so appalling
that it put everything we had ever seen in that line completely in the shade; each dog, now firmly convinced that
the other had brought his secret weapon into play, was
putting out the last ounce that was in him. And, feeling
that "this was where we came in," we started once more,
with a groan of disgust, to crawl in after them . . . . .

Backing out from under that hay-rake, dragging a dog
blinded with fury and pepper, was no mean feat. And
then, as we sat breathless, camped on what remained of
Spud and Poilu, a voice spoke to us from above. "Big
fight!" it said. "Bi-i-g fight! Ugh!" We looked up and there

was old Kenai, the Indian, safely ensconced on the roof of his ruined cabin, Winchester in hand, outlined against a cloudless sky. He had chosen this morning, of all others, to revisit his former home.

'Beautiful Joe' came in for some pretty adverse comment as we dressed the poor beasts' wounds with ointments and with olive oil. The wounds were deep, the pepper had completed the ruin, and it was a sorry-looking pair that we bedded down in the warm spring sunshine. We turned away from them towards the canoes—and at that moment the goose came into our lives, landing on the shingle on the far side of the Sikanni Chief with one portentous "honk." There was nothing in the appearance of that ill-omened fowl to warn us of the wrath to come: there it sat, and we needed meat, and a well-aimed bullet from Gordon's Mauser smote it in the head, to loud applause from old Kenai. And since we were in a hurry, it was swiftly plucked and cut up, and put, skin, fat, and all, into the mulligan —a savoury stew of venison, ducks, beans, barley, and odds and ends that was simmering on the stove. But, though dead, its career was by no means at an end.

Then we got busy with the loading of the canoes; and, by evening, it was obvious that we were going to need all our space and a raft as well. We discussed this over a hearty supper of mulligan; and something put it into my head to make not a square, but a triangular raft—one long side to lash, flush, to the side of the big canoe, and a short base at right angles to this. With this streamlined effect, I said, it would steer and travel better . . . . . And so the raft was made in this pattern, and by the afternoon of the next day we were ready to drop down the river. A 4-h.p. outboard was in position in the freight canoe, which Gordon was to take. The raft was laden with gas, traps, and other hardware: four dogs and one swollen-faced monster lay sprawled on top of the load in the canoe, while, across the rear thwart, was lashed a hard-tack box, converted into a travelling-kennel for the pups. Used, by now, to freedom, they were taking this hard, and battle raged furiously within for possession of the window, through which first one woolly head and then the other would appear for a moment—only to vanish again, with a snarl of baby rage, to cope with some fresh attack from the rear.

I was to take the small canoe and act as pilot, and on top of my load lay the husky with closed eyes, and a nose like a diseased potato. The day was perfect, and we had eaten well of the goose mulligan—it only remained to take a last look around and to shove out into the current.

The Sikanni here was just fast enough to make the canoes come alive, and for half an hour we slid easily down small riffles and long reaches of swift water. Suddenly the drone of the outboard ceased and there floated down to me the swearing of one who struggles with a starting-string. The engine started again, stopped a second time, then started once more in a hesitant sort of way. Something was very wrong back there; and I waited till Gordon drew level with me. He was shouting something, but the row of the kicker and the yiping of the pups defeated him— it sounded like "get an oar," which was plainly silly. He drew breath for one last desperate bellow, and at that precise moment the engine conked. ". . . . . don't feel very well!" he bawled into the sudden silence. "How about getting to shore?" Two small paws got a grip on the window-sill, and a black woolly head appeared. "Yipe, yipe, yipe," it shouted, and got a smack for its pains.

I was not feeling particularly bright myself, and we compared notes as we drifted down a quiet stretch of river. Spasms of pain; ominous, deep-seated growling, and a general queasiness . . . . . Had that mulligan been left standing in/ the sun? And then, like a couple of idiots, adding the goose to it, freshly killed and with all that fat . . . . . What was it people usually did with goose-grease? Water-proofed their boots, or rubbed the stuff into their bald heads, wasn't it? And what had we done? Eaten it, Lord help us, and this was its revenge! Better get to shore and make camp. But the shore was littered with the wreckage of trees and with great blocks of ice, and there was nothing for it but to travel on down-stream until we should come to a gap in the ice rampart on a good beach, with water deep enough and quiet enough to fetch the big canoe and its raft to land.

Once more I listened to Gordon talking to the starting cord, but this time there came no answering outburst from the kicker. And now began a hair-raising progress—a nightmare of canoe travel. The Sikanni quickened, to sweep round a series of sharp bends, each with its riffle and swift rush of broken water, where the current foamed against sharp promontories of ice and round the roots of dislodged trees. Except for being heavily overloaded, I was all right with the sixteen-footer. But, with the main out-fit, the triangular raft had now taken charge, acting as a fixed rudder. A mighty effort with the paddle seemed to be keeping the big canoe on her course most of the time, but, periodically, canoe and raft would swap ends and loop the loop so that the crazy argosy lurched down-stream in a series of egg-shaped circles. It was a dangerous per-formance, and a nerve-racking one to watch; and, to make matters worse, one of us—never mind which—was sud-denly and violently overcome, and laid his head over the gunwale and fed the fishes. Our hazardous position on the Sikanni ceased to trouble him, and for a little while the only sound to break the evening stillness was a series of shuddering, tormented groans—"Oh-h-h-h!"

At last a gap in the ice-wall on the right bank revealed a wide, gently sloping beach of fine shingle, and towards that we drove the canoes. The only memory that remains to me of that landing is of carrying Spud from my canoe and into camp; and then, hours later, of us lying in our eiderdowns under the poplar trees, watching the stars break into the pale northern twilight, no longer men but empty, aching shells. There was no threat of rain, nor was there any frost or dew. The weather was warm and dry, with a soft south-west wind blowing, and there were no mosquitoes—and this was fortunate, for Noah's own Deluge would not have made us pitch a tent that night. Nor did we even light a fire for two days, but lay and slept and, in our waking moments, groaned and damned the goose and fed the mulligan to the dogs, who seemed to be able to handle it. And so a night and a day went by, and a second night—and the following morning we cautiously ate a little hard tack and cheese and mixed up two mugs of powdered milk, and crept feebly down to the river to unload, and to remove the spikes and lashings from the odd-shaped raft which had so nearly wrecked us. And, while we were working at this, into sight drifted the first of the voyageurs from the Conroy—Father Gouet, in a skiff which he allowed to spin gently, round and round, as he hung over the side; absorbed, apparently, in the play of the boat's shadow upon the stones down through the clear water. He looked up and saw us and put in to shore, but would not land. "No, I thank you," he said. "They are all bad; but that bitch—she is the worst."

He went on his way, and we set to work on the next two jobs—the thorough overhauling of the outboard and the building of a new raft; and while Gordon tackled the engine, I went back into the woods to hunt up sound dry poplar and spruce. There was not much dead stuff close to camp and suitable trees were far apart, but gradually my pile on the beach grew until, towards evening, it was complete. So, too, was the outboard, but it still refused to start. All day the ruffed grouse had been drumming in the bush and, as I felled my trees, I could hear the sound of their wing-beats—exactly like the starting of a kicker, and lasting about five seconds. This would raise my hopes as I staggered back with my raft log to the beach.

"Get her going that time, Gordon?"

"No, old man. Just another bloody partridge!"

We were still very feeble, but that evening we dared
to make a rice pudding and a pot of tea.

Next morning we had porridge and coffee for breakfast,
and wondered whether venison steaks would kill us off
or complete the cure. Nobody felt like risking it, so we
played safe and went steakless back to the beach and started
to work again, feeling rather low: Gordon set about his
engine, and I began to mortise the braces into the raft logs.
What we needed now was a tonic, and that was exactly
what we were about to receive.

The sound of voices came to me and, looking up, I saw
a light, flat-bottomed skiff coming down-stream towards
us. In it were Hamilton, an employee of Olsen, the fur
trader, and another man who was a stranger to me. They
were evidently surprised to see us there, and were pulling
in close to shore. They shouted, as they passed, that Olsen's
scow was close behind—they were piloting for him and
were going ahead so that they could point the channel and
warn him of any dangerous obstacles in the way of drift
piles and sweepers.* They waved and passed on, taking the
shallow channel to the right of an island, the upstream
point of which lay in mid-river, exactly level with the
scene of our activities. The Sikanni was swinging to the
right here, and disappeared from view below the island,
and the main channel lay, naturally, on the outside of
the bend—that is, to the left and on the far side of the
island from our beach. This far channel Hamilton should
have taken had he not allowed himself to be distracted
by the unexpected sight of our camp.

We watched Hamilton bounce down the riffle at the
foot of the island, and then looked upstream where a scow
was already in full view, its engine running about quarter
speed. It drew swiftly closer and soon we were able to see
the details of its arrangements. In front of the steersman,
who stood on a slightly raised after-deck, a section of the
scow was covered by a peaked tent of proofed canvas. In
front of this tent, which would serve as sleeping quarters

* Sweeper: a tree which has been felled into the river by the action
  of the water, but the roots of which remain attached to the bank.

and as shelter for the stores, was a long stack of trade goods covered with tarpaulins, and on top of this was lashed a double bedstead complete with spring, and adorned with all those curlicues and brass knobs so dear to a bygone generation: a truly magnificent affair as it glittered in the clear sunlight. On a little foredeck was the busy figure of Mrs. Olsen, bustling about and getting the midday meal ready on a cook-stove which was set up there, with its six feet or so of smoking stove-pipe wired to a green poplar pole.

Olsen and another man, and Olsen's son, who was something of a simpleton, sat at ease in the sun, obviously very much interested in us and in the various possible reasons for our being in camp less than half a day's run below Kenai Creek. In fact they were taking far too great an interest in us for their own good, and the steersman was automatically following Hamilton.

"They'll be getting a bit too much over on this side if they don't look out," Gordon said. At that moment the same idea struck Olsen and, scrambling to his feet, he tore down the scow, kicked the engine to full speed in passing, wrenched the sweep from the steersman and swung it hard over. The pleasant tableau of domestic peace was suddenly shattered: everybody was shouting orders to which nobody paid any heed, and, as the scow made a wild lurch to port, two frying-pans, a coffee-pot, and what seemed to be a stew slid off the cookstove—one frying-pan landing in the river and the rest of the pots and pans on a terrified dog which had apparently been enjoying a siesta on the foredeck, and which fled howling into the tent. Mrs. Olsen's voice was now added to the din, but unfortunately we were unable to catch her exact words.

It was an exciting moment as the scow drove across the river in an effort to reach the main channel, but the strong current of the Sikanni was just too much for her, and she grounded with a crash on the bar that projected upstream from the point of the island. The stove-pipes flew into the river and the ruin was complete.

On all river-craft long push-poles are kept handy, and these were now brought into play. One pole seemed to resist all efforts to pull it out—and then came suddenly, in answer to a terrific jerk, and smote the steersman behind the ear, felling him to the deck, where he lay hidden from us for a while, and where, as the other two shoved and heaved on their poles, it seemed to us that they must be trampling on his body. The scow lay broadside on to the current which boiled up against the 45-foot length of her port side: it was soon plain that no two men with poles could cope with that.

"Into the water and rock her off!" shouted Olsen. He leapt over the downstream side followed by the other man, but their efforts were frustrated by the boy, who jumped into the water on the upstream side and assisted the Sikanni to keep the scow jammed on the bar. At this point Mrs. Olsen, alarmed by the flames which darted from the pipeless stove, poured a bucket of water into it, and the foredeck was immediately hidden by an explosion of steam and ashes through which her voice could be plainly heard giving her impression of the proceedings to date.

A long spar of driftwood lay on the point of the island. This gave Olsen a new idea and he clambered on board, stumbling over the prostrate steersman as he did so, and ran over to the port side to get an axe. There he caught sight of his son, whom he grabbed by the shirt and breeches and hauled on board, flinging him up on to the pile of freight. "If you can't do any good, you fool," he roared, "then stay where you can do no harm!" He jumped overboard again and splashed through the water to the island, where he cut a long pry, and this they carried back to the scow. As they were struggling in the water to place the butt of the pry beneath the rear end of the scow, the steersman's corpse sat up with a dazed look on its face, tottered to its feet, slipped on the wet deck and fell overboard on top of them. Meanwhile the boy was not letting the golden moments slip by. He had clambered up on top of the bedstead and was jumping delightedly on the springs, flying farther and farther into the air, and whooping in ecstasy with every bound.

Spontaneous buffoonery of this calibre did not come our way—or anybody else's—every day, and it was doing us a world of good. Faced simultaneously with one crackpot boy cavorting on a bedstead, one frantic woman putting on an act like the Bad Fairy in the pantomime, and three men sitting in the river, too furious even to swear, we were by now far gone in laughter. We were past coherent speech and our empty insides were hurting us. One could scarcely have asked for more: indeed, one might have thought that, by now, the performers must have exhausted their repertoire. But, no. There were still two more turns to come before the final curtain.

The pry party, sinking its differences for the time being, now started to heave. Little by little they got a rocking motion on to the scow, which started to edge towards the riffle at the head of the island. It was this rocking motion that brought about the downfall of the bounding boy, whose performance on the springs was still the star turn of the show. Landing from a remarkably fine jump when the scow, and consequently the bed also, was at an extreme angle, he flew into the air again on a slightly different course. His wail of dismay was cut short by a resounding splash as he hit the river, whence he was once more dragged by the scruff of the neck—this time by Mrs. Olsen, her face blackened with rage, soot, and wood ashes.

The scow began to grind over the shingle and her nose was now feeling the head of the riffle. The pry party was still heaving away at the stern, but getting with each shove into deeper water. It was obvious that, when they finally got the stern far enough out, the current would take it and swing the scow end for end and send them down the riffle backwards. In fact, already things were starting to happen, and the men dropped the pry and splashed towards the slowly moving scow which was pivoting on the bow end. Mrs. Olsen could be seen up there, pointing, evidently shouting something: she had wiped a wet hand across one cheek and her piebald face was registering two distinct shades of anxiety. Of course—the stove-pipes! and, as Olsen and the steersman scrambled on board, the other man picked them out of the shallows and raised them up endways for Mrs. Olsen to take from him. As he did so, he received from them, full in the face, a cascade of watery soot; and at that moment the scow swung. He made one last desperate flounder and got hold of a ring-bolt in the bow and Mrs. Olsen grabbed him by the shirt: and in this perilous fashion they passed, with their blackened faces taut and set, behind the island and out of our lives— the three whites on board being too busy to go to their assistance.

The place seemed quiet after they had all gone. As for us, we were cured. We were still speechless, and the tears were running down our faces, but even so, we understood each other in a dumb animal sort of way. What we needed now was steak, and the sooner the better. And so, arm-in-arm, we weaved our hilarious way back to the camp-fire and fell to . . . . .

In this way the spell of the goose was broken and, on a firm foundation of venison, things went well with us that afternoon. By supper-time a solidly built raft of orthodox design was finished, loaded and lashed alongside the big canoe, and before six next morning, we were heading down the river, happy and care-free and full of roast duck and bacon: everything was going well, even the kicker, and Spud and Poilu once more had spirit enough to snarl when they met.

The perfect weather continued. Out of a cloudless sky the sun blazed down, and the sudden spring of those northern regions laid its gay mantle over the valley: birch

and cottonwood, aspen and willow were bursting into a
foam of pale green and gold; small flowers, saxifrages and
anemones, greeted the sun; mallard, widgeon, and teal flew
downstream ahead of the canoes; the river gave back the
sky its blue, and the warm, sweet scent of the poplar buds
came to us on the breeze. No mountain snows had melted
yet and the river was dropping fast, making small rapids
where, at high water, there would be none. Twice we
unlashed the raft and ran it down by itself—once where
the river foamed between black limestone outcrops, and
again where it raced round a bend, swirling between great,
fallen trees; and, on each occasion, we made a short
portage, in case of a swamping, of our cameras, rifles, and
personal sacks. We lived mainly on cold roast duck, of
which we had a supply in the grub box—and then, when
we were almost out of meat, a young bull moose swam
the river ahead of us and we shot him as he landed. He
fell dead, jammed in a narrow V between two vast, dripping
ice-blocks, and a gory scene ensued as we worked away
with hunting-knives, wedged into the bloodstained ice and
with the noonday sun beating down upon us. Barring one
that fell dead at dusk in an ice-cold spring in the high
Rockies fifteen years later, that was the most inconsiderate
moose I ever met.* But when we set out again the dogs, for
once, were full—completely stuffed. We took the lid off
the travelling-kennel and laid the sleeping puppies gently
down in it, bloated and happy. Four distended and torpid
beasts lay on top of the main load, each with the shinbone
of a moose beneath his paws, and, in my canoe, there slept
a corpulent husky, his head pillowed on a juicy-looking
shoulder-blade.

We made camp that night almost within sound of Fort
Nelson. There was some little difficulty with the dogs; for,
to start with, none of them wanted to move at all, and
finally, when half-awake and semi-intelligent, each one
insisted on carrying his own monstrous bone up to camp
and to his tree. It was a lengthy and wearing performance.

* See Chapter XIII: *The Awkward Moose.*

The pups were easy—they never woke at all. And then, as I was frying some steaks for our supper and keeping one eye on the teapail, I heard a mutter of disgust from Gordon. "Come here and smell this," he said. He had been pottering happily about in the outfit, and was now holding open for my inspection the dunnage bag that contained our shore-going clothes, our finery—bright scarves, moccasins gay with Indian silk or quill work, buckskin waistcoats similarly adorned, clean khaki shirts and trousers of Bedford cord. It was a foible with us to make our entry into a fort, or trading-post, clean-shaven and dressed in our best, and Gordon had been making ready for the morning.

There was nothing wrong with the smell. On the contrary, in its own fashion and in its proper place, it was a magnificent smell, and doubly so here in these far northern forests. A staggering compound of the fumes of brandy and rum greeted my nostrils—and nothing was wrong with it except that it was running wild amongst our clothes. Which of us, we wondered profanely, had been ass enough to drop this sack, of all others, on those portages!

We had laid in two bottles of rum and two of brandy, of the finest quality and highest voltage obtainable, so that we might have a drink to offer to thirsty friends at Fort Nelson, and again at Fort Liard. These bottles had been tenderly wrapped in sweaters and shirts and woollen socks —and now where were we, after all this kindness and forethought? We were faced with the choice between shuffling into Fort Nelson looking like a couple of down-and-out ragamuffins or making a proper entry, gaudily arrayed and smelling to all and sundry like an ill-kept bar. After some discussion we chose this latter course, and, since the Spud-Poilu affair had got beyond a joke, we also decided at this session to sell Spud in Fort Nelson, if we could. We already knew that we had a market there for the pups.

As we paddled downstream in the clear, blue light of the morning a big river came in from the west. It was the Muskwa; and the Sikanni Chief was no more. From here

on to the Liard the combined streams were known as the
Fort Nelson River, and there, half a mile down-river, was
Fort Nelson. One phase of the trip was coming to an end.

We tied up below the Hudson's Bay house, and the little
company of whites, Indians, and half-breeds that came
down to greet us seemed to recoil slightly as we landed.
Then they pressed forward again with terrier-like interest,
and not without a certain respect. Contact between Fort
Nelson and the outside world as regards supplies was
limited, in those days, to one boat a year, in July, and
their drinks were long since gone. And now there stepped
ashore under their very noses (*and* with a favourable wind)
two godlike creatures exhaling this ambrosial stink!

It was no use trying to explain: far better to leave to
them, unspoilt, their vision of a lordly binge in some fire-lit
camp beside the darkly gleaming Sikanni. And so, after an
exchange of news and courtesies, we headed up the bank
and towards the British Columbia Police, reeking of firewater and closely followed by our little band of admirers.

Business was brisk in the dog line that day, and it was
not long before the Provincial Police became the owners
of the puppies. A young policeman then rashly admired
Spud. "I'd like to own that dog," he said. "He's pretty
scarred—is he much of a fighting dog?" We tried hard to
tell the truth. "Lead dog keeps picking on him," we said,
and the deal went through. The children's pet walked
demurely off behind his new owner, and it was not till
a year had gone by that the news filtered through to us
that, within a couple of weeks, he had put the young
policeman up a tree.

Among other things we bought a shocking old eighteen-
foot freight canoe from the Hudson's Bay post there. It
was battered and full of years, and its canvas hide flapped
loosely and rottenly against its ribs: it was to cause us
much tribulation—but we had had enough of rafts for a
while, and thought it would probably just do the job for
us. Here also, in the Hudson's Bay Company store, we were

asked direct by some casual stray why we were going up
the South Nahanni. It is not customary in the North to
ask a man the reason for his movements if he does not
volunteer it, and a strained silence fell on the roomful
of listeners, broken by Gordon snorting out disgustedly,
"Going in to study the flora and fauna." An hour or two
later we happened to overhear our inquisitor discussing
this with a crony—"Didn't rightly catch what he said, but
looks like no doubt there's a couple of squaws mixed up
in it somewheres!"

Late in the evening our friends escorted us to the landing
and watched us lash the three canoes together. We could
do this now, on this bigger stream, and travel as one unit,
unhitching in case of need. Long streamers of saffron and
deep orange lay across the north-western sky, and we
dropped down-river into a lake of gold. It had been a good
day . . . . . and now we were going on to something
new. The whole wide northland was ours to play with,
and we were young, and a two years' outfit was in the
canoes. What more could we need? Nothing—and so we
were happily singing, to the din of the engine, an unprint-
able little song—a song of the camp that has done duty
in several of our wars and which was, with us, a sign that
all was well:

"Now Wellington sat in his tent," (we sang)
" 'Twas on the plains of Saragossa . . . . ."

I looked back as we made the first bend, and, in the
flaring yellow light of the sunset, I could see a little group
of figures still standing and looking after us. That was
something new, too; for the first time somebody had been
sorry to see us go.

CHAPTER VIII

Fort Simpson,
*McKenzie's River

"Faille never came out," the letter said, "and I think he is finished this time. It wouldn't do much good to look for him if he is not out by open water—he is sure to be dead some place. . . . ." I was running through some old letters and browsing here and there: this one was from the Game Warden of the Mackenzie Mountains Game Preserve and it was headed "Nahanni Butte, March 20, 1952." The post mark was "Fort Simpson, N.W.T. May 20, '52."

But the Game Warden had evidently not been at all certain: Faille had vanished, in September 1950, into this one-man empire of 73,000 square miles, but Faille, he knew, had the knack of survival down to a fine art. It would be better to go and see. So in May, of 1952, as soon as the ice had gone out, the Warden took his boat and ran down the Liard River to Fort Simpson. A constable from the Royal Canadian Mounted Police detachment there came back with him, and together they rammed their way up the South Nahanni River in the Warden's boat, through the great canyons and into a country of low, bald-headed mountains with a wild-looking, jagged range ahead of them, streaked with snow—the Yukon Territory divide. And late in June, when two hundred miles of river lay between them and Nahanni Butte, they saw Faille's boat

* The spelling of the old-time fur-traders, today standardised as Mackenzie.

and canoe drawn up on the shingle and the smoke of his fire drifting out from among the trees.

He said it was real neighbourly of them to come so far, visiting; he had been out of coffee for over a year and he was almost out of tea—and he could do with a bit of conversation besides. So he came down with them to Fort Simpson—and got himself a new outfit and went back in again to his mountains to continue his search for the lost Nahanni gold.

I laid the letter aside; things had not changed very much in the last twenty-five years, it seemed. It must have been some time in February 1929 that I was sitting, one evening, in the comfortable kitchen of the R.C.M.P. barracks at Fort Simpson, alternately talking to Johnny Robb, who was cooking for the police that winter, and, when any particular pearl of thought or expression occurred to me, adding it to the letter that I was writing. Notepaper was a bit short just then, so the letter was being written on the backs of Wolf Bounty Claim forms—a scandalous but necessary abuse of government stationery.

I had just snowshoed a couple of hundred miles down from the mountains of the Nahanni, looking for my partner, Gordon Matthews, who had been stuck by a tremendous fall of snow in Fort Simpson with a dog team and a heavy load—and now I was laid up with the *mal de raquette** in one foot and it would be a few days before I could get out and break trail again.

The kitchen was bright and cheery and they were evidently particular here to the point of fussiness; for on the wall hung a notice in large, clear printing—

YOU ARE REQUESTED NOT TO SWEAR
IN THIS KITCHEN.
NOT THAT WE GIVE A DAMN
BUT IT SOUNDS LIKE HELL TO STRANGERS.

Robb was busy preparing the barracks supper: on one end of the big kitchen stove he had a large tub of water

* *Mal de raquette*: snowshoe sickness—a sort of 'trench foot.'

warming up for me. It was just about the right heat now, so we carried it over to my corner and I proceeded to steep the *mal de raquette* foot in it according to the Doctor's instructions, at the same time carrying on with the letter, one sheet of which promptly fluttered down into the bath-tub. It was swiftly retrieved, but not before the "stranger" of the moment had blotted his copy-book in more senses than one. Robb grinned. He was asking just then about Faille, and I told him that Faille had portaged his outfit over the Falls of the Nahanni and was alone in the upper country with a kingdom all to himself and not even an Indian in it. He had camped overnight with us in June 1928 and no man had seen him since.

"He'll be doing that once too often," Robb said.

Outside it was dog feeding-time. The long-drawn-out howling of the huskies rose on the frosty air, broken by the sharper barking of our Alsatians: Gordon and McIntyre were out there in the dog corrals, dishing out the feed: some of the police dogs were away with a patrol up the Liard, and McIntyre had given us an empty pen for our team. And then, suddenly, the howling and the barking were stilled; the dogs were hastening to gobble up their supper before it could freeze solid in the bowls.

Gordon came in; and with him came a swirl of cold air that eddied low down across the floor, condensing the steam of the warm kitchen into grey wreaths of mist.

"How's the foot coming?" he asked.

"Going down fast. Another two or three days and we can hit the trail."

McIntyre came in, and again the cold, grey fog crawled across the floor.

"What's that about hitting the trail?" he said. "You're just as well off here tonight—do you know it's fifty-four below already? It's going to get pretty damn cold before the night's out."

That was no dream, Gordon and I decided, as we walked back to Andy Whittington's hotel where we were staying.

Fort Simpson is built on a high island close to the left bank of the Mackenzie, just below the mouth of the Liard. The Mackenzie is just under two miles wide there and from Fort Simpson waterfront one can see ten or twelve miles downstream and about the same distance upstream. The buildings are strung out in a long line facing the Mackenzie, which changes its direction at Fort Simpson from almost due west to little short of northwest. The place is open to all the cold, uncharitable winds that sweep in from poorly heated places like Great Slave Lake, the Barren Lands and Great Bear Lake; and the trail that runs the full length of the settlement, between the buildings and the river, is no place for sweet dalliance or idle chit-chat on a February night in a cold snap.

There has been a fort at the meeting of the Liard and Mackenzie since the North Westers built the first one there in 1805. It was burnt down, and then rebuilt in 1820: in 1821 it passed, with the assets of the North West Company, into the hands of the Hudson's Bay Company, and the name was changed from Mackenzie Forks to that of Fort Simpson.

Though on the main highway of the great river, the place has always been on the edge of things. Down below, down the Mackenzie—*'La Grande Rivière en Bas'* of the voyageurs—towards the Frozen Ocean, there were other forts, even in the early days—Fort Norman and Fort Good Hope. South-westward, up the Liard a hundred and fifty miles, there was Fort Liard. But beyond that, and westward and north-westward, there was nothing—only the tangled mass of the Mackenzie Mountains out of which came new tribes of Indians bringing furs and strange tales of a country where the rivers ran "towards the setting sun."

It was from Fort Simpson that one expedition after another set out to follow the dangerous Liard River "beyond the Rocky Mountain." Chief Factor Edward Smith wrote in 1831: "You will be joyed to hear that success has

attended our undertakings in the West Branch Liard
River—Mr. McLeod junior returned the 9th September—
and followed its Waters 500 miles to its source in the Icy
Mountains. His route was through a fine Country—
abounding in Fur-bearing animals . . . inhabited by
Indians friendly and hospitable—from this voyage Five
new tribes is in a manner introduced to our Acquaintance
—the navigation is dangerous—With smart Canoe men,
care and caution, it may be navigated without the loss of
life. . . .There is no success without some loss—on the
return of the expedition and when far advanced on their
way Home, in running a rapid the Canoe filled, broke, in
three Pieces, two men drowned. . . ."

In 1838 they were still at it, and Chief Trader Murdoch
McPherson writes from Fort Simpson: "We made a small
advance in our very tardy business of the West Branch
this last Summer. . . . Fort Halkett was removed to the
very *ridgepole* of the Rocky Mountains—a region of eternal snow & barren rocks, and I do believe, literally of
nothing else. Mr Campbell was also on the Pelly's River
(Russian 'Sticken'), where, about 15 miles farther on
than the farthest point of Mr J. McLeod in '34. He found
a brigade of Russian traders with a very large congrega-
tion of Indians who meet at the same Rendezvous twice
every Summer. What kind of trade they make we know
not, for Campbell did not see or hear anything that could
inform him on the subject, but the Furs, if there were any,
might have been removed from the Camp before Campbell's arrival. He remained only a few hours at the Camp,
which I have reason to think was a good plan. The Russian
Com. in chief of the Party (a 'Mr. Monrobe') received
him with apparent politeness and introduced him to three
other ragged Officers like himself, and treated him to a
Glass of *Whiskey*. It was, however, very evident that they
were jealous of his appearance in that Quarter."

That was at the mouth of the Tahltan River, where it
joins the Stickine, and it is due to the forethought of a

bygone American Secretary of State, Mr Seward, and to his Alaska purchase, that the Russians are not there now, within our gates.

Fort Simpson today is three hundred miles by rail and eight hundred by river—with one sixteen-mile portage round the Smith Rapids—from its base of supplies, Edmonton in Alberta. But in the old days its supply base was York Factory on Hudson's Bay: well over two thousand miles of lake and river had to be covered then by York boat and canoe before the season's outfit reached Fort Simpson. The Smith Rapids on the Slave River still had to be run, lined or portaged and, in addition, there was a host of minor portages and the major one of Portage la Loche—a twelve-mile carry over the Hudson's Bay-Mackenzie divide. It was no wonder that Chief Factor Edward Smith felt bitter when he found that broken glass and crockery had been carried at great expense over the long, hard trail from the Bay to McKenzie's River, as they called it then.

"Your Packers," he wrote, "did not pay the usual attention in Packing some of the Cases—two-thirds of our plates and cups was smashed—and also the window Glass, except 18 Squares, was broke; the latter loss I think was owing to the person that nailed up the Case—the lid rested on the glass, and driving in the nails the contents was broken." That was in 1831, but his complaint has a most modern ring to it.

Things seem to have been in even worse shape at Fort Simpson in 1840, and Chief Factor John Lee Lewes penned a truly heart-rending plea to James Hargrave at York Factory: "I must now . . . point out to you, with a view of *moving* your *sympathy* to the destitute state of McKenzie's River in the articles of table furniture; I am sure if you could but see us for a moment and be an eye-witness to our beggarly display that you would not *only pity* us, but instantly *say yes, yes,* your wants are great, and *shall* be supplied; look therefore to my Indent, it will point out how you can relieve us, and in doing so I beg that the greatest care and attention be paid to their packing, for they will be in the hands none of the most careful or tender, the portage La Loche Boys are a sett of rough & terrible fellows, caring little for the contents of packages. All their *aim is* to get through the voyage as quick as possible, their cry is the *D——l take the hindermost* helter, skelter, bing, bang, the pieces here & there on the portage, pieces containing the most brittle ware are as tenderly dashed on the rocks as two or three pieces of bar iron fasted together; consequently . . . the greatest care is necessary in the packaging; it's confoundedly vexing and galling, after taking a piece from Y F to this, to find on opening everything broke useless."

But that was not the end of Lewes's troubles in this long letter of November 1840: a cheese in his voyage allowance had gone so rotten that the "Men who gathered round it in expectation of a treat found it was too much for their strong noses & stomachs," and it had to be thrown away on an island in Great Slave Lake, but not before it had added insult to injury by completely spoiling the tea and sugar which had been carelessly packed alongside it. A serious loss in that cold country.

And the wild waters of the Liard had been at their tricks again. A party of Lewes's men, coming down from Fort Halkett, had passed, as they thought, all the dangerous water and "were at the very moment of the accident congratulating each other, that all cause for dread was past, and nought ahead to create fear, blind mortals are we all, the next minute and they were in their watery grave, the Canoe tho' under the full way of the eight paddles . . . was suddenly arrested in its progress by a whirlpool, turned round twice with a velocity hardly perceptible, and then head formost commenced descending the fearful gulph, while in that state one of the unfortunates ('John Johnstone Steersman') sprang from the Gunwales into the water; his spring had no sooner been

made than the Canoe, which was a brand-new one &
strong, broke by the middle, stem and stern came together
and the vortex closed over them, and six out of the nine
sank to rise no more. . . ."

The only gleam of light in Lewes's dark sky came from
the far west: "Mr Campbell last Summer was on a trip of
discovery to the Westward of this, and I am happy to say
that his excursion was crowned with success; it has opened
to us another wide Field for extending our Trade in that
quarter, the large River he fell upon, from its course and
magnitude Mr C. judges it to be the long sought for
Colville, the country is very rich in Beaver, abounds with
large animals, next Summer please G—d if I can possibly . . . find the means I will have that new-found River
explored to its mouth, . . . and summer '42 I will have
other posts pushed farther to the Westward, and work up
the Russian Territory. . . ." A stout-hearted lot, those old
fur-traders of Fort Simpson.

Starvation often stared them in the face. McKenzie's
River in those days was a poor moose country and the
nearest first-class fisheries were those of the Great Slave;
all that was needed to precipitate a famine in a hard
winter was the periodic scarcity of the hares. Then the
lynx would leave the country and the Indian would have
neither food nor the fur to trade for what little, if any, the
posts could spare. In June 1842 Chief Trader Alexander
Fisher wrote to Hargrave regarding the previous winter:
". . . after recruiting myself a little I returned to my charge
at Ft. Good Hope and found that 52 Indians, men, women
& children had perished by famine and the surviving
living on the dead carcasses of their Relations, all within
200 yards of the Fort during my absence, my man & his
family living on Moose Skins, Pack Cords, Bear Skins,
Leather Sled Trappings, etc. These poor Indians seldom
could get sleep, they both men and women kept axe in
hand for self-preservation & if any found knapping

instantly was knocked on the head and as soon devoured by their nearest relatives. . . ."

But that was in olden times and now it was 1929. Starvation no longer haunted the forts ot the Mackenzie: it had taken itself off to the wind-swept spaces of the Barrens or the lonely uplands of the Mackenzie Mountains, lying in wait for the man whose outfit has gone through the ice or whose cache the wolverine has destroyed. There was certainly no danger of it in Andy's hotel, towards the lights of which we were making our way over the hard-packed, squealing snow.

The building faced the river, and it was the only hostelry of any kind on the twelve hundred miles of waterway from Fort Smith to the Beaufort Sea. One came, first of all, into a dance-hall—a place that had seen, and would see again, many a lively celebration. It was heated by a huge camp stove, fired with long billets of wood, and it gave refuge from the intense cold to a varying group of men and girls—Indians, half-breeds, idlers, never more than half a dozen or so at a time, and never a white girl.

There was a large gramophone with a collection of old records—square dances, waltzes and melancholy cowboy songs—and to these the assembled couples circulated joylessly and silently (for the moccasins made no sound) over the polished floor. The last mail plane had dropped off two new records—one of them a most regrettable little chanson about a young lady of singular beauty whose name was Brown, and the other a song by Frank Crumit: "I saw a robin this morning. Too-wheet! Too-whee!"

The first piece evidently touched some hidden, sympathetic chord in these children of nomad hunters, and they played it incessantly. The robin song with its birdlike whistling, Gordon said, reminded him of spring in some far-off, greener land—and he insisted on having it with our breakfast coffee and cornflakes while the bacon and eggs were frying.

One passed from the dance-floor into the combined

store, bakery, and meal counter. There Andy was to be found at work—at all hours, it seemed, for he baked the bread for almost the whole fort. He was busy, and beyond a quiet "good morning" he did not want to be bothered with anything. He worked at a big kitchen range: on it there was usually some clear space and always a big kettle of water singing a welcoming song. You helped yourself from the shelves to whatever you could see, sliced your bread and bacon and found your eggs. You laid out your meal on the counter, made your tea or coffee and toast, and cooked the bacon and eggs without speaking above a low mutter. The gramophone out on the dance-floor did not count: Andy was so used to it that the noise had about as much effect on him as water on a duck's back. When all was done and you were perched up at the meal counter with a new carton of cornflakes in front of you and a can of freshly opened cream—then, and not before, you were free to raise your voice to a sort of dim, religious mumble that could not possibly offend.

The meal cost you one dollar. It cost you a dollar if you went in and blew yourself out till you nearly burst, and it cost you a dollar if you put in there in the afternoon and had a cup of tea and some sweet biscuits. Andy had it figured out that a man who was just lying around the fort could not possibly eat two terrific blow-outs running—and that if he, Andy, only broke even at breakfast-time he would probably do pretty well out of you at midday. And the meal included the price of one's room. There were a number of rooms upstairs, simply furnished with one wooden chair, one metal cot bedstead with wire spring mattress and a few clothes-hooks on the wall. The doors were always open and the rooms were always warm: as for bedding, you carried up your eiderdown sleeping-bag and that was that.

Andy Whittington was an old Klondiker and Yukon man who had settled in Fort Simpson and built his hotel there with his own hands. He was an expert with the long,

Yukon-type poling-boat, a specimen of which was drawn up on the bank outside, out of reach of the ice. He was also an expert on the Liard and its hazards, and had trapped and prospected for years on the Beaver River in the south-eastern Yukon Territory. Some of the tributaries of the Beaver River and the Flat River head close together on the Yukon-North West Territories divide. Andy found out, somehow, that I had been up the Flat River, and he opened up to me one evening when I was alone with him in his kitchen, shaving—and doing it, as usual, very quietly for his benefit. He took me into another room and unrolled the compass survey that he had made of the Beaver River and for a happy hour we went at it, questioning each other and straightening out our theories about the headwaters of the Nahanni and those of the rivers on the Yukon side.

One of Andy's troubles was the shawl trick. The meal counter was just a shade too close to the shelves where the canned stuff was stacked; and while Andy's attention was for a moment distracted elsewhere, a lithe active Indian girl from the village across the Mackenzie could easily lean over and sweep a can of beans or bully under her shawl, which she wore over her head and shoulders much as the Northumberland fisher-girls used to do.

An unsuccessful performer who had recently attempted the trick, Suzanne, had been caught and was now due to come up for trial. On the appointed morning Gordon and I strolled along to see the proceedings. I had to be up at the Wireless Station very shortly, so I was only able to stay for the opening chorus. Gordon saw the whole show through, and it was his burlesque of it afterwards that made me realise how much I had missed.

Flynn Harris was Indian Agent and magistrate at Fort Simpson in 1929. He was sixty-nine then and had been Agent for seventeen years, but he had traded and dealt with these Indians for over forty years in all. He had a dash of Charles Laughton in him, in appearance and mannerisms, but he also had a pronounced lisp, and one of

the most appalling squints I have ever set eyes on. We all
jammed into the small over-heated room, Flynn in the
chair, Suzanne in a chair facing him, with various Indian
supporters giggling and shoving behind her, one Mountie,
and one or two white spectators who were on their way up
the waterfront and had dropped in to listen to Flynn and
also to warm up, for it was very cold.

The administration of the oath was all I had time to see,
more's the pity. Flynn called for silence in the court. Then
he fixed me with a basilisk glare from his right eye, swivel-
ling on to Suzanne a blast of equal force from the other,
drew a deep breath and said, "Now, then, Thuthanne. . . ."
An impressive pause followed. Then he drew an even
deeper breath and broke into a monotonous, rumbling
gabble that carried right on through to the end without
even so much as a comma in it: "You realithe you got to
tell the truth the whole truth and nothing but the truth or
you're liable to thpend theven dayth in jail tho' help you
God kiththabook." And with that final piece of abracadabra
Flynn whipped a Bible up from the table and rammed it
under Suzanne's nose. Suzanne was naturally a bit startled
and backed up apprehensively. One of the Indian girls said
something to her in the Slave language and she plucked up
courage, giggled self-consciously, and then leaned forward
and kissed the Book so heartily with the whole force of her
flat but cheerful Mongoloid countenance that it fell from
Flynn's hand, landing with a crash on a tray full of pens
and pencils on the table. One of the pens flew spinning
into the air and landed point first on the table, where it
stuck, quivering like an arrow—and the oath had been
administered.

Flynn let fly with a few winged words; those who knew
him can guess what they might be. I caught Gordon's eye
and knew that it was time for me to get out before one or
both of us blew up. With me came Hall who was black-
smithing for the Hudson's Bay Company.

"Old Flynn," Hall said. "You can always count on a bit

of pantomime somewhere when he's handling one of these things—sooner or later you get it. This time it was sooner!"

That night Gordon and I were asked to supper with Inspector and Mrs Moorehead of the R.C.M.P. at their house. On the way up there from Andy's Gordon besought me to remember that this was a civilised house we were going to: we would be sitting on chairs, he explained, and not on rocks or up-turned canoes. It was most considerate of him.

"None of your camp habits tonight," he said. *"Don't* gnaw the meat off the bones and chuck them over your shoulder like you do in the bush, and if you don't like the coffee *don't* say "Perfect muck" and pour it out on the floor. Remember. . . ."

However, we rallied our table manners and spent a most enjoyable evening with these two kind people who were to be our hosts again in the spring. It was pretty late when we left them and walked back to Andy's. Gordon took a look at the thermometer by the hotel door.

"Sixty-seven below, and dropping," he said as we went in. A mournful howl from the half-breed caller greeted us—

"Ba-alance your partners right and left,
And a grand right and left."

They were starting up a square dance. . . .

We came again to Fort Simpson in the spring, four of us from the Nahanni country. There were Gordon and myself from Deadmen's Valley, and Starke and Stevens from the Flat River: Jack la Flair, the independent trader from Nahanni Butte, had come down alone, ahead of us, as soon as the ice had gone out from the Liard, which had been about May 7th. That left Faille alone on the Nahanni (for there were no game-wardens then), somewhere in the huge country that lies above the Falls. Faille had found a good marten country and there was some prospecting he wanted to do in the summer-time: he showed up, bright and smiling, a year later, in the spring of 1930, not having had speech with a human being for twenty-three months. But already in that spring of 1929 men were wondering—as usual—what could have happened to him. "Sooner or later," they were saying, "the luck runs out. And then . . ." And they shook their heads gloomily, like so many croaking ravens.

Our camp at Fort Simpson was in a little clearing cut out of the willows towards the north-west end of the island: here Gordon and I set up the tent and here we chained the dogs, round the camp in a circle. They were half savage by now and unused to anybody but the two of us and Starke and Stevens: nobody in his right mind would attempt to molest our camp with those five wolves sleeping round it. The other two partners slept on their scow which was tied up on the Mackenzie River side of the island, below the waterfront; and close to the scow lay our three canoes.

Our first visitor was Jack la Flair. We were cooking supper on the evening of our arrival when I felt something come between me and the sun. I looked up to see a stranger standing there and smiling down at me—and so beautiful was this sudden vision that I completely forgot my manners and just stared and stared. The man was clean shaven and stockily built; he was wearing a well-pressed, grey pin-stripe suit with socks to match, black-and-white shoes, blue shirt and collar and a pink tie. On his head sat a straw hat of the boater variety the crown of which was encircled with a light-blue ribbon. This was Jack's annual holiday, and an essential part of it was the wearing of his best clothes. If he could not get to Edmonton (and this had been a poor fur year and the catch did not justify a trip to the outside) he intended to wear them at Fort Simpson and be damned to local custom; and so, arrayed in these splendid trappings, he was a familiar sight on the waterfront and an example to the simple Indian of the heights

to which the white man could rise when he gave his mind
to it.

Just then my fellow yokel emerged from the tent carrying a bowl of something or other; he stopped dead in his
tracks and stood there staring like a man turned to stone.

Suddenly the vision spoke: "Well fellows," it said, in
Jack's familiar voice, "Don't you know me?"

Until then the dogs had been sleeping, but the strange
voice roused them. They, after all, were just dogs and
could not be expected to recognise their fur-trader friend
in this exotic garb: plain mackinaw and moosehide was
what they were used to, and Jack's Atlantic City outfit had
startled them: they reacted promptly—they leapt simultaneously for his throat. They fell short and fell back on
their chains, snarling and struggling to get at him. Jack
had the sense to stand still, though protesting volubly
that the dogs were dangerous; and we finally quelled the
uproar and got him safely out of camp after taking him
round the circle to be sniffed and accepted anew by each
dog in turn. And in future, when he came to call on us, he
whistled for an escort and refused to approach without one.

The days slipped by and May was drawing to a close.
The catkins were appearing on the willows, and from the
water the insane laughter of the loons and the strange
calling of the "aleck" ducks* proclaimed that spring had
come to Mackenzie's River. But the upper Mackenzie between the mouth of the Liard and Great Slave Lake
remained frozen, and the lake itself would not be free of
ice until July. And until the ice was gone from the upper
Mackenzie the plane for which I was waiting would not
come.

The going out of the ice at Fort Simpson, usually in the
first ten days of May, is one of the great sights of the North.
Coming from the warmer western country, the Liard breaks
before the Mackenzie; then, smashing and driving everything before it with the tremendous force of its onset, it
opens the lower Mackenzie from Fort Simpson north to the

* White-winged Scoters.

Eskimo lands, eight hundred miles of waterway, in a furious struggle that leaves great blocks of ice stranded far above the river on Simpson waterfront. I have never seen this thing, but Chief Trader John McLean saw it from the fort in 1844 and wrote of it afterwards:—

"The River Liard has its source in the south among the Rocky Mountains: its current is remarkably strong; and in the early part of summer, when swollen by the melting of the snow, it rushes down in a foaming torrent, and pours into the Mackenzie, still covered with solid ice, when a scene ensues terrific and grand: the ice, resisting for some time the force of the flood, ultimately gives way with the noise of thunder, and clashing, roaring and tumbling, it rolls furiously along until it accumulates to such an extent as to dam the river across. This again presents, for a time, a solid barrier to the flood, which is stopped in its course; it then rises sometimes to the height of thirty and forty feet, overflowing the adjacent country for miles, and levelling the largest trees with the ground. The effects of this frightful conflict are visible in all the lower grounds along the river. The trading posts are situated on the higher grounds, yet they are not secure from danger. Fort Good Hope was swept clear away some years ago. . . ."

Great cakes of Ice, they say, weighing many tons, go driving into the bush on the flood, snapping off stout trees before them as they would so many match-sticks. . . .

But the break-up of the upper Mackenzie came with a quiet magnificence that set it worlds apart from the brawling uproar of the Liard ice. The first cakes and floes came at midnight. Gordon and I were sitting on the Moorheads' veranda, which overlooked the river, talking with the Inspector and his wife. The sun was down below the northern horizon; a few small golden clouds hung motionless in the north-east, low down, reflected in the lake-like sweep of the Mackenzie; nothing was stirring and not even the faintest breeze came to ruffle the calm surface of the river. There was no sound, only the everlasting calling of the "aleck" ducks in the distance (and it was Moorhead, on that night, who gave us that name for them); "a-a-aleck—aleck" they kept on saying, and the mournful cadence of their cry was in keeping with the pale colouring of the northern spring. But from every quarter of the tremendous sky of the plains—and how big it seemed to us who came from the valleys and the deep canyons of the Nahanni!—there streamed a radiance, clear, luminous and shimmering, beneath which every detail of the immense river and of the level, monotonous forest of the northern shore stood out sharp and well-defined. And it was in the calm light of that midnight sunset that I saw the first block of ice go sliding, white and ghostly, down the Mackenzie. I watched it for a minute or two before pointing it out to the others—it might be only a stray that had broken away from the main ice sheet. . . . But others came after it, and still more, until the farther half of the river ran white with the sedately moving galleons of the ice as they swept on into the north-west, breaking the mirror of the golden clouds, a phantom armada sailing into the sunset.

The Liard ran brown and muddy from its mountains and the Mackenzie came clear and green from its great inland sea: the two big rivers ran side by side for thirty miles before their currents mingled, and for the next two days, across half a mile of muddy Liard Water, we would see the stately procession of the ice in the Mackenzie stream.

A feeling of departure was in the air: when the Maczenzie was open the plane would come—and I began to say my goodbyes. Our fur was sold and Gordon was taking charge of our canoes and outfit; he was to come out with Starke and Stevens and that would be as soon as a channel opened between the shore and the ice in Great Slave Lake. And Starke was itching to get going. He came from a farm near Stirling and was the son who had been destined for the ministry. At precisely the wrong moment, from his family's point of view, the news of the Klondike had come

to Stirling and the spring of 1898 saw him heading down
the Yukon towards the golden river, lost for ever to theo-
logical disputation—doomed by his fate to wander end-
lessly across the North. And he had already had more
than enough of Fort Simpson: he would soon be on the
move. Tall, dark, black-hatted and smoking a black pipe,
the Klondiker was a well-known figure. To his friends of
the trail he was known as the Black Pirate.

The last morning came and the north wind was blowing
strongly; the plane would land in the mouth of the Liard
where there would be some shelter from Simpson Island.
A committee of five had appointed itself to see me off:
there were Starke, Stevens and Gordon, Jack la Flair in his
Sunday best to lend a bit of tone to the proceedings, and
our lead dog, Bloody Poilu,* who was coming up for the
exercise. Starke and Stevens took our big canoe up to the
point of the island; Gordon and I carried the stuff and
Jack kept an eye on Poilu. On the way we stopped at some
trader's place where there was a stock of dried fish and
tallow; Gordon wanted to make sure of a supply of this for
dog-feed and we went in. It took a little time to complete
the deal and towards the end of it a nondescript, varmint-
looking character stuck his head into the store.

"Feller," he said to Gordon in an irritating drawl, "if
you want to see the last moments of that short-haired dorg
of yours you want to hurry."

We looked out. Three huskies stood round Poilu, and
the situation was charged with menace. Every dog had his
hackles up and his teeth bared in a snarl, and they were all
moved slowly and with extreme delicacy. Poilu looked
savage enough but rather insignificant beside these woolly
monsters. . . .

Suddenly, and before anybody could do anything about
it, the explosion took place. Poilu did the exploding while
the huskies were still considering ways and means and, in
the briefest dog-fight on record, he killed one, lamed
another, so that it had to be destroyed and chased the

* See Chapters: Life with a Dog Team and
      The Sikanni Chief River.

survivor down the waterfront. Thus began his victorious progress down the Mackenzie to Aklavik in the frozen lands of the delta, where his descendants fight, work and breed to this day.

"My Gord," said the varmint-looking one in a tone of respect, "that dorg of yours sure knows how to handle himself!"

In the course of the uproar the plane had landed unnoticed in the Liard mouth: we retrieved Poilu and hurried on. The canoe was waiting and Gordon and Stevens took me out in it. I climbed aboard the plane and stood on one of the floats while Punch Dickens and his cockney mechanic, Parmenter, slung the mail into the canoe. The usual last-minute awkwardness descended on the party. I looked across the great stretch of water towards Gros Cap.

"You know, Gordon, there's a sort of miserable fascination about this northern country."

"There is, old man."

"One will probably be back."

"One probably will."

The engine roared and the water flashed past the windows. I had a vision of two men paddling a canoe and then of the little party on the point—the Black Pirate, Jack la Flair waving his straw hat and Bloody Poilu with a cocky-looking swagger on him. And then Simpson Island and the Mackenzie River fell away from me as we climbed into the north and I could see the others no longer.

The plane swung into the south-east, still gaining altitude, and, far away in the west, a range of mountains climbed slowly into view. It was the Nahanni Range and on the left hand of it was a mountain that was shaped like a great bell. That was the Butte, the gateway to Deadmen's Valley and to Faille's Country, and on it I kept my eyes fixed until it sank once more beneath the horizon.

Part Three

THE FOOTHILLS

1929 ~ 1946

*"I wish that it were possible for me to
see the Rockies once more for the first
time."*

"The Diary of a Dude-Wrangler"
by STRUTHERS BURT

113

CHAPTER IX

Dudes and Bears

The next step in the evolution of this new Canadian—this greenhorn homesteader whose eyes were so firmly fixed on far pastures—was in a southerly direction. Some magical stock exchange victories, plus the acquisition of a brand-new wife, specially imported from England, made this step both possible and advisable—in spite of John Petersen's kindly offer of the post office (today known as North Star) in which the "woomans" was to have found happiness, reading the postcards and minding the "schickens".

Now, with benefit of hindsight, I can see that the sane thing would have been to have stayed with the Northwest Territories and to have launched out into the river-freighting business—as Gordon Matthews and I had often talked of doing, on winter nights in the quiet of our Deadmen's Valley trapping cabin. But even we, with the eye of faith, could not foresee the immense development that was to come; and so down south I came, to Calgary and to the foothills, while Gordon went on north to Aklavik. I sold the homestead, and said (as I then thought) good-bye for ever to the care-free northern life; and I looked around among the hills, seeking for some new venture.

Unfortunately I found one all too quickly—a deal in sheep. I had just got that all nicely tied up when along came the stock-market crash of 1929, burying me, along with many others, in its ruins . . . Some fifteen months later I crawled out from under, one of the lucky ones, battered but not crippled, and cured for good and all of any hankerings after sheep. This was just as well, since a year or two later they were still further down the scale, to about a quarter of their pre-depression value. From then on, all I have ever asked of those perverse animals is mutton—on a plate.

Life looked a bit blank and the Great Depression was going swiftly from bad to worse. For a year and more my wife and I roamed the foothills, exploring that beautiful country to see what it held for us. Gradually, out of all those miles we covered, one thing emerged as certain: there was no valley like that of the Highwood River, and no place in it that had the appeal of the Buffalo Head Ranch. Gradually we became interested. Soon it was to become our home . . .

The ranch lay in the "Eden Valley" of the Highwood River—that is, in the stretch of the Highwood country that lies between the Sullivan Hill and the first range of the Rockies. Legend has it that this was called the Eden Valley by Dr. G. M. Dawson, the famous explorer-surveyor, later Surveyor-General of Canada, after whom Dawson City in the Yukon is named: it was, that far-travelled man is supposed to have said, the most beautiful valley he had ever seen. I can well believe that story. One only had to observe the effect that the first sight of the Eden Valley had upon a stranger to the country—a guest, it might be, or a dude. I remember driving, one October evening of the middle Thirties, up the valley trail with a late-season dude, Mary Pope by name, straight out from England. In the shadow we drove up the hill from the O.H Ranch flats. Suddenly we came out into dazzling sunshine; suddenly the mountains were close, with the sharp spire and rounded shoulder of Patterson's Peak dead ahead. Shading my eyes against the sun I drove across the wooded summit of the hill—and then, right at the top of the Sullivan Hill, a drag on the steering wheel and a grinding rumble from below announced a flat tire.

That flat couldn't have chosen a better time or place. This was Mary's arrival in the foothills, and the Eden Valley of old Dr. Dawson burst on her suddenly in all its autumn glory. Down below ran Sullivan Creek in its small canyon; further upstream you could see the water shining through the sheltering trees. And then, almost straight south for four miles, ran the river flats of the Buffalo Head with the line of the Highwood River winding through them, marked against the yellow grass by the dark green of spruce. To the right of the river lay the wooded north slopes of the Buffalo Head hills, a blaze of colour: rich old gold of cottonwoods, red of choke-cherries, pale gold of poplars with here and there a tree-top reddened by the frost's searing fingers. All this was lit by the low sun, slashed with belts of dark and light green in the coulees, and set against the tawny grass of the meadows. Eastward from the Highwood the open grass hills of the Bar U framed the valley, and to the south the vista was closed by the blue mountains of the Lookout Range. I have said that this mass of riotous colour was lit by the low evening sun. It would be more true to say that the whole gorgeous country had stolen the light of the sun, and now was radiant with some inner force of its own. It was dazzling to the eye. It was not *lit:* it was Light itself.

While I wrestled with the jack and the spare wheel, Mary Pope tramped excitedly up and down over the grass by the trail, an exotic figure in her English tweeds. She was talking to herself. "God," she was saying. "Oh God, but it's beautiful! And I'm seeing it—me—Mary Pope. I've looked forward to coming here, but never in my wildest dreams did I think it would be like this! It must be the loveliest valley on earth . . ."

Yes, that was what I thought too. And behind Mary was standing the silent, approving ghost of the old Surveyor-General—he also liked to hear his valley well spoken of.

This was going to be a happy visit, I could see that already.
It had got off on the right foot, if anything ever had. I
tightened the last nut and kicked on the hub-cap. Then
I put the tools away and wiped my hands and moved over
to where this ecstatic young woman with the mop of unruly
hair was prancing around on the grassy slope. I pointed
out to her the nearer mountains in the south-west—our
own mountains where our cattle ran in summertime. I
told her the names of the peaks of that range: the Holy
Cross Mountain, Mount Head, Patterson's Peak, the Dogtooth Mountains—the sun was dipping towards them now
and we shaded our eyes as we faced that dazzling glare.

"So you've got a mountain called after you," she said.
"How marvellous! Tell me all about it, now, while we
look at it."

I grinned. "That peak's nameless on the map," I said.
"It's an orphan mountain and I just adopted it. If you
ride up Flat Creek—which you'll do in a couple of day's
time—you can leave your horse and clamber on up the
valley to a lake that's hidden behind that mountain. I
did that one day around the middle of June a year or
two back. We had a construction gang on the place at
the time—some alterations to be made. Too many people
around and never a moment's peace. The old kitchen was
pulled down; our Italian cook had moved his outfit into
the living room, and the living room was open to the sky.
Just bedlam—also I was curious to know what it was like,
in behind those mountains at that season. So, without
saying anything to anybody, I got up in the dark one
morning and got my own breakfast and got out of the
place while the bunch was still enjoying its beauty sleep
—just kissed the outfit good-bye for one whole perfect day.

"It's twelve miles of a ride up Flat Creek, and then you
tie your horse in a little grove of firs and go ahead on foot.
I got into the lake basin towards midday and I found lots
of snow and ice there and a hot sun shining—and on the
bare patches a few small saxifrages in bloom. No other

signs of life, and yet that's an amazing place for alpine flowers later on in the summer. But there was so much snow that June that the lake was still frozen and tremendous drifts were still banked up at the edge of the timber.

"After lunch I took it into my head to climb that peak: I thought I could do it easily, up to the shoulder anyway, by kicking steps in the snow that was banked up against it. I had no ice-axe with me, nor even a pole, but I had good, nailed mountain-boots on. And so I kicked steps and I kicked steps, balancing there somehow as the snow-slope got steeper and steeper till I could stand upright and touch it with my hand. And I got within a few feet of the shoulder —and there I stuck. The snow came to an end and the rock above was overhanging.

"My pocket aneroid said I'd come up nearly eight hundred feet of snow. I looked down for the first time, hanging on to the rock, and it seemed an awfully long way to where I had left my pack. And another thing—the sun was blazing down on the snow, a hot midsummer sun, and I could see that even the steps near to me were melting and rounding off. And, with nothing to hang on to, I didn't dare to try to kick steps going down."

"That was a nice spot to be in. How on earth did you get out of it?"

"I had a bright idea. The rock that I was hanging on to was loose and slabby. I thought that, if I could dislodge a large chunk of this without pulling anything down on myself, I could slide down, face to the snow and using the rock as a brake. I thought it would drag and slow me up if I could get its roughest surface to the snow. So I stamped out a bit of a platform and went at it. It took me ages, but in the end I eased out a slab nearly three feet long and up to five inches thick—a heavy brute and I couldn't manage to turn it over to see what the underside was like. It seemed to take hours, wiggling that rock into place. However, there were two good handholds on it, and

finally I got the thing where I wanted it and started—ever
so gently. At least, that was the idea."

"And it worked? It must have, because you're here now,
telling me about it. What a brain wave!"

"No—it didn't work. Or, at least, it worked in reverse.
The rock travelled even faster than I did and it took charge
right away. There were some fierce acrobatics that I don't
really remember—you see, I was absolutely terrified—
while the rock by-passed me. But I had a death-grip on
the thing and I hung on—and there we were, plummeting
down that snow-slope, the rock in the lead and me hurtling
after it, too frightened to let go. Thank God I lost my grip
in time and the rock went careering on ahead. I think I
heard it bounding and clattering about on the scree at
the foot of the snow-slope; but I was feeling rather sick
and dizzy by then, and also weaving about and slowing
up a bit as the slope eased off and the snow got wetter
and softer. I just slid gently into the rocks at the bottom,
soaked—and then I *was* sick. Not without reason."

"I should say not. It must have been like a parachute
not opening. Then what did you do?"

"I walked on down to where I'd left my pack—and, as
that was above timberline and there was hardly any wood
around, I'd left the tea-pail full of snow and ice in an
angle of the rock where the sun would warm it for me.
That dodge worked; and a tiny fire, which was all I could
scrape up, had that warm water boiling in no time. Tea
and the rest of the beef sandwiches, and all was well again
. . . I got back to the ranch in the evening to find
people obviously wondering where I'd been all day. I didn't
enlighten them; and my wife was safely out of the way
—in London, celebrating King George's Jubilee. Just as
well, probably: no awkward questions, no reprimands for
behaving like an idiot. All in all it was a memorable day,
and I still feel I have a sort of a squatter's right to that
mountain."

As I finished speaking the last flaming segment of the
sun dipped behind the mountains. A chill came into the
air, and the cold blue peaks, outlined in fire, seemed to
grow taller, reaching up into the cloudless sky like fingers
of steel. We drove on up the darkening valley, meeting
nobody. It was a dead-end road then, running only to the
Forest Ranger Station—a twin-rutted wagon-trail winding
through the grass. From it the home trail turned off to
the right across the last hay-flat, and soon the lights of
the house became visible through the sheltering trees.

Mary Pope was a dude-wrangler's dream come true.
She stayed with us well into November and she enjoyed
everything. The worst snowstorm we ever had came while
she was there—and she was thrilled by it. She loved the
huge open fires that lit the old living-room with their
roaring flames, and she loved the impromptu parties that
made those winter evenings come alive. She loved the
mountains to the west and the rolling grass hills of the
Bar U to the east; and a low of thirty-three below zero
was just another marvellous experience. She invested me,
quite early on, with the title of Brigadier-General; and
the last I saw of her (till we met again in England a
couple of years later) she was still singing hymns of praise
—from the back end of a C.P.R. train this time, eastbound
out of Calgary. "God bless you, Brigadier-General," she
shouted, waving frantically, "you've given me the time of
my life! God bless the Buffalo Head and all of you!" It's
not every day that one runs into enthusiasm of that calibre,
and the usually torpid inmates of the observation car were
all wide awake, listening and smiling delightedly.

She meant what she said, too. One cold afternoon, a
year or so later, the phone rang in the veranda at the
ranch. I crammed on a fur hat and went out to answer
it. It was Mary Pope, phoning from London. "I was looking
at my photos of that wonderful month," she said, "and all
of a sudden I felt I just *had* to call you and tell you all
over again how much I loved it. My husband'll curse me

for this when he sees the bill, but never mind that. Now,
come on—tell me everything about everybody."

I told her. And at the end of it all she said, "We've only
two minutes left. Tell me—is it cold there today?"

"Oh, a dirty day—just like that cold spell when you
were here. Around twenty below, grey, and a little north
wind with a touch of powder snow in it."

There was a reverent hush at the other end, during
which I heard Big Ben striking and the honk of a London
taxi. And then Mary's voice again, as the voice of one who
is seeing visions: "Twenty below," it was saying. "How
absolutely marvellous!"

Then there was Lois—another dude from England and,
like Mary Pope, the owner of another head of unruly hair.
A scorching south-west wind raved unseasonably over the
foothills during that summer that Lois spent at the Buffalo
Head. Swept by the wind, that dark wild hair would soon
take on the semblance of an osprey's nest—a first attempt,
I mean: one that has been built by a learner. Dimly
(and when the wind was right) one could discern through
the tossing plumage two questioning eyes and a mouth
that seemed always on the point of laughter. There went
another dude who left golden memories behind her—and
it may well be an invariable rule that the tangled mop
tops off the gay, blithe spirit.

For those happy natures who enjoy everything and make
no bones about saying so, one does what one can. I don't
now remember whose idea—Lois' or mine—it was that
we should attempt to run a canoe down the Highwood
River on the ranch, from the Fideli Ford to the Sullivan
Ford—but between us we decided to put that lunatic plan
into action. It was the month of July in the drought of
1936—the hottest and driest summer we ever saw on the
Buffalo Head. Through the ranch the river ran in a low
canyon, with cliffs of around fifty feet in height. The
water was at its lowest and the river was cutting, in those
miles, across the strike of the rocks. Its very bones, its reefs,

were showing, and the passages through them were narrow. The canoe (which we used sometimes on the Bow River) was a sixteen-foot Chestnut, made of eastern cedar, canvas-covered—exactly the same as I had used on the South Nahanni. It was a tough outlook for that canoe and the project was insane.

No thought of that ever entered our heads; and, on a blazing afternoon, a wagon rolled across the flat and down to the Fideli Ford. It dumped off Lois and myself and the canoe. Then it departed.

We threw the canoe into the river and settled ourselves into it, clad in shorts and shirts and canvas shoes. Then we committed ourselves to the deep, and in no time at all we were slipping down the river—faster and ever faster. We shot around the sunny point of the little bull pasture by the ford; then the canyon walls closed in on us and the confined river ran deep and green. Stray shafts of sunlight filtered down through the trees that lined the canyon rim. A rider appeared suddenly up there. That would be one of the party that had left the corrals when we set out with the wagon. Their aim in life, of course, was to be at the right spot on the cliff edge to view the grand finale. They were people of no faith, and what they both expected and hoped was that, sooner or later, we would hit on a reef or something and spill ourselves into the drink. In this they were not disappointed; and, in the meantime, they were having a few troubles of their own. They needed horses to keep up with us, but the narrow belt of woodland along the river was getting horribly in their way.

A long, tossing race of white water loomed up ahead of the canoe. We took it plumb in the centre and rode the crest right down to the final eddies—a most exhilarating rush. The last two waves broke over Lois as we drove through them. Spluttering cries came from the osprey's nest in the bow—then we floated serenely on, down a quiet reach and into the big, gentle eddies of the bathing pool. We circled the pool once or twice, planning the next move and watching the shadow of the canoe beneath us, moving over the rocky bed of the river. Then we drove our paddles into the water and shot out of the pool, over the steep shingle spillway, bound for God alone knew what—for this was a stretch of river that one scarcely ever saw. There was no reason ever to see it: the cliffs made a perfect barrier to cattle, and all I knew of the place was from wintertime trips on foot, on the river ice, exploring those shadowy, frozen reaches, or hunting for a tall, straight spruce with which to repair some primitive bit of haying machinery.

The rush downstream continued. On the cliff top the trees had thinned out and the riders were bunched together now and level with us. I had begun to think we would make it, and I was not in the least dismayed when the river fanned out suddenly over a wide shingle bar, too shallow even for this light canoe. There was still a channel—a long, narrow, creaming chute between the vertical canyon wall on our right and a parallel reef on our left. Into it we drove the canoe. There was no room to paddle—so Lois shipped her paddle and crouched low, and I trailed mine behind to act as a steering fin. Two large isolated rocks awaited us at the foot of this hill of water. It was essential to pass between them—and in a split second, as we shot down the chute, I saw that we would not do this unless I swung the canoe a little. Without taking my eye off the twin rocks, I thrust with my paddle at the rock wall on my right hand, just hard enough to put the canoe into position. By an evil chance there was a crack just there in the rock face—and into that crack my paddle blade drove and jammed. I wrenched it out instantly before it could throw me backwards out of the canoe, but the jerk put the canoe off course and we hit the twin rocks broadside on. The river boiled up into the canoe and turned it over. Slowly we rolled out and went under, still clutching the gunwale of the canoe and our paddles.

Much to my surprise I could feel with my feet, deep down, a ledge on which I could stand, braced against the current by my rock. Lois had found a foothold, too, and up came her head looking wilder than ever. She shook the water from her hair and laughed and shouted something, but the uproar of the river made it impossible to hear a single word. Up above, on the far cliff edge, the riders had dismounted. This was what they had been waiting for, and two of them were busy with cameras, while my small daughter, aged six, was capering with delight like some agile puppet manipulated by hidden strings.

The whole force of the race was pouring into the canoe which was jammed against the rocks, bending and cracking under the strain. We were only head and shoulders out of the water and it was hard to get much purchase—yet something had to be done, and quickly. With a struggle and some rough handling we freed our craft from its watery vise, only to have it almost torn from our grasp by the current and sent whirling off on its own. We hauled it back and steadied it. Then, at a signal, we lept upwards from our underwater ledges and cascaded into the canoe from opposite sides in a chaos of kicking legs, head first. This, the riding party told us afterwards, was the finest individual turn of the whole afternoon. . . As for us, we were well out of a dangerous place, and before the canoe could run foul of anything else we once more had control.

Soon, however, we came to a place where the river ran head on into a sloping cliff of smooth grey limestone, boiling up against it and then changing course, making a right-angle turn to the right. In this extreme low water there was not room for the canoe to make that turn and get safely away downstream. Sweeping with the paddles we managed to get the canoe turned—but too late: we were already at the foot of the cliff. We felt ourselves swept up it, broadside on, on a cushion of water. Then we slid away, down and to the right, and a curling wave caught us and decanted us once more into the river, this

time with the canoe on top of us. Things must have happened quickly after that, since, without knowing how I
got there, I found myself sitting astride of the upturned
canoe and paddling it to shore, while downstream a
tangled mop of hair, looking from where I sat like an
Aberdeen terrier, was swimming gallantly in pursuit of a
twirling, floating paddle.

That finished the horse party, in more senses than one.
They were convulsed, they got off their horses and sat
down on the edge of the cliff, laughing and calling to us.
Their horses, I learned afterwards, stood for a while as
they had been trained to do, staring anxiously at their
imbecile riders. Then they backed up a few paces and
stared again. Then, slowly and carefully, but none the less
purposefully, they hit for home, trailing their lines alongside. Their riders followed as best they could. Lois and I
ran on down the river to the Sullivan Ford in peace, perfect
peace. There we cached the canoe in the bush, and then we
walked the three miles home—dripping wet and cool to
start with, drying as we went under the burning sun.

This was not the last of my ventures on the Highwood—
and, in a country where the saddle horse was king, these
canoe exploits were news. The total stock of knowledge
possessed by the denizens of the foothills regarding canoes
and their habits came, as near as was possible, to absolute
zero. This, of course, did not prevent a canoe-story from
spreading, snowballing a little as it went. Therefore it was
no surprise to me, when I met Gordon Hall by Flat Creek
Bridge one morning of a pre-war summer, that he should
feel inspired to comment on these watery frolics. Gordon,
I should add, was what you might call a free-lance cow-
puncher, working when and where it suited him. For
instance, one could count on finding him at the Buffalo
Head in October; his birthday fell in that month, and it
pleased him to celebrate it with us and to work with me
in the mountains at that season, gathering cattle. We were

friends, and to him, as to many others in the hills, my name was "George".

Gordon, in his turn, was known as "the Duke"—and the reason for that goes back to an occasion at the E P Ranch, the Prince of Wales' ranch, some ten miles away from the Buffalo Head across the Bar U. The Prince was visiting his ranch, officially incognito, and a luncheon party had been given to his neighbours of the hills. Everyone was happy—and none more so than Gordon Hall who had liberally sampled "the best god-damn whisky you ever tasted in all your life", as he always afterwards described it. After lunch a move was made towards horses, and the Prince settled himself into the unfamiliar stock-saddle and tried out the paces of his mount, rising in the saddle English fashion—oompah, oompah.

This was too much for Gordon, who by now had shed any inhibitions that might normally have restrained him. He went up to the Prince to point out the error of his ways. "For God's sake, brother," he said, "stop slapping that saddle with your behind and sit down on it. This is a stock-saddle and you've just got to forget that English stuff . . ." And he went on to instruct the Prince in the proper handling—if I may put it so—of the western saddle, in which a man sits down and accommodates himself easily to the movements of the horse.

The Prince took this instruction kindly, in the spirit in which it was meant; and from that day onwards Gordon was known in the hills as "the Duke," from his obvious familiarity with the customs of the nobility and the correct forms of address.

This season of which I speak Gordon was working for my neighbour, Guy Weadick, the owner of the Stampede Ranch, cattle and dudes. An absolute bevy of dudes had invaded Guy's place this summer: thirty head of girls, all from the U.S., plus two hard-working chaperons, all supplied complete by a sort of dude-ranch agent, Richard de

Zeng Pierce. This man had come to me first, the previous fall: would I care to handle his bunch for him? Every year, he said, he made up a party and arranged a ranch holiday for it with some dude-ranch outfit that agreed to his terms and commission. The chaperons he could absolutely guarantee: they were his regulars. Working through him, they were able to enjoy a mountain summer which they could not otherwise have afforded, and that helped to make the job attractive to them.

Financially the thing was alluring. But Hitler was already raving around in Europe and I didn't want to clutter up the place with a lot of unwanted horses (we had around fifty head as it was) to say nothing of building the extra accommodation and then being stuck with it if a war came. My wife, who had at first favoured the idea, then said we were doing very nicely the way we were, and that, furthermore, she didn't take too kindly to the prospect of having our nice home meadow disfigured by any barrack-like cook-shacks and sleeping quarters. I agreed, and that settled it—and Guy and Florence Weadick took on Richard de Zeng's bunch at the Stampede Ranch.

Gordon Hall had been hired by Guy to help herd these dudes around the countryside and tell them the tale, with local colour laid on thick—which, no doubt, he did to everybody's satisfaction, including his own. The day before meeting him on Flat Creek Bridge I had been up in the mountains, packing a load of salt to the cattle. I had ridden down the last hill and into the home meadow late in the afternoon, coming in by the Flat Creek gate—and I was surprised to see approaching me, passing the corrals, a long, slow-moving cavalcade, sixteen horses, the Duke in the lead. So this was his harem—as the valley had christened it. Deeply interested and wondering what they had been doing at the Buffalo Head, I held the heavy swing-gate open for them. My packhorse, Molly, walked straight on to the barn, taking no notice of anybody or anything, her mind set on oats. My saddle-horse, Rex, seeing his mate leaving him in the lurch, stamped, whinnied and pawed furiously in the dust.

Up came the Duke. He never stopped: just rode on through, giving me a prodigious wink and a quiet "Thank you, George." Then each girl, as she passed through, favoured me with a dazzling smile and a "Thank you, Sir-r"—so infinitely more impressive than the clipped English "Suh", that for a minute or two I fancied I really *was* somebody, and not just a foothill rancher with worn old leather chaps on, dusty, thirsty and holding a frantic little horse.

I closed the gate and looked after them, as one who has caught a glimpse of paradise. The last girl turned and waved to me and I rode off to the corrals in a daze, my head spinning . . . I soon found out what the party was all about: Gordon had brought over this lot on a visit, and Marigold and our sweet-tempered cook, Mrs. Kiddle, had filled them up with tea and creamy cakes. Pure neighbourly routine. But the beauty that had passed me by, each girl smiling like the flowers in May, each one more lovely than the last—if Guy had a straight thirty head of that Grade A 1 stuff up at the Stampede, then the age of miracles had returned and I'd eat my old leather chaps! Just wait till I next saw Gordon and I'd get to the bottom of this!

And now here he was, riding over Flat Creek Bridge. We checked our horses and greeted one another, and very soon our talk turned on the dude situation. Gordon opened the scoring.

"I heard strange tales, George, when I was over at the Bar U a week ago. The boys over there tell me you folks at the Buffalo Head have taken to drowning your dudes. May I-er- inquire how this system works out? The line of least resistance, I take it?"

"Well," I said, "we've found by experience that it's the best way of disposing of them. The technique is simple: keep them around for a week or so, lull them into a false

sense of security, then lure them on to the river and upset
the canoe. There's a certain amount of risk attached to it,
of course, and I can see it's going to come heavy on canoes.
Apart from that—fine. You should get Guy to try it. You'd
look just right in a canoe with a couple of yesterday's
beauties."

Gordon's weatherbeaten face wrinkled into a smile.
"Me? Heavens, no! That'd be outside my line of endea-
vour, completely. Besides, I might overplay the act and
drown myself, too—and just think what a hell of a lookin'
corpse I'd make, going down to High River on one of
these thunderstorm floods we've been having and landing
up in Sam Smith's garden. Sam wouldn't thank me for
that at all." Sam Smith was our fishery warden and his
house stood just above a channel of the river.

"Well, think it over. And now you can just tell me a few
things about that bunch of beauties you brought over to
the Buffalo Head yesterday. Damn it—surely they can't
all be like that?"

"Oh God, no. No. That lot you saw me with—that was
hand-picked. I cut them out in the corrals before starting,
and believe me, I really topped off the bunch. There was a
few that stayed home, and the culls I sent ridin' up Sullivan
Creek, to hell and gone out of sight, in Sandy's care. I
wouldn't pack *them* around on exhibition. Now if you was
to corral the whole thirty head and let 'em mill around
till they was well mixed, and then take fifteen head as
they run—you'd get just a fair average bunch of heifers . . .
Hell, no, George! What you're asking for is miracles, even
if they was all pure-breds. No complaints, mind you—and
if a man could just get rid of two hopeless culls out of the
thirty, then he'd have quite a nice little herd . . ."

Too bad—and bang went another lovely dream. Still, it
was nice to have a word with the Duke: his views on life
were always his own and never machine-made, and the
solemn nonsense he talked was always entertaining.

Not every female dude had a bird's-nest tangle of hair

and the disposition that seems to go with it: there were other types. There came to us one summer a woman whom nobody loved—and whom, for the sake of a name, we might call Miss Harris. One by one, people swore off having anything to do with her; and that left me—I cannot accurately say, "holding the baby", but words to that effect. I could get along with Miss Harris: she was at her best *not* in a mob, she rode well and she was careful of her horse's feet, which was more than you could say for many.

I took her out one afternoon across the river and up on to the Knife Edge Ridge, a thousand-foot ridge, wooded here and there, narrow at the top and with a grassy trail running the full length of it. We rode south until we were above the spot where Flat Creek falls into the Highwood, and there we dismounted and sat down, leaving the horses loose to crop around in the bunch-grass that clothed the ridge.

The view from that spot is magnificent, and I pointed out to Miss Harris the lay of the country. That was Flat Creek, shining in the afternoon sunlight, flowing straight towards us out of the blue mountains to the west. And there south-westward through the Highwood Gap, were the peaks of the Continental Divide. They might mean, I realised, nothing to Miss Harris but they meant a lot to me. I knew what lay beyond them: meadows and forests, lakes and glaciers, all the unspoilt wilderness of the East Kootenay. I sent up one trial balloon—but, no: Miss Harris was "not interested in the bush".

All right, then—beyond the river and a thousand feet below us they were stacking hay on the Stampede Ranch, one could see the rake and sweep teams moving in their patterns like performing fleas. Miss Harris stared at them while I told her a story or two about the well-known owners of this ranch: how Guy Weadick and "Flores la Due" had met in the show business and teamed up together—trick roping and riding and the line of talk that

went with it: how Guy had built up and managed the
Calgary Stampede till it was the best-known rodeo in
North America: how his long room, whose gable I pointed
out, was hung with interesting and valuable things—the
letters of Charles M. Russell, the cowboy artist; gifts and
trophies and fancy bridles, and signed personal photographs of famous people: Colonel "Buffalo Bill" Cody, the
Prince of Wales, Lord Lonsdale, Mae West, Will Rogers—
a truly catholic collection. I might have roused a flicker of
interest—nothing more.

This was getting desperate—surely there must be *something*, somewhere? And I switched to the rounded Bull
Creek hills, to the west there, in front of the Holy Cross
Mountain, and to the Bull Creek Pass that cut through
them. I talked about the red-legged grizzly who lived up
there, an old friend of mine, I had seen him often. I took
a look to see how this was going, and lo, the lady's eyes
were shining! Here was something at last! This woman of
leather and granite had a passion for bears! And I launched
out wildly into the Saga of the Bear, as seen on and from
the Buffalo Head.

I told Miss Harris about the grizzly on Bull Creek (not
the red-legged one) that Nancy Bennett and I had ridden
right up to in a roaring south-west wind—a narrow shave,
that one, and I wouldn't try that trick again for all the gold
in the Klondike.* I told her about the grizzly that my wife
and I had chased on horseback in the meadows at the foot
of the Holy Cross Mountain,† and I told her about the
black bear I had seen dancing, one afternoon, from the
Grass Pass at the head of the South Fork of Flat Creek. I
had been looking down the Pack Trail Coulee with the
field-glass, searching to see if any Buffalo Head cattle had
strayed down that way; with a good glass you could read
the brands on cattle a thousand feet and more below and
save yourself a lot of riding. The Pack Trail Coulee ran
steeply down to the Highwood, bunch-grass in its upper
half, timber below—and something was moving down

* "The Buffalo Head," pp. 144-146.
† "The Buffalo Head," p. 138.

there, on the edge of the trees. I watched; and a black bear loped out on to the open grass, rose up on his hind legs and danced his version of a Highland fling, dropped on to all fours again and galloped back into the trees. This performance was repeated three times and it was most entertaining to watch. I never saw the like of that again: could it have been a wasp's nest that he was into, hunting for grubs?

The woman appeared to be fascinated. "Go on," she said in a low voice; and I, confident that this time I had hit the pay streak, babbled happily of bears.

There was the time, up Cataract Creek, I said, when I had ridden away from camp one October evening, following an old Indian trail up a small, dark, rock-walled valley, curious to see where it went. The spruce were thick on the flats of that valley and the slopes below the rock were clothed with pine. The creek looped and meandered round beautiful small meadows, each one a camping place for horses—and over everything was the rush of the Chinook wind. The trail became fainter and fainter. Then, as a horse trail, it petered out, though there were signs that at one time it had gone on. I hunted around on foot for a time, looking for stray axe-cuts. Then, filing away for future reference, in some mental pigeon-hole, the lay of the little valley, I turned and hit for camp.

As I was riding quietly along over the thick carpet of pine needles, thinking of supper and nothing much else, I heard a snuffling noise. I looked up; and there were two black bear cubs, obviously twins, bounding excitedly about a few feet ahead of me, while off to one side an agitated mother bear was making small rushes in various directions, rising up on her hind legs at the end of each rush to get a better look at me. Her movements were light and quick and absolutely silent; there was never even the snap of a twig underfoot. I pulled my horse up, and the mother let something between a snort and a snuffle out of her which was evidently a command. Each cub promptly went up the nearest tree; and of course the little beasts had to choose pines that grew one on either side of the trail, four feet apart at the most and no way round for a man and horse owing to the growth of pines and their interlacing branches. The cubs went sky high and then just hung there, clutching the pine trunks and still snuffling, peering down at me from behind their trees, first on one side, then on the other.

Here was the classic situation: a bear with cubs in between the rider and home. And the little valley was fast darkening in the October dusk . . . The last thing I wished to do was to shoot the bear: all I wanted was my supper, and that soon. The horse that I was riding, Rex, could go in a second from a walk into a mad gallop; I decided to put my trust in Rex, who was well used to bears and was showing no sign of fear. I rode forward quietly and passed between the two pines. The snuffling from up above became continuous. The soundless loping of the mother bear ceased, and she watched me carefully from about six yards range, standing up to see and giving one questioning, coughing grunt. I rode on towards camp, turning once in my saddle to see the cubs still further up their trees and the mother, now on all fours, standing in the trail and looking after me.

There was a sort of a sequel to this. My ranch foreman and hunting partner, Adolf Baumgart, was with me on that trip and we had seen a lot of bears. Now that we were getting near home we had decided to shoot one and take it in, the meat of a young bear being good to eat, something like domestic mutton. Females with cubs were out, but otherwise the next bear we saw was for it.

Next morning, as we were packing the horses, we decided to take a new way home—a new trail that we knew had recently been cut out by the forest ranger. We started, and I was in the lead, eyes down and searching in the bunch-grass for signs of travel. Suddenly Adolf's voice came from behind, tense and excited: "Look out!" it said.

"Quick! A bear!" I didn't wait to examine the scenery. I had Rex trained so that I could dismount on the off side where my rifle was slung. I swung out of the saddle and landed with my back to the black shape that had shown fleetingly in the tall grass on the edge of my vision. The Mannlicher carbine came slick out of its leather scabbard into my hand and I whirled round to face the bear. The bunch-grass was moving a little in a small hollow just ahead: then it parted, and the trusting, innocent face of a fat black steer looked out—one of Thorpe and Cartwright's, they ran up here on Cataract Creek. And there was I, alert and poised, rifle half raised—and Adolf, crimson-faced and rocking in his saddle with laughter.

"Blast you, Adolf, and your tricks! How did you know that one would work so well?"

"Because you were so wrapped up in the trail, and because we saw so many bears yesterday that I knew you would first go for your rifle. Oh-h—ho! ho!"

I told Miss Harris all this, and she just stared at me, completely absorbed and not a bit amused. "And so your man was deceiving you?" she said.

"Well, to tell the truth," I replied, "I'd never thought of it like that. But he certainly took a rise out of me that time."

The lady looked a bit blank. "Took a rise?" she queried hesitantly. Remembering that she was an American, I translated hastily: "Put a fast one over on me, I mean."

But Adolf's transgressions were not what Miss Harris was worrying about. "These bears," she said, "do you have them outside the mountains? I mean, near home?"

"Oh, yes," I said brightly. "With a bit of luck you might see one any day. Only last week Adolf and I were going out of the home meadow around five in the morning, and we stopped to open and shut the Flat Creek gate. And there, walking across our trail behind us, went a bear— right between us and the corrals, and leaving a trail in the dew till you'd think an elephant had passed by. He was taking not the slightest notice of us, and our horses weren't paying one bit of attention to him . . . Then last summer my wife and Mrs. Kiddle were picking saskatoons in that big patch of saskatoon brush above the kitchen garden—you can see it from your cabin. They were in our end of the patch for quite a time before they found there was a bear busy picking in the other. I think that must have been the bear and cub we used to see nearly every day up there last fall . . ."

Well—I was doing my best, wasn't I? I mean, how was I to know that, with every word, I was building a small private hell for Miss Harris?

Her cabin was about a hundred and fifty yards from the house. There was another cabin quite near to it, and a short lane through the poplar trees linked the two. The cabin nearest to the house was inhabited by a liked and valued inmate of the Buffalo Head, "C.M.B." This girl had come to the ranch originally for a couple of weeks, to look after the children while Marigold and I were away, travelling in the mountains. She fell in love with the place, and the two weeks extended themselves into twenty years. Amongst other things, C.M.B. badly wanted to see a bear—and, literally for years, bears avoided her as though she were bewitched. Anybody else could run into them, but not she. And when finally she broke the spell and achieved her ambition, she did it in style: it was not just *one* lonely, niggardly bear that met her delighted eyes, but a female with two whacking great cubs!

It was to C.M.B. that Miss Harris turned in her hour of need. She never said anything to anybody else, but after my recital of the bear saga she never slept at ease. She would wait, in the evenings, till C.M.B. left the house, and the two of them would go together. Then, on some pretext or other, she would inveigle C.M.B. down to her cabin; and, when C.M.B. had said good-night and departed she could hear Miss Harris slamming her windows shut and shoving the furniture about as she barricaded her veranda door and the inner door—all this, mind you, on a summer night and on account of our inoffensive Highwood bears . . . Finally Miss Harris decided to put her defences to the test. She confessed to C.M.B. about her fear of the bears and told her what she already knew—about the nightly barricading of the cabin. "Now tonight," Miss Harris went on, "I want you to do something for me. I'll barricade my cabin and shut the windows like I always do. Then I'm going to lie on my bed—where I'd be if a bear attacked the cabin—and scream. You go to your cabin and put your door and windows the way you always have them. Then lie on your bed and listen and see if you can hear me . . ."

Struggling with a mad desire to laugh, C.M.B. went off to her cabin and stood by her mosquito-screen door, her sole defence against the hordes of dangerous carnivores that apparently swarmed in the meadow. Slam, thud, bump came from the northward as Miss Harris went through her furniture shifting act. Then silence for a minute or so— and then faint, desperate shrieks, as of coyotes in the distance, serenading the evening star. Then more rumbles and bumps, and a voice calling through the darkness "How was that?"

C.M.B. went off to the other cabin. "It wasn't bad," she said, "but I'm not sure that it would wake me. Perhaps if you could scream a little louder . . . And, anyway, what do you want me to *do*? I can't fight off all the bears in the foothills."

Well, it would comfort Miss Harris to know that another human being was sharing her last moments; and besides, C.M.B. could always rush up to the house for help. As for screaming louder, she could do that all right. Just let C.M.B. go back and listen and she'd *really* hear something!

And she did—Miss Harris yelling like an Iroquois: an unforgettable experience, and all the more memorable

since it started all the owls of the valley hooting. "Hoo!"
they cried in chorus. "Hoo-hoo!"

Now, in telling these few mild bear stories, I had indeed
meant well. How true it is that the road to hell is paved
with good intentions!

CHAPTER X

The Eden Valley

It was the denizens who made the valley what it was, all through the years when it was my home. But today there could be no returning to it: for me there could never be another Eden Valley, simply because that particular combination of human eccentricities has ceased to exist; nor is anything remotely resembling it likely to be seen again in these overtaxed times. A great pity. The world needs a few mad valleys of that kind. It is more than adequately stuffed with the humdrum and the conventional.

I have used the expression "mad valley" because, in a way, it was forced upon me. To the neighbourhood, to High River and Pekisko, the Eden Valley was known as Loony Lane. That name, I am glad to be able to say, had been well and truly earned before I ever appeared on the scene to make matters worse. However, as both Guy Weadick and I ran each a bunch of dudes in the summertime and also entertained some interesting and unusual guests, I think we did our bit to maintain the tradition. And any gaps that we may have left were sure to be filled in by Frazier Hunt up at the Eden Valley Ranch. But through July and August the dudes could be counted on to keep us thinking. You *never* knew what a dude would come up with. One of ours, for instance, who had insisted on riding alone across the Bar U lease, turned up eleven miles away, at Walter Hanson's Chinook Ranch with her bridle inside out and upside down. That is the only way in which I can describe it: she had taken her bridle off so that her horse (luckily a quiet one—we had seen to that) might get a bite of grass somewhere along the trail; and then she had contrived to put it on again in some fantastic fashion, so that the long levers of the western bit, instead of hanging *down* from the horse's mouth, protruded *upwards,* seeming at a distance to rise out of the wretched animal's nostrils.

Walter Hanson had been at school with Rudyard Kipling at the United Services College, in Devon, in the time of "Stalky and Co." That was in the Eighties, and now, in 1939, Walter was no longer young. He happened to see this weird outfit approaching his corrals, and all the horseman and stockman that was in him was deeply shocked at the unseemly sight.

"You know, Patterson," he said to me when he was telling me about it, "I thought at first she was riding a cross between a horse and a wild boar. The way she had that bit, it looked just like a pair of tusks. So I said to her, 'God bless my soul, what the devil's happened to your horse?' And she said to me, 'There must be *something* the matter. I can't seem to get him to go straight or do what I want him to do'."

Walter sorted that one out for the girl and advised her not to take her bridle off again till she knew how to put it on. He realised, of course, that this English girl had probably only ridden riding-school horses that were produced all ready, saddled and bridled for her. But with the hired men it would be different. An apparition like that, coming from where it did, would seem to them perfectly normal: just another mad thing out of Loony Lane. And so the legend grew.

Riding once a week for the mail, we always managed to pass an hour or two en route at the Hansons'. Walter, together with Frank Bedingfeld (part of whose ranch became, when he sold out, the E P Ranch of the Prince of Wales) and one or two more kindred spirits from the hills, set out for the Klondike in the winter of 1898. They never reached the golden river. Their party was one of those that tackled it through the Peace River country and up the Liard, intending to come in to the Yukon from the southeast, by the back-door. The wild canyons of the Liard defeated them and they were forced to camp and hunt and wait for the freeze-up of 1899. They had persistence and endurance, those men—and courage. They broke up their boat and made sleds out of the lumber; and then, when winter was far advanced and the river ice, they thought, was solid, they started into the canyons on snowshoes, each man pulling a sled. Hell Gate, the Grand Canyon of the Liard, Whirlpool Canyon—they passed them all, sledding and relaying the outfit. The danger of it—the treacherous open water, snow-covered and hidden; the hotsprings that keep the river open and overflowing; the falling rocks from the canyon walls; the bitter wind! One can see them there in those shadowy depths, small specks of life where no living thing had any right to be, slowly breaking an endless trail that the wind and the drifting snow wiped out behind them —but always struggling on.

On the soggy April snow, and with the water already running over the ice, they made it through to the Lower Post near Watson Lake, where the Alaska Highway runs today. There, in the spring sunshine, they built their boat again. But by this time it was 1900. They were still six hundred miles from the Klondike, with the Frances River to ascend and Campbell's Portage to cross from the Frances to the Pelly. And two of the party were sick men: understandably so, perhaps, since they had of late been reduced to cooking with candle-grease. There was nothing for it but to turn aside and head south, up the Dease River towards Telegraph Creek and Wrangell and the sea. They had failed—but the memory of that trip stayed with Walter all his life. Useless as it might have been had they gone on to the Klondike, I know Walter Hanson would have loved to have reached that fabled river. Always he would talk to me of the North, referring sometimes to books in his library by northern travellers—Hanbury, Warburton Pike, Sir William Butler. And the bond between us was the Liard. To nobody else in this country of the horse could Walter talk of river currents and eddies, of tracking and poling and portaging—for nobody else would understand . . .

By the Thirties of this century Walter was somewhat deaf, and after a spell of conversing with him my wife and I would invariably ride away bellowing at each other, no doubt to the vast enjoyment of anybody within a half-mile radius.

Walter Hanson always said what he thought, and he also had a most engaging way of mixing some quite grand-motherly expression with a mild cussword. He told me of an occasion when, on entering the old Alberta Hotel in Calgary prior to leaving town for the ranch, he spied a brother horseman and polo-player standing hunched up at the bar, the picture of gloom and despondency. Walter ranged himself alongside the stocky little figure and clapped it on the shoulder. "Drink that up and have one with me," he said. "You look as if you need several. Anything wrong?"

"Got engaged to be married," came the glum reply.

"Bless my soul! Who on earth to?"

"Prunella Bunbury."

"Oh, my God! You poor little devil!"

Knowing them both well, I burst out laughing.

"It's all very well now, Patterson, but you know, he was quite upset about that. I can't think why: it was a perfectly sensible remark. I had quite a time, calming him down . . ."

To the south of the Buffalo Head, next in line in Loony Lane, lived an entirely different character, Guy Weadick. The strong mountain stream of Flat Creek was all that lay between us, and the two ranch-houses were a bit over three miles apart. I have already, in the preceding chapter, explained the lay of the land and said a word or two about Guy and Florence Weadick.

They were the best of neighbours and, wherever possible, we co-operated. Their guests would ride over to visit us, and many was the good party that we and our people had up at the Stampede Ranch. But best of all were those winter evenings when the dudes had gone and the Eden Valley was itself again—and we would sit by the fire in the long room at the Stampede or the living room at the Buffalo Head, and Guy would tell of their days in the show business on the vaudeville circuit, or with the 101 Ranch show in Europe, or touring, the pair of them, in Europe with "the horse" (they never referred to it by any name) and about the devil of a time they often had, getting that awkward but essential animal through the customs, sometimes as a stage property, sometimes as pedigree livestock, and once as an article of clothing. This last was due to a slight misunderstanding. Guy, driven almost frantic by French red-tape, had replied, to a suggestion that they could stage their act in Paris without the horse, by saying that they might just as well leave their clothes and lariats, too, at the port of entry and walk on stark raving naked. The French customs man was appalled. He said, in broken English, that that would certainly never be permitted. But since they insisted on leaving their clothes with the horse, he would see what could be arranged . . . French logic, no doubt, found the solution, and the horse was allowed to accompany the Weadicks (who remained within their clothes) as an item of clothing and equipment.

There was the time when the sculptor Prince Troubetz-koy was modelling Guy and the horse in the garden of his Paris house, and a green door in the garden wall burst open with a crash. In rushed a frantic little man, jabbering and gesticulating nineteen to the dozen—but still less fast than the Prince, who out-talked him, shoved him back through the door again, slammed it and shot the bolt home. "I will not be troubled by that man again," he said. "He is angry because I now model you when I have twice refused to model him. I will make him the laughing stock of Paris."

And he did: his contribution to the next Salon was simply a pig with its feet in the trough, and the sole caption was "Le Cochon". But the pig had the features of the frantic little man, and the frantic little man was a member of one of the first banking families of Europe. Everybody immediately perceived the resemblance . . .

It was on a spring evening in Paris, during that same visit, that Guy, headed for the theatre, stopped somewhere on the Boulevard des Italiens for a shave and a shampoo. He was grossly overcharged, but had not sufficient French to argue about it. Also he was late, so he paid and got out. However, he took it out on the barber during the act, ad-libbing to his heart's content before an audience that was largely English and American. They loved it, and it went so well that Guy slipped it into the act from that night onwards. But the French had evidently appreciated it also, for a voluble little delegation called round at Guy's dressing-room, on that first night, to tell him so. He could understand that much because the word "satisfaction" kept cropping up, again and again. He bowed and smiled and said, with appropriate gestures, that he was indeed happy to know that they had enjoyed the act.

But they went on and on about it; and finally, in desperation, Guy got hold of a French theatre attendant who could speak a little American. "Tell these guys," he said, "that I'm pleased they enjoyed the show. And get them to hell out of here—I want to change and go."

It was only then that it became clear that these Frenchmen had not enjoyed the act at all. They were the friends of the barber, who had been in the house when Guy was saying his piece about the highway robbers of the Boulevard des Italiens—worse, he had said, than any of the hold-up men who had once shot it out in the wild days of the American frontier. The barber's honour had been affronted and the satisfaction his friends were talking about was a duel to the death.

As the challenged party, Guy had the choice of weapons.

He promptly suggested the lariat; or, if the barber preferred it, he volunteered to knock him into the middle of next week at any given spot in the Forêt de Whatsitsname (and let the barber name it) the very next morning. Uproar broke loose at this ungentlemanly suggestion, and finally Guy shooed the whole lot out, changed out of his western finery and went his way . . .

In London Lord Lonsdale, horseman and aristocrat of the old school, was mightily taken with the 101 Ranch show. He became friendly with these Americans, examined with interest their horses, saddlery and dress, and finally asked them if there was anything he could do for them that would make their stay in London really memorable.

Yes, Guy said, there was. If it were possible, they would enjoy most of all seeing over Buckingham Palace stables —horses, harness, carriages, everything.

Very well, Lord Lonsdale replied: he thought that could be arranged. There was just one thing, he continued—and one may suppose there was a smile on his face as he spoke. He wanted them to come on horseback, in full war-paint —chaps, boots, sombreros, fringed and beaded gloves and jackets—everything just as in the show. Let them assemble at ten o'clock the next morning at Prince's Gate in Hyde Park—but casually; not in a body, but in twos and threes as if they were out for a morning ride. And so it was arranged.

The next morning the twos and threes, gay as butterflies against the quiet London scene, riding in Rotten Row, began to attract attention. Occasionally they stopped to greet each other and small, admiring crowds assembled. The crowds grew and followed the cowboys. The police intervened and said that the riders could not be allowed to create a disturbance, riding around in fancy dress. The Americans, all innocence, said it wasn't fancy dress —it was just their ordinary working clothes, all they had to ride in, and they had always wanted to ride in Rotten Row. A highlight of their English visit. The police were baffled; and slowly, and with perfect timing, the 101 Ranch closed in on Prince's Gate—just where the motor road cuts across between Hyde Park and Kensington Gardens.

A glorious traffic jam was the immediate result. Buses were stopped, the old open-top buses, and people swarmed up on top of them to cheer and laugh. The London crowd took charge, always unpredictable, this time delighted. Carriages, cars, taxis, riders in sober black or grey, nurse-maids with perambulators—everything came to a standstill. It was a good-natured riot. Only Kipling's pen could have done justice to it, as in *The Vortex* or *The Village that Voted the Earth was Flat.*

Precisely on the stroke of ten Lord Lonsdale appeared. He was probably one of the best-known and most popular men in London at that time. The crowd roared its welcome; and soon, by the magic of his smile, his lordship had everybody soothed—police, bus-drivers, taxi-drivers, even, let us hope, the orthodox, bowler-hatted riders and those who, by now, had quite certainly missed their trains. Soon, with Guy Weadick and the other top men of the 101 Ranch, he was riding easily towards Buckingham Palace— the whole gorgeous cavalcade following behind him, guests, for the morning, of the King . . .

Above the fireplace in the long room at the Stampede Ranch there was an old buffalo skull set into the rough river-stone of the chimney. Red electric lights were set in its eyeless sockets and the thing grinned ghoulishly in the flickering light of the log fire. Undeterred by this horror—or possibly even stimulated by it—Guy would tell tales of the Dolly Sisters, or of the days when he and Florence were on the same bill in vaudeville as Rosa Ponzillo and her sister—was the sister's name Luisa? Until that tour the Ponzillos had been billed quite low down, but at some eastern theatre Rosa's wonderful voice drew the attention of a discerning manager. He moved the sisters up on the bill and gave them full-stage instead of only the half-stage that they had had till then. That first step on the ladder of fame temporarily turned their heads, Guy said. He was a born mimic in voice, hands and bearing, and soon we had the pleasure of seeing him mincing about the long room in the character of the future Rosa Ponselle or her sister on their first full-stage set, ordering the re-arrangement of piano, chairs and other properties, and objecting, now, to being sandwiched in between the animal act and the monologist. He would then become the owner of the performing dogs, complaining that his terriers were as house-broke as any one else on the bill, and good enough so that nobody need be ashamed to follow them. Then the soft, southern voice of the monologist would come out of the wavering shadows of the long room, saying that he'd been happy once till the manager messed the bill up, and now he wished to God he was back home in Georgia where there was peace. The monologist did not end there, but most of what he said was strictly libellous and best left alone . . .

The one thing that the Weadicks were scared of was an English dude—or, worse yet, a pair of them. They were sure they never gave them the right food, and they felt that at frequent intervals during the day (but just exactly when?) they ought to be offering them cups of tea. Then there was their passion for exercise—how was one to cope with that when the American or Canadian guests just wanted a gentle ride? So, when desperate, they sometimes turned a couple of the English over to us for a day—though not without prayers for their horses' feet. Their dudes could count on an energetic time with us: up Flat Creek in the early morning, tie the horses in the shade, and then forward on foot and climb. We met some delightful people on those mountain days, and they saw the alpine meadows, ablaze with flowers and rippling in the summer wind, that they would never otherwise have seen. I have a picture of one of those expeditions: my wife and two English girls from the Stampede Ranch, and a guest of ours, walking over a vast snowdrift at the head of Flat Creek one hot July day. Our only difficulty was to prevent some of these people from galloping the whole ten miles home in the evening—downhill and over all the rocks. The horses, headed homewards, were eager to lope or gallop; they needed no urging, and what did they care about their feet? The one thought in their heads was oats—and the sooner the better. The dudes, for their part, were only too happy to oblige the horses ("Surely the horse knows best?"). But *we* cared, for we well knew what Florence Weadick would be saying next day if we sent her guests in with chips and chunks hammered out of their horses' hoofs: "Out all day with that wild bunch from the Buffalo Head, and God only knows where they've been! I knew it! Serves me right for taking the easy way out! Never again . . ."

We co-operated in other ways, also: when we had a few head of cattle to get rid of we would try to time it so that the Stampede and Buffalo Head bunches went together, each of us sending a man or two. Usually that worked well, but not invariably—and here let me introduce my foreman, Adolf Baumgart, once of Aulowöhnen in East Prussia and a man in a thousand. Adolf had come to the Buffalo Head in the time of my predecessor and friend, George Pocaterra. He had liked the country and liked the people, and so he had stayed. He was capable, reliable and a good shot, and having been brought up with livestock, he had an eye for a cow or a horse. And more than just an eye: I once saw a horse of his that he was breaking, Soldier, bolt with him—through the corrals and into the old work-horse barn. Leaning over like a Cossack, or an Indian attacking a wagon laager, Adolf somehow stayed with Soldier through the low doorway of that barn—and then came a tremendous crash. Killed, I thought—but no: that was the pair of them fetching up, head-on, against the saddle-room door. There came to me, running up to pick up the pieces, the sound of more bangs and crashes and a great pounding of hoofs.

The Eden Valley in the Fall.

George Robertson, complete with "super-sombrero," on Midge.

The *"Greenhorn homesteader."*
R.M.P. Christmas Day, 1924.

"My cabin on the ridge."

"*Mamselle's head was thrust, serpent-like, through the lacings.*" *Gordon Mathews and the team, ready to start. Spirit River, Alberta, 1928.*

R.M.P. and Spud, Fort St. John, B.C. Background: the outfit and toboggan loaded on McLeod's sleigh.

"A beautiful Husky, a child's pet . . .". Gordon Mathews and Spud at Fort St. John.

Gordon Mathews and R.M.P. at Fort Liard, N.W.T. 1928.

"The last two waves broke over Lois as we drove through them." The
Highwood River on the Buffalo Head at that precise spot.

"The big, gentle eddies of the bathing pool." C.M.B. diving.

The author on the Bow River, Stoney Indian Reserve.

"Struggling with a mad desire to laugh, C.M.B. went off to her cabin."

Marigold and Raymond Patterson in the home meadow, booted for the trail to Calgary.

R.M.P. on Rex. The home meadow, Buffalo Head Ranch.

Paul Amos, the Stoney, the old hunter.

A riding party on the Grass Pass. Reading from the left: second—Guy Weadick: fourth—Frazier Hunt: fifth—Marigold Patterson.

The Eden Valley. Extreme right centre: Stampede Ranch buildings (Wea-dick). Against far hills and to left of pine tree: Eden Valley Ranch buildings (Hunt).

"It's twelve miles of a ride up Flat Creek . . .". "Patterson's Peak" on the left—the twin Dogtooth Mountains on the right.

Albert Faille at Irvine Creek, N.W.T. 1951.

R.M.P. in a burnt muskeg, Flat River country, N.W.T. 1951.

The end of a perfect day! R.M.P. and the Beaver at the Asarco float, Quartz Lake, Yukon Territory. July, 1955.

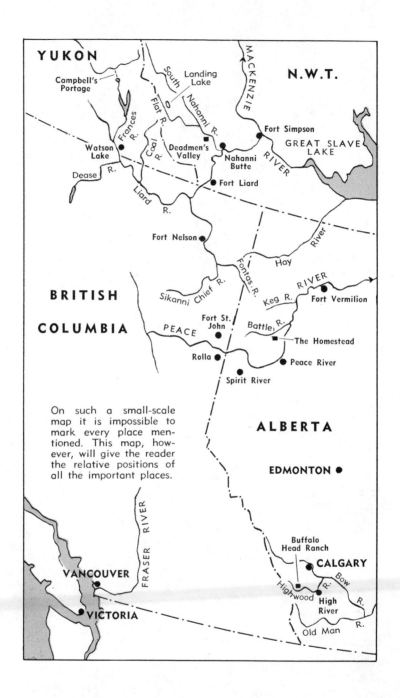

YUKON

Campbell's Portage

Landing Lake

South Flat R.

Nahanni R.

MACKENZIE

N.W.T.

Frances R.

Coal R.

Deadmen's Valley

Fort Simpson

GREAT SLAVE LAKE

Watson Lake

Nahanni Butte

RIVER

Dease R.

Fort Liard

Liard R.

Fort Nelson

River

Hay

BRITISH

Sikanni Chief R.

Fontas R.

Keg R.

RIVER

COLUMBIA

PEACE

Fort St. John

Battle R.

Fort Vermilion

The Homestead

Rolla

Spirit River

Peace River

On such a small-scale map it is impossible to mark every place mentioned. This map, however, will give the reader the relative positions of all the important places.

ALBERTA

EDMONTON ●

FRASER RIVER

Buffalo Head Ranch

CALGARY

Bow R.

VANCOUVER

Highwood R.

High River

R.

VICTORIA

Old Man

R.

Then Soldier shot out through the barn door (it was something under seven foot six) with Adolf still in the saddle giving him the basting of a lifetime with a heavy quirt. Through the corrals they went at a mad gallop and out by the Flat Creek gate, all gates open, out into the blue; and, by the time they returned, Soldier was very glad to be allowed to walk soberly and quietly. He'd had his fling; only he'd had it with the wrong man on his back, and from now on he was just going to be a good, well-behaved little horse.

Thoroughness in all he put his hand to was second nature with Adolf, and he gave a special demonstration of this in September 1934 when he took a bunch of Stampede-Buffalo Head cattle down to High River, to sell there over the scales to Swift's. Adolf's English was still a foreign language to him then, and you must imagine him speaking slowly and precisely and giving to each word its full value.

The arrangement was that I would send Adolf and one other man, Patrick Ryan, with the cattle; and Guy Weadick would send a man that was working for him at the Stampede, Paddle River Smith. My wife and I and Guy would ride down with the bunch till we got them out of the hills and to the edge of the farming country. There we would leave the cattle with the three men and ride back home together, calling on Johnny Brown at the OH and Jim Bews at Sullivan Creek, and generally making a day of it. The evening before we started I gave Adolf fifteen dollars (the equivalent of about forty-five now) and told him to be sure to stand the other two riders a few drinks after they had handed over the cattle. I also suggested that a little dissipation would do him no harm, and possibly even a power of good after long months on the place.

Adolf thought that one over and said: "I have read in the books on the old-time cattle drives that the cowboys always got tight when they got in to town. It is evidently the correct thing to do. If it can be arranged I will get tight, as you so kindly suggest, and I will make the other boys tight also. But first I have a little shopping to do. I need new riding-boots and we are out of four-inch spikes."

I have no doubt that everything was done in the proper order and with due deliberation. But, for all this caution, Adolf went at it with true Prussian thoroughness and staged a memorable bender. They roped the fishery warden —English and a great friend of ours—into the earlier stages of the binge; they did the St. George's tavern a bit of no good; and they slept on their saddles in the old Astoria Hotel—an empty, windowless and dilapidated building. Adolf rode the thirty-odd miles back home the next day, and appeared to be in the full bloom of health. He was without Patrick Ryan, who, however, was quite safe and cooling his heels in jug for assaulting the local policeman. But Paddle River had vanished completely from human ken. I could only pray that this vanishing act was not permanent, since Guy Weadick, who was a hard man to dislodge from the telephone, kept calling me up at all hours of the day to see if I had word of him, and also to ask "what the devil it was that Adolf got those fellows into?" I could well imagine Florence's comments in the background: "*I* knew it! *I* told you— that wild bunch at the Buffalo Head. Never again . . ."

Adolf was with us for eight years, and his character is best summed up in his own words in the following incident. A certain spring of the early Thirties found me alone on the place—that is, minus family but with a most variegated gang of about fifteen head all told: Danish, Irish, English, Norwegian, Prussian, Italian, Scotch—even, since this was Canada, a Canadian or two. We were trying to get some improvements and alterations done by the end of June, hence this human zoo. Into it one morning blew the census taker, wanting birthplace and every kind of foolish detail for every soul on the place. My brain reeled; and furthermore I knew Adolf was waiting for me with two saddled horses to go out and do something with the cattle. So I told the census taker, without much ceremony, to go on up the valley and bother Hunt and Guy Weadick and the forest ranger, and to come back in the evening. The census taker, full of his own importance, flew off the handle and started prating about the law and penalties and so forth; so I suggested that, if he didn't want to go as far as the ranger station, he could always take a jump in the river instead, and *still* come back in the evening. With that I walked off to join Adolf and left the furious busybody talking to the hitching rail.

We rode off towards Flat Creek and I was still mad and muttering, under my breath, about the damned census. Adolf's English was correct and precise, but had not at that time the fluency and range of later days; and I, completely absorbed, failed to notice that he was becoming scarlet in the face with wrath.

Suddenly he gave tongue. "Senses!" he burst out angrily. "You go on and on about senses! It may indeed be that I have no senses, but at least I DO MY BEST!"

Looking at me out of the shadows I can see the strong features of an Indian friend, Paul Amos, the Stoney, the old hunter. That was his "white-man" name. The English translation of his Stoney name was Spotted Wolf. Paul was blood brother of Pocaterra who had trapped and hunted with the Indians in the early years of this century,* ranging beyond the Divide and far into British Columbia—the old hunting country of the Stoneys, now closed to them. There had always been a welcome for Paul and his people on the Buffalo Head and it was fitting that this should continue. Moreover, I learnt a lot from Paul. He would come to the house with a present of mountain sheep meat or venison, and he would depart carrying away with him sugar, tea, tobacco—anything his camp was short of. On those visits, or while driving down with me to

*"Among the Nomadic Stoneys," by George W. Pocaterra. (Alberta Historical Review. Summer, 1963.)

Longview or High River, he would tell me of the mountain trails, of the ways of the wild animals, of old hunting trips when the Stoneys still lived the wild life of nomad hunters.

The borderland between fact and dreams was often hard for me, knowing only a few words of Stoney, to determine. The Indian is by nature an orator and an artist. Once he is started on a tale he becomes carried away by the sheer vividness of his imagination. All the glory and the wonder of the West lie handy to his tongue: who but a fool would waste his breath and bore his audience with plain, unvarnished fact? The Indian ends, of course, by believing the tale he tells, no matter how wild and wonderful—just as many white men can, and frequently do.

I chanced on Paul one summer morning on the summit of a high hill in the valley of the South Fork of Flat Creek, close under Mount Head. I was riding up to look at a high spring, and he was just sitting there, motionless, his rifle lying beside him on the grass, his horse grazing nearby. I sat down beside him and he told me a story about the great dome of rock that thrust out from the range, a mile or so to the south of us, between Mount Head and the Holy Cross Mountain—how his grandfather (who may have been any remote ancestor) pursued the king of all Bighorn rams up there, cornered him and fought it out on the edge of the drop. "Eh-h, koná!" he said—and his eyes were shining. "Oh-h, my friend! My grandfather, he's grab'um by the horns — fight — then throw'um down!" And he pointed to the precipice. "All the way! Piff - paff - *pah!* *Kill!*"

There was Paul, now up and kneeling on the kinikinik, tense, his hands reaching forward, his fingers hooked like an eagle's talons—and you knew that he was no longer with you: he had gone back into the red past of his race, and he was up there, himself, on the dome of the rock, hurling the ram into the abyss with his bare hands.

I have heard more about that "grandfather" of Paul's: how he was a magician as well as a mighty hunter, and a man cunning in battle, giving himself the appearance of three men and arranging it, by his magic, so that his enemies shot their arrows at the false images and not at him—a very practical device, that one, and disheartening for the foe.

Paul hit the long trail three years ago, to the hunting grounds where the game never fails and the white man can never come. He was old and it was time, and the things he loved were no longer as they used to be. His way would be an easy one for, in his active days, the old hunter had sent ahead of him a hundred grizzlies to break the trail . . . . .

Most welcome of all the summer migrants on the Buffalo Head was our fishery warden from High River, Sam Smith. When the crocuses were in bloom and the last snowfalls were melting, then we would look for Sam's arrival. Usually we would hear the warning thud of horses' hoofs over the bridge in the lane below the house, and then Sam and one or two of his horses—Pink Eye, Sailor or Big Medicine—would appear at the hitching-rail. Now at last, when both Sam and the blue-birds had turned up, we would know it was really spring. But the most spectacular of all Sam's advents was on that dry April day when Ernest Cox and I and the Major (a Boer War veteran and friend) were extracting the car-battery in order to take it down to the saw-engine with an afternoon's sawing in view. Tools and a tool-box were lying scattered around on the grass—when suddenly a terrible hullaballoo came to our ears from the lane through the woods. It grew louder and changed its note as it swept round the hill below the house. Then a vintage car surged into view over the crest with, of all people, Sam at the helm—Sam whose second home through all these years had been his saddle!

He shot past us, heading for the ice-house, but with his head turned towards us, looking for a welcome and for applause—which, indeed, he was getting. Then he pulled

back on the steering wheel, as if driving a team, shouted
"Whoa, Lizzie!", trampled on the brake and fetched his
skunk-wagon to a standstill with a final roar of the engine
and a splintering crash of wood—one wheel plumb on top
of what had been our best tool-box but which had obviously
not been constructed to stand up to this sort of thing. Sam
then bowed regally from his car and cut the engine, and
silence fell on the place with a thud, broken only by the
laughter of Ernest and myself.

The Major was advancing slowly towards our fishery
warden, one finger pointing to the ruin under the front
wheel. "You supply these by the dozen, I suppose, at places
where you visit regularly?" he enquired of Sam.

"What's that, Major? I don't quite—."

"Get out and have a look at the crime you've committed."

"Oh, the devil . . ."

From that day onwards Sam's car stood, in summertime,
on the north side of the storehouse, used occasionally to
supplement his horses when he wanted to reach some far
corner of his big district. Sometimes he would vanish for
weeks on end. Then one morning he would be seen, a welcome figure, walking over to the house for breakfast from
the old cabin on the knoll that we kept for him and where
his outfit was stored.

Many a day's help did the ranch get from Sam when his
skills as a stockman or a blacksmith were in request. And
if there was anything I wanted to know that had anything
to do with the ranch—from packing an awkward load on a
horse, all the way to bygone weather freaks and dry seasons
—then I would seek out this man who had sailed the seven
seas before taking root at last on the Highwood River.

Here, too, was a man who had tales enough for the
Thousand and One Nights. With Sam we fished and sailed
from Galiano Island in the Strait of Georgia to the eastern
Mediterranean where the giant octopus has his lair: saw
with him the silent tentacle reaching over the gunwale to
fasten on to "old Panty", the old Italian fisherman from

the island of Pantelleria. With this Derbyshire Englishman we wandered over Europe with Lord George Sanger's Circus, set up the "big top", drove in the Roman chariot races "with a little, itsy-bitsy Roman kilt on, a scarlet cloak that streamed out in the wind, a tin breastplate, and tin cricket pads on my shins . . . "

Best of all were his stories of the early days in the foothill country. He told us of the first time he met Pocaterra. He had heard of him, of course, but had never seen him; and then came the winter's day when, having some business to see to up the Highwood, his way took him through the Buffalo Head. At a place where the trail came near to the cliff edge Sam heard the pounding thud that a crowbar makes on solid ice. He dismounted and walked to the edge of the drop—and there, down below on the frozen river, he saw a man working furiously, cutting a hole in the two feet or so of ice, presumably with a view to fishing. The description seemed to fit Pocaterra: big sombrero, silk scarf, fringed buckskin jacket, breeches, moccasins—and the dynamic energy that this man was putting into the job. But Sam couldn't see the man's face because he never looked up or took his eyes off the flying splinters and growing hole. So Sam lit his pipe and waited.

The man was using a straight crowbar, and not an ice-chisel, which would probably have had a circular handgrip on it. If this fellow goes on at this rate, Sam thought, it's about two to one there'll be a sad ending. He'll punch a hole clean through the last bit of ice, and most likely that crowbar'll slip straight on through his mitts and go to the bottom of the river. Then he'll swear and I'll get some idea what he is—white man, Indian or what.

The chips flew and the hole widened. Then, suddenly, there came a different sound, a sharp click—and zoup! the crowbar had vanished and the hole was filling with water under pressure from the small black aperture at the bottom. And the figure below was swearing all right—only not in one language, as Sam had expected, but in four or five:

Italian, French, German, English and Stoney, anything that came handy. Not much the wiser, Sam tactfully withdrew, and the official meeting took place later.

Another winter ride up the valley in another year brought an even stranger sound to Sam's ear—that of a piano being played with both touch and feeling. This was on the Snowdon Hill, where the trail dropped down on to the old O H Ranch. There was no house for miles, and the brilliant sunshine of a warm winter's day poured down out of a cloudless sky on to an empty world of dazzling white. Sam thought of mirages and wondered if the same sort of thing could happen with acoustics—but this was as clear as a bell and no faint echo of a sound. Then he decided that, well, he'd probably gone daft at last, and he might just as well make a complete fool of himself and look over the grade to the left where the sound seemed to be coming from. He knew, of course that there was nothing there—only the steep slope to the flat below and the river.

He was much relieved to find that there actually *was* a piano down below there, propped upright in the snow. At the keyboard sat a young English rancher from beyond the river, Rigg. Rigg was sitting on a piano-stool of packed snow, on the top of which he had laid his folded saddle-blanket. Nearby stood his horse with his lines down, and on the top of the piano stood a bundle of music and a bottle of whisky. Rigg was playing happily and contentedly like a man long starved of music . . . The piano had been on the way out to Rigg's place when, on the Snowdon Hill, the sleighs had overturned, decanting the piano unharmed into a deep snowdrift. Unable to get it out till he had assembled sufficient helpers, Rigg was nevertheless unable to keep his fingers off the keys. Hence this angel music in the snowy wastes. Thankful to discover that he personally was sane, whatever Rigg might be, Sam gratefully accepted a drink and stayed to enjoy the concert . . .

In one of his many incarnations Sam had worked as fireman in the Calgary Fire Department. In its day this public service had been known to produce the light-hearted incident, and never more so than during the captaincy of a famous local character, "Cappy" Smart. Of one such incident my wife and I had the story from Sam one cold October evening, when the three of us were sitting before the fire in the ranch living-room. We sat there without lamps, in the fire-light and the dancing shadows, the two of us listening while Sam explained for our benefit how the old-time Calgary Fire Brigade and the funeral business which Cappy Smart operated as a side-line could, in an emergency, become all tangled up together till only luck or genius could get things straightened out again . . .

And this *was* an emergency. The funeral was an important one and, for some reason, the usual pair of horses was not available for the hearse. Trusting that, on this afternoon, the citizens were going to be more than usually careful with fire, Cappy hitched up two of the fire-engine horses that had deputised in the hearse before—and, praise be, everything proceeded according to Hoyle.

The cemetery lay south of the city, on the Macleod Trail. There had been some controversy about its position, and one well-known editor, musing on this in his paper, had declared himself puzzled why so many prominent Calgarians had lately been 'moving out of town and taking up real estate on the Macleod Trail with a view to establishing permanent residence there.' It must be the view, he thought, or the bracing air—and he expressed concern, if this sort of exodus went on, for the future of the city.

And now one more prominent citizen was heading south on the Macleod Trail to take up his final bit of real estate, followed by a long line of horse-drawn vehicles; and Cappy Smart was on the box of the hearse, handling the lines, and Sam was sitting solemnly beside him with folded arms . . . "and we had stove-pipe hats on our heads, and black gloves, and crepe bands on our arms. And we'd got our faces set in about the right shade of gloom, and everything was going swimmingly. And then, all of a sudden—what should we hear but the fire-alarm sounding back in Calgary!"

Marigold was leaning forward, fascinated. "What on earth *could* you do?" she said.

"That's just what I wanted to know, ma'am," Sam replied. "I said to Cappy out of the corner of my mouth —like this—still looking straight ahead as if nothing had happened: 'And what the hell do we do *now*?'

"Well, ma'am, he was quick. He said, speaking just the same way as I'd done: 'When I give the word we'll stop the outfit. Then down with you and we'll pull the stiff out of the show-case and shove him under the fence. Then we'll whip the horses round and hit for town, hearse and all . . . NOW THEN!' "

They must have moved like R.H.A. gunners on parade; for in a few seconds the chief participant in the funeral went sliding under the fence into the long grass, and Cappy Smart and Sam were hurtling back towards the city, clinging to the hearse as gunners to a lurching limber.

The mourners, on the whole, seemed to have been a pretty tolerant bunch. Heads popped out of carriage windows and a few shouted queries came from them—but the owners of the heads realised that Cappy had his business problems like everybody else, and they knew from experience that he was not a man who would see them stuck. Trusting in his integrity they composed themselves to wait.

It was a lively afternoon, Sam said—all mixed up till a man hardly knew what he was supposed to be wearing —stove-pipe hat and a face a mile long, or fireman's helmet and prancing around like a drunken dragoon at a Guy Fawkes party. Still, they got the fire dealt with—luckily it was a small one—and then, with a couple of half-dead horses and their faces all fixed as for a Methodist prayer meeting, the pair of them got back on to the main job again before any riot had broken out among the mourners.

"And how were they doing?" I asked.

"Oh, they were doing all right," Sam said. "They were nicely primed to start with, and some of them must have had something on their hips as well, because, when we got back, they were holding a highly successful wake, all crowded round the dear departed. They were quite sorry when we gathered him up and they had to move on again . . ."

The truly amazing thing about all that, of course, is not so much the genial tolerance of the mourners—we can find a reason for that—but the fact that the grain-fed, and consequently dashing, horses of a fire-engine could be held down on the plodding pace of funeral cortège. Sam did say that they started to get up in the air a bit when they heard the fire-alarm sounding, and that it flashed through his mind, before Cappy Smart announced his sudden decision, that this was liable to be the first galloping funeral in history and how was that going to go down with the bereaved? But, as we have seen, all went merry as a marriage bell—and it is, in the end, not to the mourners but to the mechanised generations of today that one's sympathy really goes. How much fun they have missed!

About two miles up the river from the Stampede Ranch a lonely garage stood by the trail. Close to it, anchored to the solid rock and spanning a chute of rushing water, a light suspension bridge crossed the Highwood. That was one way of reaching the Eden Valley Ranch of Frazier Hunt—political journalist, war correspondent, author, and one of the best hosts in North America.

Another way was to cross the river on the Buffalo Head and ride the five miles or so up to the E V, coming in over the hay flats. One could make a spectacular approach that way: the going was good and one could come in to the corrals at a gallop in full view from the veranda of the house. One was liable to make a spectacular exit also, leaving in the small hours of the morning with everybody laughing and talking and the horses excited and eager to go: up in the pitch blackness on to a horse you couldn't see, and then off like a bullet from a gun. Thank God the horses were sure-footed because we certainly put our trust in them.

There was a third way of reaching this roadless place —by a ford some distance up the river from the suspension bridge. The main hazard of that ford was a deep hole into which a driver, ignorant of the crossing, could put his team. A democrat of ours found that hole once, and two of its occupants cascaded into the cold, wet river, to be dried out later at the E V, miscellaneously clothed by Emmie Hunt. Crossing the river there in a California cart driven by Guy Weadick was a thing to remember. Going was all right, even though the cart might be grossly overloaded. Coming back was the thing—again in the small hours, sometimes by moonlight, sometimes in the darkness of a cloudy night. The E V lay well over half a mile back from the river, close under the high hill which Spike Hunt had christened Spike's Peak. From the ranch buildings to the river one descended, in a series of steps, from bench to bench. So the return was most exhilarating, whether you flew down over the benches in California cart or democrat with Guy driving, or were driven by Spike in the ranch flivver, Leaping Lena, to the suspension bridge. It was particularly so for those who were packed like sardines into the backs of these vehicles. They could not see what was coming—and then, suddenly, the democrat or the old Ford truck would float out into space and fall (or so it would seem to anybody sitting on the floor behind). A mixed wail of terror and delight would go up . . . and then everything would flatten out and we would be flying along again on the new level. On reaching the ford Guy would become extremely cautious, restraining the one of his team that was apt to pull. "Whoa, Nigger," he would be saying. "Whoa, Nigger—gently there —whoa, Nigger."

Everybody in the back would be laughing and helping

him with a mixed chorus of "Whoa, Nigger," variously rendered, until Guy, in desperation, would give tongue: "If some of the damn fools behind there would just shut up and give the horse a dog's chance, we *might* get across." There would follow an abashed silence, broken only by the clatter of the wheels on the rocks and the rush of the river.

But if the party had been taken by Spike, in Leaping Lena, down the other trail to the river, there still remained the suspension bridge. It was just wide enough for one person. In summertime it carried a set of slat treads, but in the fall, with an eye to the coming Chinooks, the E V boys would take the slats off and you just slid your feet sideways along the cables, keeping also a firm grip on the upper, hand-rail wires. It was not the best of places for the timid, and Marigold and I used to delight in getting a certain nervous friend of ours into the middle of the bridge and then sending waves through it by bouncing up and down in turn, one at each end. I wonder we didn't turn this poor man mad with terror: he would stand there absolutely rigid, clutching the hand-wires, swaying up and down over the white water. Entreaties, prayers, imprecations—nothing had any effect on us. It was part of the Eden Valley to us (or do I mean, part of Loony Lane?) and we were not going to be done out of it.

You never knew whom you would meet in that house: editors and army officers, Helen Keller and her companion, some stray wanderer from the wilds of Asia or South America. One and all, they fell beneath the magic of "the Squire." That was the name we had for Spike, for he is a tall man, red-faced and hearty in those Eden Valley days, and with a liking for red-brown English tweeds . . . He must always have been the perfect host. He has the gift of setting people at their ease and getting the best out of them—getting out of them, at least, anything they have to give. He told me of an evening he had once passed with two men in his rooms in London—the Irish

author, Donn Byrne, and another writer who could match
Byrne in erudition and in conversation. The name of the
second man has gone from me, but if you will look at one
or two of Byrne's books—*Messer Marco Polo*, perhaps, or
The Power of the Dog—you will see the standard of schol-
arship that would be involved. "Their talk was far, far
above my head," Spike said, "but it was so damn marvellous that I couldn't let them go. So I just hovered around
and put in a word or two once in a *very* long while. And
any time I thought they might be burning a bit low, I
would pour them a drink—just the right amount to keep
them ticking. And when the dawn was breaking over London's river those two were still talking . . ."

Knowing that a man gives himself away the moment
he writes a book, I used to look at the ones that Spike
had written, and listen to him speaking of the book of the
moment that he was working on. There was *One American*—that was his autobiography. There was a light-
hearted book on the exploits and travels of the Prince of
Wales, later Edward VIII, and there was *Custer, the Last
of the Cavaliers* and *The Tragic Days of Billy the Kid*.
In these one could sense Spike's love of the West and his
desire to own, like the Prince only a few miles away, a
ranch—or, if that were not possible, at least a rahnch . . .
There were other books; and to come, in later years, were
two on General MacArthur—and I think that, if Spike will
own to having a hero, it is that man.

Ranch problems crowded upon him in the summertime,
as with the rest of us: drought, low cattle prices, water
problems, or the tragic day when a skunk fell down the
E V well, and, as Spike put it, "sank with his colours
nailed to the mast." But in the wintertime Spike and
Emmie were never there at all. All through the Thirties
they would be wandering over the troubled face of Europe,
their headquarters the Savoy in London or the Adlon in
Berlin. Spike would be interviewing the so-called great
ones of the moment, and now and then a postcard would

come with something weird and queer scribbled on it:
"Have left Savoy and am
Now on the Staatendam
Headed for Rotterdam
And I don't give a damn.
Next, the Kurfurstendam . . ."
When the fit took them they could go on indefinitely, writing nonsense by the yard.

Two pictures come instantly to mind when I think of those Eden Valley days. The first one shows the Major at the piano at the E V. Around and behind him stand Spike and Emmie, Guy Weadick, Norman Luxton from Banff, a charming U.S. Army officer and the rest of us. Our voices are raised in song, each person—American Canadian or English—employing what he or she firmly believes to be *the only* authentic Cockney accent:
"Dahn our alley comes a toff,
Nice old geezer wiv a narsty cough,
Sees my missus, tykes 'is topper orf,
In a very gentlemanly way!"
And on it went—Albert Chevalier's famous song in a dozen different dialects. They'd have lynched us in London for less than that . . .

The singers fade, and I next see Marigold and myself sidling across the slatless suspension bridge on a perfect autumn evening with a touch of frost in the air. The blue mountains have come very close, and, on the far bank, out of Leaping Lena gets the Squire. He walks down to meet us through the golden-leaved trees. "There you are, my dears. Come on, now; jump in, and away we go for the ranch. Dinner's ready and Emmie's waiting."

Away, indeed, we go—as on many a happy evening—delighted to see Spike again, but with the sadness that comes from doing a cherished thing knowingly for the last time . . .

Beyond the E V Ranch, right up against the Forest Reserve and practically in the gap by which the Highwood issues from the mountains, sat Ed Marston, a small rancher, English and ferociously independent. Over long years Ed had slowly built up his place on very little and by the time I got to know him he was well established. Long as the Marstons had been there, there still had been men before them—Englishmen, Ed told me, Tytler and Tanner. And a lively pair they must have been, for I gathered from Ed that, if one dug down anywhere around the house, for a foundation or for any other purpose, champagne bottles were likely to be encountered, common as gold on the Klondike.

The first time I met Ed Marston was on the Grass Pass at the head of the South Fork of Flat Creek. We rode down the South Fork together that afternoon with the Mount Head Range close on our left. Marston was talking about hunting in his early years on the Highwood, and I was asking him about the game in the country in those days. Pointing to the high bit of sheep ground west of the Pass, or to some deep coulee, blue in the afternoon shadow, new to me then but so familiar in the years to come, I would ask if he had ever tried his luck in that direction. The answer was always the same: "Oh, yes. Often. I used to hunt sheep in there in the old days."

This went on piling up, and I was getting more and more envious. God, I thought, what a country it must have been! Absolutely dripping with sheep, and here I've missed it by a beggarly thirty years! Born too late, that's the trouble . . .

"You must have seen a lot of sheep on that range in your early years, Mr. Marston?"

The weatherbeaten face with its Viking moustache and blue, far-away eyes turned towards me, and the level voice came expressionless and unchanged: "I never saw a single one."

So much, then, for the old days. Later on I saw quite a few sheep in there myself, and mountain goats as well.

As Sullivan Creek is at the lower end of Loony Lane,

so Ed Marston's place is at the head, up against the mountains; and so I suppose that, in a way, its owner was our senior citizen. We saw little of him down at the Buffalo Head. We met one Christmas morning at the Stampede Ranch. Ed had ridden down for his mail, and he accepted a Christmas drink from me there—a potent hot-rum-and-lemon. He then shot a hole in Mrs. Weadick's best carpet with a rifle that was being passed round and into which he had somehow managed to slip a cartridge, fiddling with the lever. Shortly after that he vanished, unnoticed in the general hum of conversation until the crash of something falling came from the back porch. That was Ed displacing a little of the Stampede hardware. Deciding that the tribes might be up, and painted savages watching the back door, he was taking all reasonable precautions and getting out through a side window. We watched him riding away, a Charles M. Russell figure against the snow and the bare tracery of the winter trees. I was sorry that I had made that rum so strong.

Strange stories occasionally came from the Marston ranch. One spring day, for instance, Ed did something rash with sooty stove-pipes. At that precise moment the west wind chose to blow a mighty blast—and in no time at all Mrs. Marston had a raving blackamoor for a husband. Of the man she knew, only the furious eyes remained, and a set of, by contrast, snow-white, gnashing teeth. Not unnaturally she laughed—and laughed and laughed. She couldn't stop, and who would blame her?

Ed, however, didn't see it that way at all. He snatched up his laughing spouse in his sooty arms, and walked away with her and dropped her in the spring—into which he might far more usefully have thrown himself.

Drastic treatment . . . yet well in keeping with the traditions of the valley.

It must have been after one of these little family tiffs, many years ago, that the driver of a lumber camp tote-

team found Mrs. Marston sitting on a large boulder that
lay by the main trail, above the sheltered ranchhouse.
Asked if he could give her a ride into High River, forty
miles away, he gladly assented and off she went.

On his return the same teamster found Ed Marston
sitting on the same boulder with a rifle across his knees.
Ed walked slowly towards the wagon and the teamster
pulled up his horses.

"Was it you that gave my wife a ride into town early
this week?"

"Why, yes, Mr. Marston—but that's nothing. She's no
trouble. Any time I'd just be too pleased—"

"I've a good mind to shoot you. And next time I will.
If ever you see her sitting here again and wanting a ride—
then, damn her, let her walk!"

Down on Sullivan Creek, at the lower end of the Eden
Valley, there sits a sheltered, contented, sun-trap of a
place, the Y Cross Ranch. It belongs to Joe Bews, the son
of that Jim Bews on whom Guy Weadick and Marigold
and I called in the day of Adolf's party. The character
of its owner is best summed up in a remark he made to me
once: "I like to see my cattle contented. That makes me
feel contented, too."

I don't wonder at that. Joe's cattle, when I last saw
them were big and beautiful, and I have no doubt they are
that still. To look at them would make any man content.
And when their owner is contented, a happy smile spreads
over his face—and when *I* see that smile, then *I* feel the
same way, too!

There must be a sort of a chain reaction to that smile
of Joe's, and I well remember it functioning one branding
day at the Buffalo Head. The job was done and the gang
had demolished two large rounds of beef and all the
beer and whisky it could conveniently hold. Joe had ridden his horse into the living room, round the table and out
again, and now he was sitting plumb in the middle of a

large, red-leather sofa, head back, eyes half-closed and smiling happily.

Outside in the bright sunshine a robin was singing furiously. Up in a tall poplar tree he sat, an unmistakable robin with a flaming red waistcoat on him; and the row that small bird was kicking up, you'd think he'd been on a branding party, too. His song cut clean throught the conversation and the laughter—and every so often Joe would open both eyes wide and smile and say, "I do like to hear the meadow-lark!" That may look a pretty ordinary remark on paper; but it pleased everybody, and it became a byword that summer—a sort of greeting between friends—and never mind the natural history of it. If Joe wanted that robin to be a meadow-lark, then a meadow-lark it was as far as the rest of us were concerned, and to the crocodiles with the bird-books.

That is the best way to remember a friend, a man who gave a home once to two homeless little horses when the Buffalo Head was sold—by some small remark or gesture that will remain for always . . .

The chief characteristic of that "mad valley" was that you never knew what would happen next, or what you would be doing in an hour's time. Things could change in a second from peace to bloody war, or some infernal thing could materialise out of a blue sky and completely change a well-planned day for you. I came to the conclusion, long since, that there never was and never could be any "even tenor" in the life of a rancher.

The sort of thing I have in mind is a certain Sunday evening in the month of June. A sabbath calm reigned over the Buffalo Head. Everything was in perfect order; and down in the trees below the house a baby boy was blowing dandelion clocks, his sister was urging him on, and Marigold was directing operations. I was walking up to the house to get a camera when I gradually became aware that a furious din was fast approaching. Shouts, yells, the thunder of horses' hoofs—then a swirling cloud of dust swept down into the home meadow and horses flew around in all directions. More yells, more galloping— until at last the corral gates were shut on eight or ten horses, and a group of riders, plastered with sweat and dust, rode up to the house. That was Tom McMasters corralling a bunch of his horses that had run out for some years up Flat Creek and were now practically wild animals. And our corrals had been the handiest.

What the riders now wanted was tea, supper, beef, ham, eggs, anything—and above all, help to get these brutes over the half-flooded river and into Tom's corrals about six miles away. So we all mobilised and had supper. Every available horse was grabbed and saddled, and in under an hour's time, instead of leading a quiet domestic life at home, we were all careering hell-for-leather across the open country of the Bar U in pursuit of Tom's horses, having come very near to drowning the smallest member of the party at the Fideli Ford en route . . .

That's the sort of thing I mean. It's bound to be an unquiet life, anyway, when you have animals around— and what makes it worse is that a fracas of this description, intruding into a peaceful day, seems somehow to start things rolling; so that, from then on till bedtime, you can bank on it being just one damn thing after another.

But that, for better or worse, is ranching.

CHAPTER XI

Springtime in the Rockies

Day-old chicks may be, for some fortunate people, just a matter of a telephone-call from the station or the bus depot, and then jumping into the car and running in to fetch them. In super-civilised communities they may be, for all I know, delivered by the hatchery straight to one's door. But the Buffalo Head Ranch in the foothills of Alberta, in the days when we held it, was far beyond the reach of such luxuries—as it still is, today. If you wanted a thing you went to town and got it, and only two conditions were allowed to govern these visits: firstly that the frightful roads should be more or less passable, and secondly that the weather should be such that the absence of one or two men would make no difference to the work of the ranch. That usually meant in summertime a dirty day which would not interfere with haying, and in wintertime a good one which would not interfere with feeding. Spring was betwixt and between.

This 29th March counted, nominally at least, as spring. The grass was clear of snow and there was no outside feeding to be done. But the day was grey and cold, and out of a leaden sky fine particles of snow eddied down on a bitter north wind—a wind so purposeful and keen that it would have chilled even the proverbial brass monkey had he been present that morning on the Buffalo Head. Still, it was not getting any worse, and there was nothing to be gained by just riding around and looking at cattle that had all the grazing in the world, the blessing of open springs and the shelter of protecting trees.

Sheltered by our woods and with the view blocked by the hills in every direction except to the south, it was impossible for us to know what it was like 'outside'—that is, on the open flats. It just seemed like the right sort of day to drive the sixty-odd miles to Calgary and get the few things that we needed, plus seventy-five day-old Hampshire Red chicks which were on order from the hatchery. Jay would come with me. Jay was foreman on the ranch; he had business of his own in town and would take this chance of getting in. This killed two birds with one stone since, on any winter trip where there might be trouble, having Jay along was like having a sort of extra accident insurance policy: broad-shouldered, slim-waisted and active as a cat, he was also very strong, and what he could not do in the way of shoving and heaving in a tough spot just simply could not be done. Together we did the final chores: we filled the feed-racks and saw to the water in the corrals; we stuck our heads into one of the dude cabins where the Major and Ernest were busy in great warmth and comfort on a job of carpentry, and took their orders for screws, mouldings and fittings. Then we got the cook's orders from the house—and finally we started the car with the usual cold-weather ceremonies and hit the trail. . . .

By midday things were far from merry in Calgary. The wind was rising and it had a nasty, threatening whine to it. Trailing wraiths of snow were driving through the half-deserted streets, and respectable business-men, their multiple chins well buried in muffler and coat collar, skipped with a rare alacrity along the sidewalks—a storm signal that it would have been foolish to ignore. Impressed, I hunted up Jay and we got the chicks and drove out of town.

The first twenty-six miles of the homeward journey were not too bad—we were travelling with the wind. At Okotoks we turned west, thereby getting the wind on our right hand, and from then on our troubles started. The wind had risen to a screaming blast, the temperature had risen to about 30°. Many of the bare wintry fields to the north were in summer fallow, and a mixture of dust and snow was hurtling through the air, blotting out all visibility beyond fifteen or twenty feet. Somehow we crawled on for mile after deserted mile of this usually busy road. Then a vague shape loomed up out of the smother and there was a glancing blow on the car. We came to a standstill and Jay peered through the back window. "I think we've knocked them into the ditch," he said. "Now there's a guy trying to climb out—now the wind's slammed the door shut on him again and I can't see anything. Wait till this gust blows over. . . ."

"Peep-peep-peep," went the chickens in their carton on the back seat. "How are they doing?" I asked. Jay looked in. "Doing fine," he said. "No stiffs yet. But we'd better keep that heater running."

A horrid, gory face appeared at my window on the south side of the car. It seemed to be streaming with blood from its wounds like Banquo's ghost and I heard Jay mutter to himself, "God Almighty—we must have killed them!" I rolled down the window.

"We've got a good tow-rope," bawled the owner of the face. "I think you can pull us out backwards."

"Your face," I shouted back above the bellowing of the wind. "Are you badly hurt?"

The man wiped his gloved hand over his face and looked at it in a puzzled sort of way. "No," he yelled at me. "I don't think so. We fell soft. That ditch is full of drifted snow. For God's sake let's get out of here before we drift in." And he went away to get his rope, his face now uniformly smeared to a deep mulatto colour with the flying mixture of snow and the rich soil of Sheep Creek valley.

It was a red Packard with two men in it, and somehow

we pulled it out, nearly getting run down by an oil-truck in the process. My own impression was that Jay and the truck-driver, a mountain of a man, disdaining its owners, threw the Packard back onto the road with their bare hands and the tow-rope slack. It could have been that way. Nobody spoke during the struggle—it was useless; for words were plucked out of one's mouth and swept away on the howling wind. Only the chickens, completely unperturbed, kept up their ceaseless peep-peeping from their carton on the back seat. And when all was done the various contestants faded silently away into the storm. No arguments started up—nobody asked for numbers, names or addresses, and nobody was fool enough to suggest informing the police about the collision—as the law required. We were only too glad to get going again, and the sole comment I heard was Jay's as he got back into the car: "Seems to me the Major and Ernest got the best of us today."

We turned south at Black Diamond and climbed higher through the oil-field. It was getting colder and the snow was powder snow again, coming in blinding whirls and eddies. Only the very tops of the derricks were visible; the bases and all buildings were hidden by the driving scud.

After what seemed like hours we ran into a drift and Jay got out to investigate. He vanished utterly and for some time. The chickens peeped, the heater hummed and the car shook and rocked in the furious wind. I was just getting out to look for Jay when he appeared at the near window. "I had quite a job finding you," he shouted. "This drift's fifty yards long and there's a guy stuck in the other end of it. But we're right up alongside the garage we want. Follow me and I think we can make it."

We could go no farther without chains, and the idea of lying down and putting them on ourselves with our bare hands out in this blizzard was repellent to both of us.

The car growled its shuddering way through the snow after Jay, and the dark mass of a building became visible.

But the portcullis, as it were, was down. Jay kicked and pounded on the big sliding doors but nobody seemed to want to open them. Faint voices came from within. "Go away!" they shouted—and "What the hell d'you want?"

From Jay I heard a furious cry of "I'll damn soon show you what we want!"—and he rushed in through the office door. About five seconds later the sliding doors flew open with a crash that nearly threw them off their tracks, and Jay stood revealed in the gateway like some giant condottiere of olden times at the in-taking of a fortress, beckoning wildly. The chicks and I rolled in and the doors shut behind us with a clang.

The place was crowded with men, trucks and cars sheltering from the storm. In one corner the natural gas flared and roared in a great drum-shaped stove that was red hot and glowing. We got the chains out and men came with a huge jack and put them on. "But you'd better stay here now you're in," the proprietor said. "I've room for no more, but you can stay. This storm can't go on for ever and it ain't safe to be on the road right now."

"I can't stop," I said. "I've got a bunch of day-old chicks in the car and I've got to get them into a brooder. Thanks all the same."

"Chicks!" One heard the word on all sides and men came crowding round. The rear doors were opened and heads peered into the car. A brave, reassuring piping and peeping issued forth.

"Well for God's sake—chicks!"

"Chicks on a day like this! They must be nuts, both of them!"

"Hey! Come over here. These guys've got chicks with them!"

"Chicks? Well I'll be jiggered! Some folks don't seem to have any sense. They should'a left them at home. . . ."

And they asked why we had chosen this day of all days to fetch these poor innocent birds from their hatchery. Jay put them straight on that point: "Did you think we chose it specially?" he inquired. "We've got the bull by the tail and we can't let go!" With that he flung wide the gates and leapt for the car; the wind, entering with a blustering roar, put the assembled bird-watchers to flight, and we rolled out into the storm with our chirping freight, plainly branded in popular opinion as the afflicted of God. . . .

Ten miles from home we turned west again. Another mile or two and we would be in the shelter of the hills; five miles more and we would be into the blessed trees and on the Buffalo Head. But it was not to be. On the north side of the road and just ahead of us stood one solitary willow, bowed and quivering before the storm. In the lee of it a drift had formed across the road, and bang in the middle of the drift an old Model T Ford was firmly stuck. Around this Ford an ancient man was shovelling furiously. He was dressed in blue overalls, a bright-red scarf and a fur hat—and, from a face that matched his scarf, a snow-white, Uncle Sam-type beard streamed out in the wind. All this we discovered by degrees; at first we could only see that something stood in our way, blocking the road.

"No use fooling around with him—we've got to get these chicks somewhere pretty soon or we'll lose them."

"Not a particle of use. Stupid old goat—at his age he should know enough to stay home on a day like this."

So we lightly spoke, separated, on an average, by the secure distance of some thirty years from this aged gaffer who was digging so frantically while the driving, relentless snow filled in his tracks behind him. And we got out and prospected around to see if we could get by on the lee side between the Ford and the ditch. On inspection there seemed to be the shadow of a chance if the luck stayed with us, so we decided to have a go at it.

Plugging back to the car Jay hailed the struggling patriarch: "Hi, grandad!" he shouted. And then, with a fine disregard of geographical fact, "Any signs of China yet?" As a cat's-paw of wind ruffles the calm waters of a lake so did a sudden spasm of rage sweep over the old man's face, and we could see his lips working busily, framing words that were, unfortunately, snatched away from us by the wind—words that mostly seemed to begin with B.

Almost we wriggled our way round that antique jalopy. The chains chewed away at the snow and the car thrust and corkscrewed forward with Jay on the edge of the ditch, on the lee side, holding the outfit on the road. The ancient ceased from his digging to watch as I made the last swing; the open road lay before me, victory and the Buffalo Head—and then there came a despairing cry from the ditch where, in spite of Jay's great strength, the near hind wheel was slipping over the edge. Slowly the car tilted, and gently it came to rest at an angle of 45° in deeply drifted snow. I switched off engine and heater and, in the silence that followed, an angry note could be plainly heard in the cheeping of the chicks. Hastily I set our little charges on an even keel again—there were only seventy-four of them now, one had been trampled to death by the mob.

Up on the trail grandad had laid down his shovel. Around and about it, with his hands raised above his head as one sees the hands of frenzied dancers at Braemar or Aboyne, he was executing a cross between the hornpipe and the highland fling. Rather a childish exhibition, I thought, as I drained the radiator and made ready to go.

We locked the car and set out on foot, westwards, doing our best to ignore the triumphant capers of the ancient. Walking was not easy, leaning against that wind; and with both hands engaged in holding a carton out in front, level, it was hard to keep hands and face from freezing. We changed over frequently.

The only thing to do now was to head for Bertie Sheppard's home ranch and spend the night there—and that meant crossing the Highwood River. This, I felt sure, could still be done on the ice, late though the season was. The difficulty, in this blizzard, was to find the right point to drop over the cliff edge—some place where we could get down to the river, and not too far from the Riverbend Ranch.

Somehow we got down that cliff—swinging from poplar-tree to choke-cherry-bush, grabbing on to bits of buck-brush, cascading down in showers of stones, passing the chicks from one to another. The main feeling was one of relief—we were out of the wind. Overhead we could hear the screaming rush of it, but here all was quiet and still except for the eddying snow. This hid the river from us and we climbed happily downwards with our minds all set on warmth and water and feed for the chicks, and tea and perhaps some ham and eggs for ourselves. Then, in the gathering dusk, a new obstacle appeared—black, swirling water rimmed by ice that was four feet thick, penned in a deep, racing channel. Spring was on its way and the river had cut out in the centre. Upstream, as far as one could see, the river was open. Downstream the open water faded out of sight round a bend.

"Hold these chicks, Jay, and sing them a lullaby or something while I go down-river and see if there's an ice jam we can cross on." And I shoved the carton at him and left him there, stamping his feet on the ice.

About four or five hundred yards downstream and round the bend I found not a jam but an ice bridge. It was not very wide and it did not look very strong, and the black, cold water of the Highwood rushed under it in a riffle that would easily sweep a man off his feet. There was nothing else in sight. I thought of trying it to see if it was safe—and then I thought, no, better not. Jay would never know what had happened and we might as well at least see each other drown. So I went back and got Jay. Then I took off my heavy overcoat and walked over the bridge—sliding my feet along so as to avoid even the shock of a footstep on the ice.

I turned and waved Jay over. He had the chicks and he, too, came over treading delicately. When he was almost across, the bridge gave a horrid crack, but that was all. It

never moved. I watched it for a minute to see if it would
fall into the river behind us, as a certain ice bridge in
the north had done for me ten years before. But no—
nothing dramatic happened. The snow went on falling as
before, the ice stayed where it was, and we walked on
up-river to the angry rush of the water and the scream of
the wind overhead.

I walked on the sloping bank of the river; Jay took an
easier course over a nice, wide, flat expanse of snow down
below me. It struck me suddenly that, whatever he might
think he was walking on, he was actually on the ice of an
eddy—probably thin ice covered with snow. I had just
opened my mouth to shout to him when, without the
slightest warning, the ice gave way beneath him and he
disappeared in up to his chest.

"Oh! Oh! Oh!" I heard him call out. "It's cold! It's
cold!" And he stood there motionless with the chick carton
raised high above his head—a sombre, suppliant piece of
statuary against the unbroken whiteness of the snow.

Somehow, with the help of an old cotton-wood branch,
I got the chicks and then Jay out of that mess and we
pushed on. Bertie's bullpens heaved into sight, then the
corrals and finally the lights of the house—and none too
soon, for Jay's clothes were starting to stiffen and freeze.

Late that night Fred Crawford, who was working at
Riverbend then, hitched up a team and drove me in a
sleigh to the nearest telephone. I had to get back to Calgary
in the morning to be at the Bull Sale in time for the
Herefords and I still had to make arrangements to get the
chicks to the Buffalo Head. By a miracle the wire had held
against the wind and I got the Major on the phone, but
the connection was terrible: there were four ranches on
that party line, two of which, especially in times of storm
and stress, could be counted on to 'listen in.'

"Buffalo Head Ranch. Hallo? Is that you, George?"

"Yes, it's me. I'm at Bertie's and the car's in a ditch
somewhere . . . No, nobody hurt . . . Yes, we got the chicks.

They're all fed and watered and mostly asleep now behind
Bertie's stove. Look here—Jay will borrow a horse and
ride up in the morning. Tell Ernest to have a team harnes-
sed and the sleigh ready. Got that? . . . And we want something to shelter the little brutes in. Go to the storehouse
and get a big carton. Better tip out that enormous great
toilet-paper carton—can you hear me?"

"I'm most frightfully sorry, old man, but there's a
shocking buzzing on this phone. Half the country must be
listening in. It sounded like 'boil a paper carton,' and I'm
sure you couldn't have said that?"

"I said, 'Toilet - paper carton.' Must I scream every
word?"

"Steam every *what?*"

This was altogether too much for our two friends who
were listening in. One American voice from up the valley
and one very Scottish voice from down the valley burst in
simultaneously with: "What he said was 'toilet - paper
carton,' Major."

"Oh, thank you *so* much! I'm *enormously* obliged to
you! And now, if you'll both damn well get off the phone
and hang up, I might even be able to hear for myself!"

That cleared the line a bit and we managed to get things
arranged. Fred and I then drove back to Riverbend. Arrived there, we hunted out a crowbar with which we
pried loose four large, round rocks from the frozen river-
bank. These we placed in Bertie's oven, and before the
little company of stormbound travellers—which had grown
larger since Jay and I came—fell asleep as best it could, on
sofas, in beds, rugged up in deep armchairs, we made up
the fire.

The morning was sunny and cold and still. Jay hit the
trail for the Buffalo Head in a glittering cloud of snow
dust, returning at midday with the sleigh. In it the chicks
rode their last ten miles up to the ranch. Their own carton
was placed, with a hot rock at each corner, inside the
large carton which had been sent down for them, the

whole affair being covered over with a horse-blanket. In the genial warmth so provided it is presumed that the chicks snoozed the whole way up to the Buffalo Head, caring little for the zero temperature of the outer air. Quite certainly they arrived in the best of health and spirits—so much so that we raised them to become grown-up pullets and cockerels without a single further casualty.

I set off in the opposite direction, headed for the Bull Sale. Fred drove me in the sleigh as far as the main road, and on the way we stopped at the abandoned car. Not much of it was visible, but we dug down till we could get one of the doors open. An attache case that I wanted lay on the front seat and I was surprised to find it buried under a foot and a half of snow. So fine had been the particles and so strong the wind that all this snow had been forced through tiny, imperceptible cracks and crannies in the tightly closed doors and windows. One would scarcely have thought it possible. We brushed the stuff out, locked the car again and went on.

The drift in the lee of the willow had piled up to a mountainous size. Rounded and smoothed off by the wind, it still showed faint signs of a frantic upheaval in the centre, whence that ancient and violent man had somehow managed, in the end, to extricate himself and his old Ford. Nobody I ever met could tell me who he was or where he came from. He vanished utterly—and I have wondered, sometimes, if we did not meet that day Something that was doomed, like Vanderdecken, to haunt the roads in times of storm and to be seen by men only to their undoing. Be that as it may, his was the victory.

CHAPTER XII

The Bow River

Kipling saw the Bow River and approved of it. He knew what he was talking about for his hosts put him on the train at Calgary, and for the next hundred and twenty miles the river is never out of sight for long.

Hills flank the Bow valley near Calgary—big grass hills to the north, low wooded hills to the south. Then, somewhere around Cochrane, as the long line of cars rounded some bend in the track, Kipling would get a sudden view of the Rockies—a blue wall of mountains, at first sight unbroken. And then somebody would point out to him the Gap in the outer range by which the Bow escaped into the foothills, and by which the train would enter the high mountains. The Gap lay in the south-west and the train crawled uphill towards it, "whistling", Kipling wrote afterwards, "to keep its heart up, through the winding gateways of the hills." And all the time down below, now on one side, now on the other, flowed the Bow River, foaming down some riffle with the crest of the white waves tossing like the mane of a running horse, swirling strongly past the points of rock, rippling down the quiet reaches with the coils of the eddies shining in the autumn sunshine like silver snakes. The Bow, Kipling wrote, "does not slide nor rustle like Prairie rivers, but brawls across bars of blue pebbles, and a greenish tinge in its waters hints of the snows."*

*"Letters of Travel," by Rudyard Kipling.

That was in the fall of 1907 when the Province of Alberta was only two years old. Thirty years later the Bow was still the same fast, green foothill river, and I bought a Swedish-made faltboat which was to teach me many things. Before that, however, I had thoroughly explored the Bow outside the mountains in conventional Canadian canoes, made of eastern cedar, canvas-covered. The first one was a sixteen-foot Chestnut, the "Prospector" model. It was a beauty and I loved it dearly because, in that country of the horse, to step into it was to step back into the shadowy canyons and the old, moss-bearded forests of a river that was far away in the North-West Territories—and where the treasure is, there will the heart be also.

I got that canoe just after a dam had been thrown across the Bow below the inflow of the Ghost River. The water of the new Ghost Lake was rising, and it was pushing also up the drowned valley of the Ghost. I could see that this arm of the new lake was going to reach the lower end of some land that I had, about two miles up the Ghost—hence the new canoe. With it I ran the Bow from below the Ghost Dam to Calgary, a distance of nearly forty miles. Delighted with that, I ran it again—and then certain stretches of it again and again. There were some lively bits of river in that forty miles, and on them the canoe also seemed to come alive. One could slide down a riffle—which is a chute through or around a shingle bar—and drive the canoe close alongside the big waves; or through them, riding wildly on the crest of the mane. On rare occasions I would meet a Canadian Pacific passenger train crawling slowly up into the hills. Nobody ever used that river; and the unexpected sight of a canoe never failed to cause a furore on board the train. Cries of delight would come from the observation car and a rush would be made for cameras. That was the time to give them their money's worth—and an extra drive on the paddle would lift the fore end of the canoe far out of water as it leapt over some big wave. Then would come the smack and the flying spray as the canoe came down

again, to land on the next wave and repeat the performance.
Quite apart from the fun of showing off, there is a thrill
about that which I have only found equalled when riding a
fast horse and trying to corral a bunch of wild and obstrep-
erous horses.

Then there was the upper river, above the Ghost Dam,
where it wound through the lonely horse and cattle country
of the Stoney Indian Reserve. The riffles were stronger there
and the standing waves were bigger; there was no sign of
habitation or cultivation, and somehow the sun always
seemed to be shining on those open flats and points where
the bunch-grass bent so gracefully before the west wind.
Here the road on the north and the railroad on the south
had each bent some miles away from the river, and one
seemed to step back into an earlier time when things were
as the Lord made them and the land was wide open and
the grass was free. Old Fort Creek was the limit of my
wanderings in that direction. At that point one met the
first rock rapid on the Bow River—a couple of sharp reefs
cutting across the stream and the water creaming over them.
It was—and still is—a lovely spot, with the leaves of the
aspen poplars dancing in the wind, with the old firs standing like sentinels on the cliffs and the rock points, and with
the wall of the mountains rising across the west only five
miles away.

Above the rapid came stretches of white water and more
and more reefs—and then, towards the Gap where the Bow
cuts across the strike of the outer range, one met with an
impassable stretch of water with falls and cascades, and
now two dams thrown across the river for power. So that
for me, as for the old fur-traders who built Bow Fort, Old
Fort Creek was the head of navigation outside the mountains. I am certain that that was why they built that post
on that open headland above the Bow. They planned, one
reads, to bring the trade goods to that fort by packhorse
from the north, from Rocky Mountain House. But to the
voyageurs from Lower Canada the birch-bark canoe was

home and the rivers were their highways. Here in the west they were in the country of the Blackfoot and the Piegan —horse Indians—and, if the sudden need were to come upon them to send a message or to abandon the fort and escape with their lives, there below them was the way, the river road, unimpeded by rapids or portages, hard for mounted warriors to follow. . . . .

Most likely it was never used. The Piegans had the Hudson's Bay Company men out of there in five short months—just after New Year of 1834 when the Bow would be frozen and the canoes useless. The fur-traders never came back; and now only the chimney mounds and the faint outlines of the buildings remain to tell the tale: the saskatoon bushes and the grass and the wild roses have that site today.

Downstream from Old Fort Creek, stretching from Morley which was the Stoney Indians' headquarters to the Ghost River, was the Ghost Lake—the water of the dam. In the first years of its existence, when living vegetation still made green the verges of the dam, tremendous flights of wildfowl would alight upon its waters in their migration from the north. Shooting from a canoe is good sport at any time, and on the Ghost Lake one could count on putting up birds from any sheltered bay, especially along the south shore—which was the sheltered shore and the Indian Reserve side. But one had to keep an eye open for the west wind, which meant watching the western sky and the Gap in the first range. The wind cloud would form over the Rockies, and then through the Gap the wind would come raging. In five minutes there would be whitecaps on the water; in ten minutes the lake would be a stormy sea. Twice I was caught out on it in a blow, and each time with one large and solid passenger in the front seat, a fellow shooter. One was a sailor and one was a landsman—and neither of them knew a thing about canoes. There each one sat, calm and unperturbed, perched up on that seat; centre of gravity far too high for an unloaded canoe but acting splendidly as a sail. And each time I wondered whether to shout above the wind and the hiss of the waves: "Kneel down, can't you? Get your weight on the floor!" But each time I thought —no, they think it's perfectly safe to sit like that; better let them think it and feel secure. If they once start getting anxious and shifting about to kneel down, wadded up in all that shooting gear, God knows what may not happen in this frail craft whose proper home is a river.

So I slipped forward off the stern seat and knelt and crouched, sweeping with the paddle to keep the canoe from broaching to in the trough of the waves. That was not easy: on each occasion the man in the bow was heavier than I, and when I slid forward off my seat his advantage in weight was increased. Nose down, tail in the air like a wind-vane, we tore down the lake. Only ducks flighting across our direct course were shot by the forward gunner; I did the picking up, missing each time a valuable paddle stroke as we slid past the floating bird. The worst seas were round the points, and the last point was the worst of all. Then came the shelter and the peace of the Ghost Arm, and I said "Whew!" and wiped the spray off my face—and each one of my friends, sailor and landsman, in two different Octobers, said exactly the same thing: "Hullo! Did we have something to worry about? Why didn't you tell me?"

For the shooter there was one further particularly local hazard on that lake. As the waters of the dam rose, the knolls and hummocks of the old river flats became islands. Some of these eventually disappeared for good and all— but others remained above high water as permanent islands. We named them, my wife and I—just any names that happened along: and one of these was Tortuga.

Creeping into the lee of Tortuga one gorgeous October evening of sun and light west wind, I ran the canoe gently aground in the shallows. I stepped out quietly into the water and picked up my gun. Mallard were at the west end of the little island, down in the long, floating grass and the willow seedlings that were already appearing at the new water level. The sun was almost touching the mountains and everything flashed and sparkled, from the golden leaves of the dwarf poplars to the small shining wavelets at my feet. I walked on through the water, straight into all this dazzle—and suddenly the mallard rose and came straight over my head. I got off one barrel and down came one bird. I turned to follow with the choke and was already pressing the trigger when I realized that my right foot was meeting with no resistance. With a defiant but futile "Bang!" I floundered ignominiously backwards and sank beneath the waves—into what? I have often wondered. . . . . A neat square hole had been dug down into the gravel there for seven feet or so; and the excavated material had been carefully levelled off. Concealed, as it was, by the water it was the perfect booby trap. But what on earth was it for? Had some Stoney Indian planned to build a cabin there before the dam was made, and was it into his cellar that I had fallen?

Not that I cared just then. That last wild shot was the sunset gun, and with it the sun vanished behind the Rockies, and the Ghost Lake became still. The islet of Tortuga is 4000 feet above sea level and the chill of evening comes quickly in that high country. Dripping from head to foot I waded out and picked up the mallard. Then I squelched back to the canoe, shoved off and let drive with the paddle for the Ghost Arm, for the cabin we had built up there and the roaring, crackling warmth of a red-hot stove.

The cabin stood on a grassy point of the Ghost River, in a natural meadow that was fringed along the water's edge with spruce and poplar. The site was in a deep glen that was flanked by steep bunch-grass slopes to the north-east, and by cliffs and thickly wooded slopes on the south-west. As always in the foothills, the woods grew where the snow lay in wintertime, and the open, grassy slopes were those that faced the Chinook, the warm south-west wind.

No road ran to that cabin. We came to it by water, leaving the canoe at the head of the Arm and then walking upstream with the little brawling rapids of the Ghost on our left. An old wagon trail ran along the crest of the grass hills on the north-east. By that trail we brought up the lumber and the window-sashes, the stove and all the fixings for the cabin: then we slid or rolled the stuff down the bunch-grass slopes into the glen—and well do I remember seeing two rolls of tar-paper and one bundle of sheet-iron and stove-pipes all in turn hit the same ant-hill (it was not easy to miss that one), and then take the wrong turning, leaping gaily over a rocky spur and down a sheer cliff into the Ghost. Nothing was damaged: the bundles fell in a deep pool. Dripping and laughing, we fished them out and splashed away downstream with them to the grassy point where the cabin was to be.

We could have cut the logs for that cabin close to the site—but it was (and still is) such a lovely place that we did not want to fell any of the trees. So we waited till the spring when the Eau Clair Lumber Company would run its winter cut of logs down the Ghost. We obtained the company's permission to pick out a set of building logs—and then, when the time came, we borrowed a team of horses and stationed on the shore a boy who was handy with a lariat. As the logs jammed or slid past the point my wife and I would indicate to young Hamish the ones we wanted. Hamish would drop his rope into the water just ahead of the required log, which then slid into the loop and could be drawn to shore. Then, with much splashing, I would get a light logging chain around the log while Marigold backed the horses up so that I could hitch the chain on to the double-trees. And so the logs were skidded up the low bank to the cabin site—and that summer the cabin was built.

Though that glen of the Ghost was only a bit over two miles up from the Calgary-Banff road, yet it was like some little piece of the wild mountains that had wandered out into the foothills and liked it there and stayed. We saw bears on that place, and deer often, and sometimes an elk. And once on the edge of the high cliff beyond the Ghost we saw a mountain sheep: the low sun of October was behind him and he appeared to be outlined in fire. What did he think he was doing there, almost twenty miles from the nearest mountain? We never knew. Returning to the lands of his ancestors, probably; dreaming of the days before the white man came and took up his winter range.

That point round which the Ghost River swept on its last descent to the Arm was a garden of flowers. There were blue pentstemons in the stony coulees, and Jacob's ladder. The slopes in some years would be blue with lupins—and down below, around the cabin, there were larkspurs and delphiniums, fireweed and wild geranium, lace flowers and forget-me-nots. Under the trees there were tiger lilies—and, in the spring, the whole place would burst out into "crocuses", which were the pasque flowers. That deep glen had never been grazed and it was a perfect picture of the Bow River foothills at their untouched best. We loved it, and it was from that cabin as a base that we shot on the Ghost Lake, went adventuring up to Old Fort Creek, and ran down from below the dam to Calgary.

A mile or more down the Ghost Arm, and on the same side as the cabin, there stood one lonely white house, high up on the grass slopes and by a splendid spring. With its barns and corrals it was the centre of a small ranch. For years we tried to buy that property and add it to other land that we owned adjoining—but we were never able to agree with the owners on the price. That was no barrier to friendship—and many a good high tea, with eggs and scones and whisky on the table, greeted us there after long days on the lake or the Bow River. At the head of the table always sat the lady of the house, old Mrs. Gillies. She could remember the coming of the Canadian Pacific Railway to Calgary in 1883, and she could remember the Riel Rebellion of 1885, and all the worry and the wondering which side of the fence the Indians would come down. She still spun the wool off her own sheep on her own spinning wheel, and to her the right language was still the Gaelic. There was a Gaelic name that she had for a grassy knoll close to the house, a knoll that was purple with crocuses in the springtime; and I am certain that old Mrs. Gillies thought in Gaelic, for you could almost see her translating. That was a table to linger at and hear stories of old times—and one October evening I lingered there a bit too long.

When I went to the door with John Gillies the day had departed and the sharp clip of the frost could be felt. There was no moon, only the stars. I said good-bye to John, felt my way carefully down the slope to the canoe and shoved off up the Arm. I drove the canoe as hard as I could, and it was a strange feeling, slipping silently over water that you couldn't even see. It was like sliding over a black mirror, and but for the feel of the paddle against the water one might have been suspended in space. Yet, if you looked behind where the paddle and the canoe's wake had broken the stillness of the Arm, you could see the stars caught and reflected like splinters of fire on every ripple. What with the strangeness and the beauty of it, and the spur of the frost—and not forgetting the whisky—it was a night when one felt pity for "folk in housen".

Suddenly there was a splintering crash and I felt the nose of the canoe ride high and then subside again. There was a sudden snatch of fear at the unexpected sound: and then I realized that I was into shell ice—and how was that going to be for the skin of the canoe? And if I went on, would the ice ahead get thicker while the splintered ice froze again behind me? Or what?

But in the silence around me, which was broken only by the faint tinkling of the ice as my wake caught up with me, I could hear, away ahead, the roar of the Ghost where it hit the Arm. Up there, perhaps half a mile away, there would be open water. And in the canoe there was a spruce pole lying along the thwarts—a ten-foot pole for poling up the riffles of the Bow. I felt for it in the darkness, and then I moved carefully forward into the centre of the canoe.

From there, flailing away with the pole at ice I couldn't

see, and then driving forward into the channel like an ice-breaker, I made my way through several hundred yards of ice-barrier. The uproar of the Ghost came nearer. On my left I thought I could see the outline of trees, high up and cutting into the stars. But of the grass hills on the right there was no sign. Then the ice became thinner—and then I rode out into living, moving water and went on through the blackness towards the Ghost and the cabin. The night was getting colder—but soon now, I thought, I shall be lighting the candles and touching off a crackling roar of fire in the stove. . . . . And that was my first experience of canoeing in utter darkness.

The second was some fifteen years later, by which time we had left the Ghost River country and moved down south to the Buffalo Head Ranch on the Highwood River. Canoeing on that stream, in the small canyons on the ranch, was murder on canoes and a strong chance of suicide for the canoeman. We tried it thoroughly, wrecked one Canadian canoe completely and gave it up as hopeless. However, the Swedish faltboat remained intact—a sixteen-foot two-seater; a kayak type of craft, a beautiful thing that fairly flew over the water when driven by the double-bladed paddles. Sometimes we still used it on the Bow, breakfasting at the ranch at about three a.m. and then driving the hundred-odd miles to the Ghost River, meeting the sunrise on the way. Below the Ghost Dam we would assemble the canoe and throw it in the water. Then away down river to Calgary, lunching en route in the shade of the cottonwoods somewhere on the Bow River Horse Ranch, and combining all this with some late afternoon shopping in town. One way and another it made a well-filled day, and the arrival home around midnight was as that of sleep-walkers, sun-soaked and comatose. . . . .

We also discovered that a very quiet pack-horse would pack the broken-down faltboat into the mountains for us; and we took it with us on several month-long trips into the Rockies, assembling it on the shores of lonely lakes,

close under the glaciers of the Great Divide—lakes that
rarely saw a human being and which had never before
seen a canoe of any kind.

That sort of thing came to an end with Hitler's war.
There was no longer any time for mountain trips involving
a cavalcade of horses, and the trustworthy and capable men
that one could leave in charge at the ranch were gone. But
every year, when the hay was all up and the stacks fenced,
we would take ten days or so and drive into Calgary—and
then up the Bow valley to Banff and to Lake Louise. From
there we would turn north on the Jasper road, still following
the Bow till we saw through the trees, in the autumn
twilight, a jade-green lake and the lights of the lodge
shining across the water; and, dimly against the evening
sky, the glacier that gives birth to the infant Bow. There,
for one magic week, we would enter once more into the
peace of the mountains—and there, in the bays and the
shallows towards the outlet of the Bow Lake, we would
glide in the kayak right up to the giant moose as they
browsed on the water weed. You moved only when they
were not watching: you made the paddle-stroke when their
great heads were under water, and then sat rigid and hardly
breathing when they raised them and regarded you—
strange, heraldic, almost prehistoric beasts, dripping and
festooned with weed. . . . .

It was on these visits to Jimmy Simpson's lodge at the
Bow Lake—and also on train journeys to and from the
Coast—that I began to look at the Bow River between
Banff and Lake Louise. There it was—fifty miles of lively
river with never a boat or canoe on it except on the seven
or eight miles of quiet water just above Banff. I could see
bits of the river from vantage points on the road, and other
stretches of it from the observation cars of Canadian Pacific
trains; and then I began to look at the maps of the Rocky
Mountains National Park. The Bow, according to the
contours, dropped 500 feet from Lake Louise to Banff—a
nice fast river, one might have said, of ten feet to the mile.

But there was more to it than just that: in the first sixteen miles to Castle Mountain it dropped 375 of that 500 feet —and in the last eight miles above Banff it dropped only about 20 feet. Somewhere in that first sixteen miles, then, there had to be some pretty wild water. What was it like? Was it impassable? Owing to the bush and the distance from road and railroad it was impossible to tell without running it.

As for the thirty-six miles or so from Castle Mountain to Banff, I found out what that was like by running it twice, in two different Septembers, on the way back to the ranch from the Bow Lake. There were plenty of fast riffles and a few boulder rapids on that stretch. But it was a lovely bit of river, with splendid views of Castle Mountain and the mountains down toward Banff, seen from different angles as the stream swung from one side to another of the big valley. The odd black bear might be seen ambling along the low banks, moving softly and silently with his shuffling, deceptive gait. And, as the afternoon wore on, beavers would appear, their blunt noses cutting through the water; diving, when the canoe came close, in their queer, humped-up fashion and with their flat, heavy tails slapping down on the water with sharp cracks like the sound of pistol shots.

And then, as the sun sank lower, the bull elk, the wapiti, would appear on the points and on the shingle bars, bugling their challenges. There they stood, each one alone and magnificent, their heads stretched out and slightly raised, giving vent to their incredible, long drawn out call—which is a cross between the agonized cry of a man being murdered slowly and painfully and a donkey's bray. They paid no attention to the canoe as it slid past within a few feet of them. Probably they took it and its motionless occupant for a drifting tree. . . . . Only Carl Rungius, North America's most famous painter of big game, could have rightly set that scene on canvas—the rippling water of the Bow and one of those great beasts standing in the shallows, caught in the evening sunlight with the black wall of the spruce behind him. Here and there on Carl's canvas, among the dark trees, would shine the golden flame of a cottonwood or an aspen poplar in its autumn colour. And beyond, and all around, the snow-powdered mountains cutting into the blue of the September sky. . . . .

That was the Bow below Castle Mountain. But from Lake Louise down to the bridge that carried the Vermilion River road—that challenge remained. It did more: it rankled. We discussed it down at the Buffalo Head; and it eventually became clear that, while the trip obviously had to be made, it would be a bit rash for both parents of our children to charge blindly down that steep and unknown stretch of river together in one frail canoe. At this point Cecy Margaret volunteered to go as bow man— it would be a change, she said, from ranch work and the eternal horse. Her offer was gratefully accepted and then, secure in the knowledge that the children would not now be wholly orphaned, we made our arrangements. Weather and some work with cattle threw us back a bit and it was not till the first of October that Cecy and I could get away. We drove in to Calgary early that morning; and there we went our separate ways, meeting again around eleven p.m. at the C.P.R. station.

The train drew in from the east and we marched towards the sleeping cars, followed by a redcap trundling our packsacks and the faltboat on a barrow. Here trouble met us. We had reserved two standard lowers, and the redcap charged in ahead of us with the various bundles. I said to the darkie porter as we boarded the train: "If you have an empty upper, how would it be to sling these packages into it?"

The porter was obviously nonplussed by the shapeless bundle of the ribs, the long bundle of the side and floor pieces, and the floppy packsack affair that held the seats and the canoe's skin. "What are they, sir?" he said. "Hand baggage?" And I thoughtlessly answered: "No—a canoe."

That pretty nearly fixed the expedition there and then.

The porter said he'd been railroading for over twenty years and this was the first time anybody had tried to bring a boat (as he chose to call it) into his sleeping car. It was an outrage, he said.

At this point the conductor appeared and took a hand. "That thing should have gone by freight," he said. To which I replied—no it shouldn't, it was camp equipment; and if it couldn't go in here, then what were baggage cars for? Meanwhile, ignoring the fracas, Cecy walked off to her bunk carrying the ribs, and some woman from down east—from Toronto probably—said it was a disgrace, blocking the gangway like this with a boat when folks wanted to get to their beds—though, she added, it was just the sort of thing you might expect in a crazy place like Calgary. And more and more people came, all wanting to go to bed, and they all talked at once and the train was getting later and later. By this time we had got the entire canoe cached in our beds, and the conductor had given it up as a bad job because, with all that mob trying to get aboard, getting the canoe out was a physical impossibility. Then the signal was given and the porter shouted "All aboard!", herded the rest of his bunch into the train like cattle into a corral, raised the steps and slammed the door shut, and went off down the car muttering to himself. He brightened up, however, when I gave him a good tip and told him to call us for Lake Louise. And away we went, up the Bow.

It had been a long day, and 120 peaceful miles lay ahead of us. I fell asleep gratefully, all mixed up with my packsack, the wooden sections of the canoe and the paddles. The clutter of stuff in my bed mattered absolutely zero to me—I could have slept that night with a bunch of porcupines. I woke only once; and I raised the blind to see where we were. The moonlight showed me a mountain, snow-streaked and precipitous. That was Castle Mountain. Thank God, I thought, there's still another fifteen miles or more—and I snapped down the blind and fell asleep again. But it seemed that only a minute passed before the porter's hand was through the curtains, shaking me, and I heard his voice saying: "Lake Louise in five minutes."

Four a.m. on the second of October is a poor sort of a time to be decanted at a lonely railway station, five thousand feet above sea level. The tail lights of the train vanished round the bend, headed for the Kicking Horse Pass, and Cecy and I picked up our stuff and the canoe and walked up the tracks to the trim, log-built station building. The place was dark and deserted, but inside it was warm and the embers of a fire still glowed on the hearth. We raked them together and put a log and some more coal on. Then, by the firelight, we fixed up to sleep through the remaining hours of darkness—I on the floor by the fire, in my parka and rolled up in the canoe skin—she, wrapped in everything she could lay hands on, on a table dragged up to the fire, on the principle that heat rises and every little helps. Silence fell again on Lake Louise station and the camp slept. . . . .

A sort of grumping noise gradually penetrated into my dreams—and every now and then the harsh rattle of metal on stone. "Grump, grump, grump" the sound came, steadily and rhythmically; and then this strange rolling of iron wheels. I opened my eyes. The grey light of dawn was coming into the station waiting room; the fire was almost out, and on the table a shapeless bundle lay motionless: you couldn't tell which was its head end and which its feet.

Damn it, I thought, the section man's got a maintenance crew at work out on the tracks already—and I untangled myself from the canoe skin and went to one of the north windows to see what was up. I was a bit anxious because we had the idea that park wardens, not being canoe-minded, and probably regarding the Bow River as certain death by drowning, would do their best to prevent us from starting if they happened to spot us assembling the canoe. The plan was to get going before anybody was about—and here was Lake Louise coming to life far too early.

I need not have worried. Twenty-three elk—bulls, cows and big calves—were on the platform and on the main line tracks just in front of it. They had made themselves completely at home there—standing up, lying down between the rails, horning in a sociable sort of way at each other. The grumping noise was a big old bull polishing his horns on a corner of the station building—up, down; up, down; steadily and without stopping. The noise of wheels came from another bull who seemed fascinated with a baggage barrow. He was weaving his head around and about it, and every now and then hitching the tines of his antlers under the end-rail and giving the barrow a shove along the platform. Altogether an unusual sight—and it was interesting to see, for once, a zoo in reverse, as it were. From the animals' point of view, I mean: from inside, looking out. I went quietly over and shook the bundle on the table. Life stirred in it. Then it disintegrated and Cecy swung down off her perch without a word and joined me at the window. We watched the elk there for a while.

"And now what do we do?" Cecy asked. "I mean, those animals can be dangerous sometimes, can't they? And isn't this the season?"

"Let's wake the fire up and have our sandwiches and thermoses and see what happens next. They may go."

So we did that; and, as we ate, the elk, as if at a signal, moved slowly away up the tracks towards the pass. Then they turned and vanished into the bush, heading north, and Canada's great artery was once more clear.

On the other side of Lake Louise station ran the main Trans-Canada Highway. Then a short stretch of grass with scattered spruce and pine. Then the Bow River, shrunken on that day to its October low, purling over its bed of waterworn stones. We observed all this, reconnoitering with caution from the door of the station building. Not a thing was moving on road or railroad; the place was dead. Hurriedly we got our stuff over the road and down over the low bank on to a patch of river sand. On that we assembled the faltboat. Then we gently laid it in the river, loaded our packs into it and arranged the seats, paddles and trackline. Then we got in and shoved off without ceremony or fanfare of trumpets—and for a time all went well.

The morning was grey. The high springs and the glaciers were frozen, and the Bow was very low, even for October. The rounded river stones flew past beneath us, plainly to be seen through the clear water and so close that one found oneself trying to sit lightly, expecting any moment a smash from below. Almost immediately the Pipestone River came in from the north, and that helped. Then the Bow picked up the creek that comes in from the Horseshoe Glacier on the south, and then Corral Creek from the north; and each succeeding access of water gave us a bigger river with more room to keep the canoe clear of trouble.

The riffles were close together and steep; we were dropping fast. Once or twice I ran the canoe into an eddy and landed, to walk ahead and pick a course down some noisy riffle which fell away out of our sight as it made its drop. Then, knowing what lay ahead, we would run the canoe out on the tongue of unbroken, racing water, to rush wildly down the slope of the riffle and ride triumphantly through the tumbling white waves, the tail of the race. Sometimes we ran through a wave, but that mattered little in that decked-in, kayak type of craft—only a sudden surge of water slapping against us; and with the "bow man", I observed, taking the cream of it. And, as usual, success brought confidence and I walked ahead no longer.

Rock outcrops appeared on the left, and then low cliffs. Suddenly the river took charge, and we found ourselves racing down a narrow chute with a right angle turn at the bottom where the full force of the current hit square against a cliff, boiled up furiously and then swung away to the right. There was no stopping in this place—and we swept madly with the paddles to make the turn and avoid piling end-on into the cliff. Had that happened at the pace we were travelling, the park wardens would undoubtedly have found themselves stuck with that least wanted of jobs—combing the river bars for the debris and the remains.

We turned the canoe, but had no time to get way on it in its new direction. There was a slam and a scrunch of breaking wood as the river hurled us broadside-on against the cliff. Then we fell back into the maelstrom and for whole seconds the water boiled and surged around us and over the canvas decking, whipping the paddle blades this way and that. I heard my voice saying: "Drive her for God's sake"—but there was really no need; the slight figure in the bow was already doing its best. Suddenly a boil of water from beneath lifted the canoe and gave the paddles something to bite on; we gathered speed and left the roar of that turbulent place behind us; we went on into the quiet lapping of fast, unbroken water; and in that calm, so still that we could hear the hiss of the air bubbles beneath the canoe, we compared notes and shook the water from out jackets. But a river never sleeps, and we never ceased to keep our eyes skinned for the next bit of trouble.

Moraine Creek came in on the right bank, bringing the water from the Valley of the Ten Peaks to swell the Bow. We landed on the downstream side of it for breakfast— a real breakfast this time, and not before it was needed. Soon the smoke of our fire was drifting away down the river and the tea-pail, suspended from a green willow stick, was coming to the boil. I made porridge with raisins in it and Cecy fried bacon and eggs. Buttered toast followed as soon as the flames died down and the embers reddened to a glow. Who, if sufficiently stuffed, gives a thought to the greyness of an October morning? Not even the heaviness of the snow clouds that seemed to be pressing in from the north-east through the gaps in the Castle Mountain range could dim our spirits, and we ate and lazed by the fire and let an hour go by. Later in the day we agreed that that had been our first mistake.

The canoe lay upside down, draining out a little water that we had shipped. A rib had been broken when we hit the rock wall but the five-ply rubber skin was not holed. When we loaded up again we jammed a packsack against the broken rib, and the canoe, braced in every other direction, remained streamlined and rigid.

More riffles followed with more or less trouble, and then some magnificent straight reaches of strong, rippling water, without a break in it, but flowing downhill so fast that we could easily see the slope. No animals appeared—it was the wrong time of day for them—and all through that day we never saw a human being.

The miles went by; and then, somewhere below Castle Mountain and the Vermilion River road, we spotted the perfect landing—a sandy beach backed by a nice flat covered with small alpine growths and a scattering of pines. As we made for it there came a breath of warm wind from the west: that was the Chinook trying to break through against the heavy cold air from the prairies. Another puff came—and soon the Chinook had its way, blowing, for once, gently instead of the usual hurricane which would have made it impossible to control the canoe. Blue sky appeared as we made lunch, and the sun came through. Soon the snow clouds were dispersed or rolled back into the north-east, and Indian summer reigned once more within the mountains. The canoe was lifted out to dry on the sandy beach in the sun and the wind. Meanwhile on the flat, amongst the pines, the voyageurs drank their noonday tea and then, in the drowsy autumn sunshine, they slept awhile. That siesta proved to be the second error of the day . . . . .

The westering sun laid the shadow of a pine across my face. It was like a cold hand, and I awoke and realised that the afternoon was on its way. Twenty miles and more of river lay between us and Banff. But it was river that I had run before and there should be nothing desperate on it. We had the affair in the bag, we thought, and lightheartedly we slung the outfit into the dry canoe and shoved off.

The pattern was as on my previous runs from Castle Mountain down to Banff. The animal world had had its siesta, and soon the elk appeared on the beaches—and then, all too soon, there seemed to be beaver at work. We raced on down the green river with the valley glowing under the October sun. It felt as though summer could never end, and I was confident that we could at least reach the quiet water before dark. Once we got that far time and darkness would matter no longer.

The Bow split up into several channels, making big islands. Taking one of these channels which I had never run before, we found ourselves flung right across the valley, close in to the C.P.R. track where it rounded a rocky spur. Blasting their way around that spur in the eighties, the construction gangs had hurled masses of rock in wild confusion into the river. There is plan and method in all that nature does, but little rhyme or reason in much that is perpetrated by man. Sixty years of floods and driving ice had not been enough to sort out this man-made mess. There was no canoe channel through it and there was nothing for it but to line down.

We stepped ashore and I picked up the trackline—a hundred feet of light line, one end fastened to the ring in the bow, the other to the rear seat. We shoved the canoe out on it and I started to steer it with the line down the riffle. Lining a canoe downstream is a lot harder than lining it up—one has less control—and Cecy followed behind me carrying one of the long, double-bladed paddles in case of trouble. And, sure enough trouble came: the canoe slid gently up on to a large boulder and refused to be wiggled off it with the line. Cecy stepped into the water to shove it off with her paddle. The paddle slipped on the wet canoe and she lost her balance on the rounded river stones. In one dire second her feet flew out from under her and she landed plunk in a sitting posture in the Bow River, the Minizni

Wapta—the "Cold Water River"—of the Stoney Indians. And not so named without reason.

A chill ran through me at the sight. It was cloudless now and still, and it was going to freeze as soon as the sun set. And that river was never a place to sit in, even in July. I helped Cecy up. "Hurt at all?" I asked. "Want to change into a skirt or something? I'll light a fire if you like."

"No," she said, and there was wrath in her voice. "It'll be dark soon and we've got to get on. I'll go back into the bush and wring myself out. I'll be all right, don't worry."

She did that while I lined down the rapid; and she reappeared a bit later, still damp but no longer dripping, and with equanimity partially restored. I knew the reason for her annoyance: she hated inefficiency and to slip was inefficient. Through that slip more time had been lost, and now the day was dipping towards evening . . . . . I also was kicking myself for having taken the unknown channel that had led us to this ill-fated boulder rapid below the C.P.R. tracks: that was inefficient, too, and it was the third error of that day.

We went on. The sun vanished behind the western mountains and, with the dusk, the roar of the riffles became louder as we approached them. The crests of their waves flashed white in the twilight; the green river was no more, and water that was already black streaked past the hurrying canoe. The beavers were busy, for this was their hour and they knew that winter was not far ahead; and in the bush, and sometimes out on the bars where we could see them, the elk kept up their eerie calling. There is the howl of the timber wolf, the cry of the cougar and the wild laughter of the loon—but of all the strange sounds in the Canadian woods commend me to the bugling of the elk at close quarters at evening time. A blood-curdling sound . . . . . Then a star appeared in the south-east— and then another, and soon the touch of the frost could be felt. Sometimes I thought of the horrid wetness of the

bowman and shuddered, but mostly I kept my mind on
the river, which was giving me more than enough to think
about . . . . . Then we ran a riffle that we couldn't see—
close in to a bank and under big old cottonwoods—and
we knew that at last darkness had fallen.

We pulled in to what seemed to be—and was—an eddy
and held a council. We were far from the railroad and
we could only guess, from the nature of the valley, what
lay between us and the Banff-Lake Louise highway which
was further yet: two miles at least of bush and beaver
dams, springs and snyes (which are subsidiary channels
of the main river), deadfall, potholes and moose meadows.
A sweet prospect in the dark, with a strong chance of a
sprained ankle or a broken leg, and ten miles of lonely,
empty road to walk if we ever managed to reach it. Or
we could light a fire and camp where we were with nothing
much but tea to see us through the night. There remained
the river—and it was not long before we were afloat again
on water that we couldn't even see, just like the Ghost
Arm years before; and once again I had that strange feeling
of slipping silently over a black mirror.

But this time we were on living water and we sat tense
and motionless, moving with the current, dipping the
paddles only to keep the canoe heading straight down
river. The roar of a riffle was approaching—the first one
in the utter blackness—and I was doing my best to determine its nature from that sound. All I could see was the
dim outline of trees moving against the stars, and that
not clearly. Even the drip of a paddle was an unwanted
noise, and when Cecy ventured some perfectly normal
remark all she got for her pains was: "Keep quiet, for
God's sake, and let me listen!"

Suddenly an elk screamed in the bush close by. We had
forgotten the animals, and a tremor shook the canoe as
we both started. The appalling sound went on and on,
to die out in a desperate groan—and when it ceased the
riffle was close and I knew that the bar was on the right

and the channel lay to the left of it. Then the water began to break and the wavelets caught the starlight, and I could see them racing from right to left as the river gathered itself for the drop. We swung the canoe and in five short seconds we were into white water and racing downhill, following the crest of the waves and praying that no fallen tree lay across the channel. Then came the swirl and pull of the eddies, and then the blackness again of the unbroken river. Slowly the roar of that riffle faded away behind us —and then the distant mutter of the next one came from down river on the still night air.

The pattern for each riffle was the same: first the sound, coming closer, getting louder; then the course, predicted from the sound; then the last minute confirmation as the stars flashed in the broken water—and lastly the sudden rush of the canoe. There was a tremendous exhilaration to it. One's every sense was tensed and taut; and there was also the feeling that it was too good to last—that you couldn't possibly go on running fast water by ear alone, with just the sparkle of a few dancing stars. But you can—and we did it, though with nerves stretched to the breaking point like drawn bowstrings.

The elk had a hand in that—and also the beaver. The elk must have sensed our silent passing; I can only account for it in that way, for never before or since have I heard them, in such numbers, kick up such an unearthly din. But the beaver were worse. To them, as they swam about their business, we were, naturally, just a floating tree. Then, suddenly, they would realise that something about this particular tree was not as it should be. And then a strong, heavy animal, of whose presence we had been till then utterly unaware, would bang the water with his tail and dive, perhaps only three or four feet from the canoe. There would be a shattering report, and out of the black water into the black darkness would rise a white column of foam, perhaps two feet high. It would hang for a moment like the column of spray from a shell that has missed its target and fallen into the sea. And then it would vanish, leaving the darkness again and two shattered human beings voyaging determinedly down a black, unseen river.

Much more of this sort of thing and we should have been right round the bend. But the end came, as it had to. A riffle approached and from it there came strange noise, one that I didn't like at all. It was the sound, I thought, of water rushing through a tangle of fallen trees —snags embedded on the river bottom, and sweepers, which are trees fallen into the river but with the roots still adhering to the bank—the most dangerous obstacles of all on a wild river.

The moon was rising behind the mountains and a faint light was growing stronger. It shone on what appeared to be a bay of tranquil water, a refuge from the noise below. "Sweepers ahead," I said. "Drive her hard for that bay before the current catches us, and we'll land and line down."

We did that—and we hit the "bay" with a thud: it was a beach of damp sand. No matter: we were safe on shore, and soon the canoe was bobbing gently down the riffle on the trackline, well clear of all the sweepers, while we walked beside it down the bar. And that—the one place where we would have met with certain disaster— was the last of the riffles. Below lay the calm water and a seven-mile paddle in to Banff in full moonlight and with a rising west wind behind us.

We were content: we had done what we set out to do. Nevertheless, we were by now cold and hungry, and even I was far from dry. We laid our plans carefully for a prodigious feed when we got to Banff, and debated what we should do with the canoe.

"We'll leave it in Jimmy Simpson's garden," I said. "His is one of the first few houses we come to. The garden faces the river. I don't know which it is but we can probably spot it—and for heaven's sake don't let's put it in Wresterby's garden by mistake. He lives somewhere there, too."

"Why not in Wresterby's garden?"

"Well, he went to a tremendous lot of work and trouble once to put a boat on a certain mountain lake. The day after he got it there I turned up on the opposite side of the lake with a string of packhorses and made camp. About half an hour later, and much to Wresterby's disgust, this canoe shot out of the bay where we were camped and on to the sacred waters of his lake. A pure coincidence, but I heard afterwards that he was convinced that I had done it on purpose, just to wipe his eye. Said there ought to be a law against me and another one against faltboats. What I rather feel is, we've had all the fun we want for one day, so let's leave Wresterby out of it and throw ourselves on Old Jim's hospitality . . . . .

Banff, when we got there, seemed to have gone to bed early. We landed a bit stiffly and prowled around houses and gardens, but there was nothing anywhere to tell us who they belonged to. Finally we chanced it: we just picked a nice house with a nice lawn wide open to the river, and laid the canoe there with its gear all neatly stacked under a well-branched spruce. Then we slung our packs and headed for ham and eggs and, above all, coffee —lots of it; about a quart apiece anyway, we thought. Probably more . . . . .

In the morning and well before train time I got hold of a taxi. I told the driver to go to the road by the river where the houses faced west, up the valley. When we got there I pointed out the canoe under its tree and asked the driver to give me a hand with it. "Why, certainly," he said. "And you couldn't have put it in a handier place. Mr. Wresterby's house that is, and on that good lawn of his we'll have your boat to pieces in no time . . . . ."

Well—there you are. If there's anything like that lying around you can trust me to land in it with both feet. Not just *not* in Jimmy Simpson's garden, but *in* Wresterby's —dead centre every time.

And that is the very end of the Bow story. There will

never be any more to tell because that classic performance, though I did not know it at the time, marked the end of my days of canoeing on the Bow River.

CHAPTER XIII

The Awkward Moose

The stalk had been a failure. The sheep had seen us, and now they were leaving the country in a hurry. Nobody was to blame—there was practically no cover on that open, stony summit and it was a miracle we had got as close as we did. Still, it was a pity; there was a good head in that bunch.

I put the glass back into its case and we rose and looked at each other. "That ram's name," Henry said, "is on no bullet of mine. Where do we go from here? Some place where we can eat, I hope: it's nearly three already—and these weird hours the Colonel keeps are getting me down."

Henry and Kathleen Jackson had been the Colonel's guests on a month's shooting trip up on Ram River, and now the trip was almost over and we were on our way out to the Colonel's ranch in the foothills. Jim Boothby and I were the guides. A picnic spirit had fallen on the party in these last days; the normal crack-of-dawn breakfast and early start had been suspended in favour of a long drawn out, hilarious feast that started late and lasted most of the morning. The Colonel would preside over the fire and make the hotcakes, while Henry fried the bacon and warmed the maple syrup—and camp would be kept in an uproar by the sallies and stories of the pair of them. The bright October sun would climb slowly into a sky of cloudless blue and the glittering hoar frost would take refuge in the shadow of the trees—and still we would sit there round

206

the fire, propped against our saddles, drinking more coffee, loading up fresh relays of hotcakes with still more butter and maple syrup, laughing helplessly. It would be midday before Jim and I had the horses packed and got the outfit on the trail the three carefree riders had taken an hour or more earlier . . . . .

Travelling thus, on what Jim chose to call "the Rip van Winkle system," we naturally made camp late. Only the night before, darkness had caught us away up Scalp Creek and we had crossed the great flats of the Red Deer River in the light of the full moon—thirteen hungry horses and five hungry, suffering humans, with our black, distorted shadows swaying silently along beside us over the frozen grass. On all sides of that hidden parkland, as if to protect it from men, the mountains thrust their dark ramparts into the star-strewn sky, dwarfing the little cavalcade that crawled across the meadows.

The horses had been unpacked and unsaddled in silence. Somebody made a fire. Some genius routed out the coffee, sugar and rum, and soon we stood around the blaze with coffee royals in our tin mugs and smiles creeping back on to our faces: things were once more looking up. But midnight still heard the sizzle and splutter of the last moose steaks in the pan—and, what with that and yet another riotous breakfast, the morning had been well on its way when the Jacksons and Jim and I had ridden out of camp. The Colonel had gallantly stayed behind—"to keep an eye on the horses," he had said, "and have supper ready for you when you get back."

This was Kathleen's first hunting trip and this last day was to be devoted to getting her a mountain sheep—a prized trophy to take back with her to New York, and one that would set her far above her fellow women. So we had ridden south up a long valley where there was a faint Indian trail and then, winding through the trees, up a vast hillside that barred our way to the west. We came to timberline, and there the last little clump of alpine fir was found to grow in a densely walled ring with a tiny meadow in the centre—an ideal place for tying the horses, and we left them there. Then we had parted company, Jim and Kathleen heading north-west over the stony eight thousand foot summit and Henry and I south-west over the hump and down into this new valley . . . . .

Now, with the ram lost to us, we moved down and across the mountainside till we came to a grassy, rock-walled hollow—a perfect sun-trap and sheltered from the wind. There we laid down our rifles, stretched ourselves on the grass and fell to on the sandwiches. Over our heads sang the Chinook, the warm south-west wind, spinning its summer clouds across the blue Alberta sky.

Presently I rose up with a sandwich in one hand and my Zeiss monocular in the other: there was no time to lose if Henry was to get a shot at something before evening drove us back to the horses. But in all that great green and gold country there seemed to be no living thing: there were no sheep on the open slopes and no bear pursued his inquisitive way through the timber. Far below a stream glittered in the low rays of the October sun: it ran due south, to the Panther River probably. I followed it northwards, with the glass, to its head in an amphitheatre of grassy hills, and there, black against those tawny slopes, I spotted a bull moose browsing. He had a good head on him as far as one could see—but I knew Henry didn't want a moose: he had set his heart on a bighorn ram. A moose head, he said, was only fit for a hotel or a railroad station; it would make a wreck of any private house. But he would enjoy seeing this moose: soon I would point it out to him and give him the glass. And then another movement caught my eye . . . . .

"Henry."

"Yes, Ray? Seen something?" And he took a bite out of a moose sandwich that would have done credit to the Mad Hatter.

"I surely have. There's a moose on a hillside at the head of the creek and Kathleen and Jim are after him."

He jumped up and an agonised cry, muffled by sandwich, broke from him. "No?! Oh, my God! Here, give me that thing—" And for a while he peered up the valley in silence.

"They must be mad," he said. "Take another look. See them scuffling across that slope in full, plain view of that animal? Of course they won't get him . . . . . But the moose must be crazy, too. Why, in heaven's name, doesn't he run?"

The shadows were lengthening as the sun sank towards the mountains. Between the moose and the two hunters the faintest suspicion of a wrinkle was appearing on that sunny hillside. There was a shallow coulee there and Kathleen and Jim were hitching themselves down into it in a sitting posture, much after the fashion of puppies hitching across a lawn. The moose had turned and was facing west, otherwise they would probably have had to roll. Once down into the coulee they began to crawl.

"They mean business, Henry," I said, and I handed him the glass and pointed out the lay of the land.

"I can't see it! I can't see it!", he cried, after a prolonged study—and it certainly did look odd if one ignored that slight creeping shadow. "No," he went on, "I'll tell you what it is. Just by sheer bull luck they've blundered on to a moose that's not only mad but deaf and dumb into the bargain. And Kathleen's going to get him, and home's going to be ruined with that monstrous head in it—"

"You mean, she'll want to take that thing home with her?"

"Of course she will—what else? She'll be the proudest woman in New York. Oh, please Lord, let her rifle jam! No—I don't mean that. I want her to look back on this as a wonderful trip, something she'll always remember —which it will be, for both of us, if she gets that moose.

How unspeakably awful! Here, take your glass and don't let me have it again; just tell me about it . . . . ." And he went back to his seat under the rock wall, bit a chunk out of his last sandwich and groaned. And the minutes slipped by . . . . .

"They've crawled up the west slope of that coulee, Henry, and now they're looking about for the moose. Now they're on to him again—he's turned north, uphill, broadside on to them."

"I told you he was crazy. Do you realise, Ray, what this means to me? I've been thinking it over and there isn't a room in the house that wouldn't be utterly ruined by a moose head. No—it means enlarging the sunroom, and with building costs what they are and plate glass worth its weight in gold that's going to be a ten thousand dollar job—all for a fool of a moose that's paralysed and—"

"Kathleen's sitting down to shoot," I broke in. "No, she isn't: must be something wrong. They're up and crawling again. That's odd."

Henry leapt up. "Give me that glass, Ray. I know I said 'Don't' but I can't stand this . . . . . My God, she's going to shoot! This is it! And Jim's just behind her, pointing: irresponsible idiot—egging her on, probably. Just wait till I get a word with him!"

A long pause followed and then Henry said in a flat tone of voice, "Take the thing. I give it up: they're crawling closer and even now that moose doesn't know enough to run."

Jim told us later that they could see the moose when they were on their hands and knees, but that, when Kathleen got into a shooting position, the bunch grass and the dwarf willows obscured the view: hence these weird manoeuvres.

At last the two tiny figures were still and I raised the glass again. Kathleen was rigid, with her rifle levelled and Jim was just behind her: the moose suddenly swung his great head, and a fraction later the crack of a rifle floated down the valley.

Henry was tense. "Any damage, Ray?" he said.

"No. Clean miss as far as I can see."

Henry rose to the occasion. "Oh, moose," he bawled with the full strength of his lungs, "RUN! Oh you great antediluvian, prehistoric, Roman-nosed brute, lumber into a trot for Pete's sake and save your silly hide . . . . ." But the moose was too far off to hear him and his words were carried away by the Chinook to be lost in the barren uplands to the eastward. And even as he spoke the great beast crumpled and fell and the sound of the second shot came down to us.

By now the sun was almost touching the western mountains and we lost no time in getting to the scene of action. I take my hat off to Henry for the way in which, with a false but charming smile on his face and black despair in his heart, he greeted his triumphant wife. "A fine head, Kathleen," he said glibly, "and a master shot. We shall remember this little valley all the days of our lives." Nicely put; and his whole heart was behind that last bit about remembering this little valley.

While the Jacksons were talking Jim and I held a conference. Only two men could work at the same time on that moose to any advantage: it would be best, we decided, to get the Jacksons headed east over the hump and, if possible, down to the horses while there was still some daylight. We would follow as soon as we could with the trophy, and the best of the meat. So we gave Henry his bearings, wished them both a happy reunion with the horses and then set to work. Looking up a few minutes later I saw them climbing steadily—two small figures already becoming indistinct on the great, stony slope of the mountain. They were heading, I was glad to see, in the right direction.

Fixing up Kathleen's moose proved to be a cold, bloody and watery job: worse by far than cutting up that moose that Gordon Matthews and I had shot, fifteen years back, on the Sikanni Chief River*—the one, I mean, which fell wedged between the ice blocks. Then we had at least enjoyed warm sunshine, and it was noon and the canoes were close at hand. Now it was the last day of October and already evening, and we were on the wrong side of a mountain from our horses and from camp. And that was by no means everything.

It was an unusually bloody performance because the moose had fallen in such a way, jamming his right antler into a boggy place, that we couldn't move him at all and had to work round and under the head as best we could. Fortunately, in addition to our hunting knives, I had with me a light and very sharp axe. The job was a cold and watery one because the big animal lay across the hollow of a little spring, damming it completely and far better than any man could have done using rocks, turf and a shovel. As Jim truly said, that moose had thought of everything except running.

We worked fast in the fading light. The flaring autumn colours had gone from the valley with the setting of the sun: all that remained was a few torn fragments of cloud, high up, flame-coloured against the evening sky. The Chinook had died down and a dead silence had settled on the timberline country. But, fast as we worked, the lake formed by the blocked spring rose still faster: soon it lipped and began to flow in an ice-cold stream over the moose, drawing winged words from Jim who was busy skinning back the hide and cutting out the tender back-strap meat from each side of the backbone. I had the cape skinned off and turned up as far as the bogged antler would allow. One last stroke of the axe drove through the vertebrae at the base of the skull and then we were able to roll the huge head out of the hollow on to dry ground. As we did so, destroying the dam in the process, a crimson torrent rushed down the watercourse, filling Jim's boots to the brim for him with a mixture of blood and

* See Chapter VII: *The Sikanni Chief River.*

water as it passed by—and I, listening with awe to his comments, waited for the heavens to fall on the pair of us.

But we were spared—and soon we had the cape skinned
off and rolled into a wet, soggy bundle tightly bound
with leather thongs. A few more nicks with knives and
axe and the antlers came away with the plate—the bony
structure of the brow and nose. All that remained to do
was to pack up and go while there was still light enough
from the western sky for us to see our way.

Jim eyed the antlers with distaste. "Miserable load, that,"
he remarked. "Not only the weight of the things, but
there's always some bit of bone or horn that's trying to
dig a hole in your neck or pry your ear off. I'll take it
half-way to the top."

"I'll take it the whole way to the top," I said. "Then we
can change over on the divide. How's that?"

"It's a deal." He took me up quickly on that offer and
he looked pleased. I was pleased, too: it seemed to me
much easier to carry an awkward load, especially in the
dark, up a mountain slope of loose rock than it would be
to carry the same load down. Now, if I slipped and fell
going down the east slope, I would merely be squelched
by the heavy bundle of green moose hide instead of being
gored or impaled by the antlers. All Jim wanted was to
carry the lighter load uphill, and so we were both
happy. Helping each other to shoulder our burdens, we
started . . . . .

About twelve hundred feet above the spring the steep
hillside eased off: the slope became gentle and the walking
good over packed gravel and alpine turf. By now it was
dark: all that remained of this day of Indian summer was
a faint gleam of light in the west, cut by the black line
of the mountains. The stars were shining and it was
freezing hard with the dropping of the Chinook—but there
was nothing odd about that for in a few hours it would
be November and we were over eight thousand feet above
sea level. Ahead of us the crest of the ridge cut across

a reddish glow in the east: that would be the rising of the moon; but why, we wondered, was it red? In front of us and quite close a flat outcrop of rock, about four feet high, stood out against this strange light: it seemed designed for the easy laying down of loads, and we made for it and rested and changed over there.

Since the pace was set by the man carrying the worst load this put Jim in the lead. In carrying a set of moose antlers a man places the great, palmated horns between his shoulders, almost at the base of his own neck. The tines curve upwards as in their natural position on the animal, but the antlers are carried by the hunter in reverse for the sake of balance, and the man's arms are outspread so that he may grasp with each hand some convenient tine. All one can see, following behind in the dark, is the outline of the man and of the great antlers that seem to sprout like reptilian wings from his shoulders.

As we walked on upwards the red light in the east grew stronger. Cutting sharply into it, and a few paces ahead of me, strode Jim, a black silhouette against the glowing sky—a demon figure, half man, half beast, like some strange god of old Assyria. It was the weirdest sight that I have ever seen, one that I shall never forget. It reminded me of a picture of Arthur Heming's—a man on snowshoes carring a set of moosehorns, crossing a frozen lake against the streaming fires of the aurora.

Soon we reached the level summit. We walked easily forward across the little stony flat and fetched up on the edge of a precipice where the mountain fell away sheer some six hundred feet into the basin where the horses were tied. We had come a bit too far to the left.

We were greeted by an enormous moon hanging low in the eastern sky. It was climbing, blood-red, through a smoke-haze that had drifted down, with the shifting of the wind, from some prairie or forest fire in the distant north. Under the moon and a thousand feet below us a heavy mist was creeping into the mountains: it was the cold front meeting the warm south-western air and it was coming from the prairie and from the foothills where, with the dying down of a Chinook, the cold always strikes first: it writhed and twisted like smoke and it was reddened by the moon to the colour of fire. Out of this heaving, fiery sea of cloud rose the black peaks of the outer range like barren, saw-toothed islands in a crimson sea. The whole unearthly setting had a devilish quality to it.

Against that fantastic backdrop the winged demon that was Jim moved forward, sure-footed, on to a point of the precipice and stood there looking down into the fiery pit of the valley.

"Damn me," he said, in most fitting language, "if that ain't one hell of a lookin' sight. I never seen anything like that in all my days." And then, after a reverential silence: "We'd ought to give the Jacksons a holler. Where the devil they've got to in that red mist is anybody's guess and if we have to look for them as well as for the horses this'll be a night we'll surely remember."

So we hollered—and, a few seconds later, there came to us, from out of the boiling vapours, faint yells, curiously remote and smothered. But the Jacksons were putting heart and soul into this yelling business: they thought, they told us afterwards, that we were trying to get a bearing on them—for they had found the horses, getting to them in the dusk and just before the fog crawled over them. So they stayed with it and hooted and bellowed all they knew how in a desperate effort to make us hear. Muffled by the fog and echoing against the cliffs, their howlings blended into one long-drawn, wolf-like note, and came to us out of the lurid glow of the pit like the wailings of the damned . . . . .

Somehow we got down to them. We loaded the antlers and the cape on to our packhorse and then we hit the trail, following downhill, in single file, the stream that drained the basin. Soon we came to the edge of the timber where we were forced to dismount. Jim then went ahead, leading his saddle horse; the Jacksons came next with their horses and mine turned loose, while I brought up the rear leading the packhorse. Slowly the red light turned to silver as the moon got clear of the belt of smoke: without that ghostly radiance we could never have made it down through the thickly-growing spruce and pines, and even with it we kept running into ravines and gulches that we could easily have avoided in daylight. When that happened and we found ourselves stuck, the little column would reverse itself and try to find a way around with me in the lead, and the led packhorse—especially when plunging up the side of some steep and gravelly gulch—doing its best to tread upon my heels. In this way, reversing again and again, we got down to the old Indian trail we had followed in the morning, and about midnight we splashed across the Red Deer River and into camp. The water, I noticed as we passed, was already freezing in the eddies.

A sleepy figure rolled out of its eiderdown beside the fire and greeted us. It was the Colonel.

"My God," he said, "I'd almost given you people up. I was beginning to think you'd decided to bush-whack it for tonight and turn up in the morning."

"Where's that supper you promised to have ready?" we asked him.

He became almost shy in his manner, which is unusual for the Colonel. "Well," he said in a small voice, "it's been a long, cold night and I had mine early and then about ten o'clock—"

"You ate ours!" Henry roared, amidst a shout of laughter. "Oh, what a dirty trick!" And, ignoring the Colonel's protests that you couldn't keep a mulligan hot for ever while a bunch of benighted greenhorns floundered about in the bush, Henry went on to say what he thought of a man who would do a thing like that. He was warming nicely to his subject when the Colonel spotted, back in the shadows, the packhorse that was carrying the moose antlers. Turning a deaf ear to Henry's nonsense he let a whoop out of him that an Apache would have been proud of and went happily off to hunt up a steel tape and the rum . . . . .

Some time later we all stood around the blazing fire with steaming mugs of coffee, well laced with rum, in our hands. It was down to about zero and a thin, cold snow was drifting down out of the north, so fine that it was little more than particles of frost. But nobody minded that: we were thawed out, warmed and well fed and the talk flew back and forth across the fire. Kathleen alone was silent. She seemed to be deep in thought and it was only absently that she replied to some cheerful sally about Diana the Huntress, or her markmanship.

Suddenly she spoke. "I've been thinking it over," she said—and at those remembered words I saw Henry look up anxiously. I knew that the hope that she would abandon the trophy, or give it to the Colonel for the adornment of a ranch gateway—or, indeed, do almost anything but take it back to New York with her—was not yet dead in his heart.

"There's only one place it can go," she went on. "It's so big and magnificent it would spoil almost any room in the house—dwarf everything. But there's the rumpus room, thank heavens: Henry can take down that Stone Sheep head of his from over the cocktail bar and put it somewhere and my moose'll look just glorious there—why it'll be the making of that room . . . . ."

And she went on to tell us how splendidly it was all going to work out; and at the end of her recital the Colonel, rushing in where angels fear to tread, patted her on the back and said, "It'll be *wonderful*, little lady—just *wonderful!* Henry, you must be proud of your wife!"

. . . . .

But it was the moose that had—and, so far as I know, still has—the last word in the matter.

For one thing, when the coffee royals had been dealt

with and we came to lay the steel tape on the antlers, what Jim and I had already guessed became a certainty —that first shot of Kathleen's had carried away the point of the very tine that gave the head its "greatest spread" measurement: there must have been two and a half to three inches of horn missing—enough to put the head away down in any list compiled on the point system. Kathleen was in deep distress. She was not allowed to estimate the amount of missing horn and I honestly believe that if it hadn't been for the snow that was gently powdering down we'd all have been up by the little spring in the hidden valley, next morning, looking for that shot-off point.

Then there was the little affair of the rumpus room. A year or two after all this took place I ran into a man who had met the Jacksons. He didn't know them well, he said, but he had been taken to their house by some friends whom they had asked to a cocktail party. We talked about the Jacksons for a while and then I asked him if he'd happened to notice a moose head anywhere about in their house.

"Notice one?" he said. "I'll tell the world I noticed one. There's some sort of story attached to it, apparently: Mrs. Jackson shot it under rather peculiar circumstances or something—Henry Jackson told me a long history about it but there was such a row going on I didn't really get the point. But the people I came with told me afterwards that that moose almost broke up the home. The party was in a kind of a rumpus room-cocktail room place that they have. Over the bar was a mountain sheep head which, apparently, was the apple of Jackson's eye—the result of a trip he made once to northern British Columbia. Well, to cut a long story short, Mrs. Jackson wanted the sheep taken down and the moose put in its place. Jackson wouldn't hear of it—he offered to build on to the sunroom and put the moose there but she wouldn't have that —she said it would wreck the look of the house and people would think they were in the market garden business. So they got the head mounted by the finest taxidermist in North America and set it in the middle of the rumpus room floor while they argued. And there it was when I saw it and there it still is, I'm told. A menace if ever there was one."

"That very evening," he went, "I was shouting at a most attractive woman that I met there—telling her something about fishing—and I just backed up a step to get room to illustrate a point I was making when I tripped over that monstrosity on the floor; how was I to know it was just behind me? I might have been killed by those damned horns but this woman sort of grabbed me and swung me aside, and we crashed together more or less over the beast's great ugly nose. What a mess! I spilt my own drink over myself and she threw hers over me. The Jacksons, of course, helped us to get straightened out. None of the other guests seemed to see anything unusual in this and our hosts took it as pure routine—in fact Henry Jackson quite definitely implied that the moose head was a risk you assumed if you came to the house at all—a sort of local hazard. I imagine no party at that house is really complete unless somebody half kills himself over those frightful horns . . . . ."

There the matter rests until some further bulletin arrives from New York. In the meantime that moose literally holds the floor at the Jacksons'—no less awkward now than he was on that night of the blood-red moon and the crimson cloud.

Part Four

THE MOUNTAINS
OF YOUTH

1943 - 1955

A man in an open shirt
Sat gazing out to sea;
A young man, a hale man,
And I wished that I were he
And that the things I loved
Were as they used to be.

What did he see
As he sat there?
Some woman's shining hair,
Or the rosy sunset clouds
That burned in the air?

A laughing goddess
Rising from the foam?
Or a tall barquentine
Come home,
Her tops'ls tattered
By the North Wind's comb?

St. Brendan's Isle
On the sea's rim,
Unseen by other men
But clear to him
Whose eyes were shining-bright
Not dim?

I only know I wished that I were he,
And that the things I loved were as they used to be.

"Mirage" by GEOFFREY HOLDSWORTH

221

CHAPTER XIV

Alaska Road

As the years went by on the Buffalo Head I would often think of the North. There would be hot days in mid-May or early June, when the sweet scent of the poplar buds came drifting on the breeze: one waft of that, and into the mind's eye would come a picture of men by the river's edge, on the Sikanni Chief or in Deadmen's Valley, loading canoes and shoving off for some far-off Eldorado, not yet found but no less sure. "This time," I could hear them saying, "we'll nail her down. This time we'll make the big clean-up." It was only the never-failing optimism of the old-time prospector and fur-hunter, I knew that; but nevertheless my heart was with them. The swaying of my saddle-horse would become the rocking motion of a canoe; the cattle ahead of me would fade, and I would see, instead of them and their drifting cloud of sunlit dust, a strange, unknown river flashing in the morning light, flowing towards me from a gap in a nameless range. And the chink of a shod hoof on a rock would become the muffled click of a shod canoe-pole on the stones, down through the brown, rippling water. Most unsettling visions for a man whose job is on the back of a horse . . .

Or the flaming glory of October would set the Highwood country ablaze, ridge upon ridge of rolling gold right up to the blue-shadowed mountains standing guard against the western sky. From some moist, trickling spring there would rise a smell of damp earth and freshly fallen willow leaves—and I would see again the Nahanni country under the autumn sun, and the Flat River foaming down through the little canyon above Irvine Creek. Downstream the scarlet-topped mountains seemed as clear as yesterday (only yesterday was fifteen years ago) and beyond the river I could see the blue mass of the Granite Range, fading away into the unmapped north-west, headed for God-knows-where. Of course, I thought, *that's* where the stuff is. If only I could get back to it—that would be the real killing!

No rancher should have thoughts like these.

Then war broke out and danger seemed to threaten the north-west. Men decided to build a road through that vast hunting park—through to Fairbanks in Alaska. They started—and a ponderous screen of secrecy descended upon the project. A child could have penetrated it, I found later, and no doubt the Japanese High Command was fully informed; but in Canada most people couldn't have cared less where that road went, and the few, like myself, who knew a bit about the country and were interested, were too busy to take the time to find out. Then one cold January evening the phone rang at the ranch. An oil company, it seemed, had a contract to fill a string of storage tanks along the Alaska Road with gasolene "before break-up." A party of the company's officials, of whom I knew one, proposed to drive over the road and size up the possibilities—but when, they were wondering, would break-up come in that country and what would it involve? Would it take the road out in places and flood it elsewhere? Or what? Who was there who could tell them anything about the god-forsaken country? And some inspired genius said, "Patterson's your man. Get him to go along."

The weather that January was perfect: a Chinook blowing softly over the hills, no snow, and the cattle had unfailing open water. I snatched at the chance and away we went—to Pouce Coupé, Fort St John and the Sikanni Chief River, partly following the old trail that Gordon

Matthews and I had driven the dogs over in 1928, partly in new country west of that, and which I had only seen from a high, lonely winter camp on an isolated mesa. I was thrilled. This trip might have been a chore to the oil men but not to me. There was the place, on the Kiskatinaw River,* where the first furious dog-fight took place in March 1928—the one where I fell on top of Sammy, and where Gordon and Spud and Poilu rolled bloodily down the hill and fell on the river ice. And that was the camp where Clay Martin, dazzled by the firelight, mistook Gordon for a fighting dog and, with a stout willow pole, fetched him a crack on the bottom that sounded like a pistol shot—oh, happy days! Well—happy, anyway, for me, if not for Gordon ...

The Chinook, as is common with Chinooks, overdid it: it became almost a hot wind. This is one sign of a dying Chinook, and it invariably upsets the apple-cart and brings about a reversal of temperature. This took place at Fort St John, and the thermometer dropped, with the dying down of the west wind, from over sixty degrees above to a few degrees below zero. That night it so happened that I shared with my friend, the head of the party, the owner's suite in a most palatial construction camp. As we undressed for bed I saw that what I had mistaken for a cupboard in one corner of this large, warm room was, in reality, a well-appointed shower. "My God, Jim, look at this," I called out. "A shower! We'll probably never see another. Who'll have first go? You or me?"

Jim was half-undressed, and at my words he clutched his remaining clothes around him as if I'd tried to tear them from his body. A look of horror came over his face. "Do you realise," he said sternly, "that it's ten below outside? Nothing doing: catch me opening my pores at this temperature! Why, it's downright dangerous!"

Some of these city dwellers took cold weather pretty seriously. For them, death lurked in the blue-shadowed forest with its frost-rimed trees, and in the black night sky

* See Chapter VII: *The Sikanni Chief River.*

with its myriad stars. For them there was nothing friendly in this enormous country through which the road ran, a tenuous thread of safety and of life. Only a dumb, frozen, relentless hostility, biding its time, waiting to pounce. There was no arguing about this—it went beyond reason. I had that shower all to myself.

It got colder as we went north and west; the Chinook did not return. I made friends with a geologist, Henry Rae, recently returned from Badakshan in Afghanistan. In order to get a little exercise Henry and I would hit the trail on foot, right after breakfast and while the others were still thinking about crawling into an ice-cold U.S. Army vehicle and getting started. We used to walk furiously, as fast and as far as we could on the packed snow of the road, knowing that sooner or later the gang would drive along and pick us up. This worried the rest: they feared we might get lost or suffer frostbite—I still cannot see how, walking at that pace. Every vehicle that passed us, seeing two maniacs unaccountably on foot, slowed down to offer us a lift. We could have thumbed our way without question from the Sikanni to Fairbanks, set bridges on fire, done anything: security was non-existent.

And plain, ordinary horse sense was at a premium. We stopped one afternoon to warm up and arrange oil supplies at a camp high up in the northern ranges of the Rockies— I believe they call it Soldier's Summit now. Most of the U.S. troops on the road were southerners and what they knew about cold-weather insulation would not have hurt a little child. The army hut we entered was "heated" by a huge, roaring drum-stove bang in the centre of the floor; there was enough heat passing through that thing to have made a tropical hell out of that hut. Yet the place was freezing cold and it was impossible, even standing right alongside the stove, to warm feet that were chilled after hours of resting on the steel, uninsulated floor of the U.S. Army "carry-all" in which we had been riding. There was nothing at all surprising about this, however, since the engineering genius who built the hut had set it up on stone or concrete blocks, and now, beneath the thin wooden floor, there whistled unimpeded a thirty-below-zero north-west wind. I solved that problem for the party. With Henry Rae and one or two helpers I dragged two trestle tables up to the stove. On these we set chairs and in those chairs we sat, to the silent, unprotesting amazement of two U.S. officers who, in a far corner of the frozen shack and in parkas which they probably never removed, were eating some half-cold meal which they had carried in in metal mess-kits. Heat rises—which, apparently, nobody in that army outfit had yet discovered—and up above that stove the temperature was that of a summer's day. In that temperature, and toasting their toes, sat the Canadians, enthroned like strange hyperborean gods on their tables, clad in mucklucks and moccasins, mackinaws and parkas, fur hats and mitts. Toes and fingers began to wiggle freely, tongues to wag again. Over in their frozen corner the two Americans struggled in silence with their frozen food. Not a word passed between the two nations. In came a negro driver, in a long army greatcoat, to complain to his officer about a frozen steering gear. That was the first time I had ever seen a black man grey with cold. . . .

That night it went to thirty-three below zero. After supper at some camp further along the road Henry Rae and I, well fed and warm, walked back up the hill towards the pass. There was not much snow on those stony mountains where the Rockies end, and a full moon was hanging in the sky. Soon we turned aside from the road and climbed high up the mountain to the north. Then we swept a rock clear of snow and sat down to see what we could see.

For a long time we sat there, saying hardly a word. I don't know what Henry was thinking of: comparing it, perhaps, with Badakshan where the rubies grow; with early snowfalls on the Pamirs, the high, clean Roof of the World. For me a door was being opened again. I had

thought that I was through with the North—but here and
now, around and below me, was this wild country of the
Liard canyons for which I had started out so light-heartedly
sixteen years ago. It was then the most inaccessible country
in Canada—it was the dangerous country from which old
John Petersen had tried to turn me back that evening on
the homestead. "We will look after your place for you till
you come again," he had said, when he saw that I meant
to go.*

But I had never got here, I had turned aside up the
South Nahanni River—and now here was the far country
with a white, packed-snow ribbon of a road winding
through it, the road by which we had come. Below us
some belated vehicle crawled down from the pass, headed
for the camp which was hidden by a spur of the mountain.
Its headlights threw a yellow glare on the glittering, moonlit snow and the insect hum of its engine floated up to us.
Then it vanished round the spur, and the silence fell back
into place again behind it, leaving us with the low,
tumbled mountains, barren and glittering like some huge,
frosted Christmas cake, stretching away into the south-
west—and the empty road, a road before its time, a road
that was a precaution rather than a necessity, for no load
of freight would ever be trucked over the full length of it
to Alaska.

Rae spoke about *ovis poli* and asked me what game
there might be in these hills. This, too, was sheep country, I
thought, trying to imagine it in summer-time—Stone
sheep, probably; somebody had told me that they ran
north to the Liard River. And we examined the open
slopes with my field-glass but we could see no living thing:
any game that had survived the construction crews had
probably hit for fresh fields and pastures new—even sheep,
who do not lightly leave their homes. . .

The next day we came to the Liard and crossed over on
the temporary wooden bridge, a long line of trestles embedded in the river ice, to the north shore. The camp was

* See Chapter V: *Itching Foot.*

known as Liard Crossing and there we stayed that night. It was colder, thirty-seven below zero when we got in; and I observed with interest a line of men in U.S. Army great-coats, waiting patiently outside a cook-tent, holding their metal mess-kits. Out came a cook's head and hands through the tent door, with pots and ladles: smack went the supposedly hot food on to the blistering cold metal, too cold to touch with bare hands, and away slouched the half-frozen recipient to some lair of his own, bearing the steaming grub in front of him, unprotected from the crackling frost. By God's truth, if there *was* a hard way of doing anything, it seemed that one could count on these people finding it!

In the officers' mess we ate in reasonable comfort. Henry Rae and I got into conversation with a U.S. captain, Connelly by name. We stood him a drink, a thing he hadn't tasted for months, and then we took him over to our room and fed him a dessert of cheese and raisins, chocolate and biscuits, of which we had each brought a small store. These things were luxuries to Connelly—it was like feeding a hungry schoolboy. The units up the Alaska Road, he told us, were the forgotten army—and it was obvious that, with all the waste and mad spending in other directions, these men did not have the simple foods that keep the cold at bay. We talked, and Connelly questioned me on the old-time stories of the Liard—particularly on the legend of Tom Smith and the tropical valley.* Then, quite suddenly, he asked us if we'd care to join him in a bathing party—an odd sort of invitation with about seventy degrees of frost hammering on the roof.

"It's our one amenity," he said. "These must be the springs you've been talking about; there's nothing else like them on this stretch of the Liard. More like a hot creek than just a spring, and we've dug the creek bed out, cribbed and floored it and tented it over. You'll love it. The men have it up to ten p.m., the officers after. It's ten now. Come on, let's get going."

* "The Dangerous River," by R. M. Patterson, p. 43 (English edition).

Rae and I rushed off to tell the others, but they recoiled in horror from the project. Sheer madness, they said. No opening of the pores for them. So up the road we went with Connelly driving, eight miles or so, and then up a side trail into a beautiful, tall mixed forest—trees glittering in the moonlight, heavily rimed with steam from the warm waters. We pulled up alongside a small tent, set some twenty yards or so from a vast marquee affair on a wooden foundation. Connelly jumped out and ran into the little tent, the changing room. We heard him strike a match and a lamp glowed suddenly through the tent walls. Then he came out again. "That's right," he said. "As usual the stove's out and the flaming sons of bachelors haven't left us a stick of wood. Into the bush with the axes and knock down any dry stuff you can!"

A furious cutting broke the silence of the forest, and soon we had the little stove roaring. "Now then," Connelly said. "What we do is—we leave our clothes and towels here and run over the snow, each man with his soap, into the big tent where the hot creek is. You'd think you'd catch cold but you don't. And mind, the top step's iced."

Two or three minutes later a comic little procession of three naked men, each clutching a cake of soap in his strong right hand, skipped nimbly across the packed snow and disappeared through the tent-flap into a blue haze of sulphurous steam, illuminated by a roaring pressure lantern suspended from the ridge-pole. The area of the bath was, from memory, about twenty-five feet by fifteen, and Connelly had not been exaggerating when he called that spring a creek: there was a tremendous flow of hot, clear and buoyant water, and the soap floated swiftly away down-stream off one's body in a milky cloud. The sound of an engine came to us as we soaked and talked, and Connelly expressed a fervent and adjectival hope that we might find some clothes still waiting for us when we got out. But all was in order: it was South Carolina, a lone lieutenant who was making his solitary way up the road

to Whitehorse, by easy stages in a small army car that he
had probably stolen. Soon a pink, bare foot appeared
throught the tent flaps—and then another foot—and then
South Carolina hit the blue, steaming water a resounding
belly-flopper, sending a tidal wave over the three of us. No
body had told *him* that the top step was iced.

They had found it was dangerous, Connelly said, to stay
in those hot mineral springs too long. It was time to be
going—and once again a comic little procession of three
naked men, each one clutching his cake of soap, trotted
smartly over the moonlit snow, dripping and steaming
this time in the crisp, invigorating snap of forty below
zero. . .

Our little party of oil experts never reached Whitehorse;
it met its Waterloo at Watson Lake in the Yukon Territory. The evening we got there it was fifty-seven below
zero, and by next morning it was sixty-three. That night,
before going to bed, I took a stroll with Henry Rae around
the vast car park. It was a weird enough sight: every
imaginable type of army vehicle was represented there,
neatly parked in rows. From each one, car, truck and carry-
all, there issued little silvery puffs of exhaust vapour—
every engine had been left running in a frantic effort to
stay mobile, regardless of cost. The effort was in vain:
one by one the engines ran out of gas or choked and died.
Those which survived were in no better shape: their steering gears were frozen solid. The odd essential vehicle
could still be limbered up by means of a hooded heating
device which forced a steady blast of hot air into the
frozen engine, but this method was too costly in gas for
even this Alaska Highway picnic—and our party of oil
engineers and distributors was not essential.

The road was dead. Only the planes still came and went:
transport and freight planes headed for the Yukon River
and Alaska, returning to Edmonton and the south; war-
planes destined for Siberia and the Russian front. One by
one and two by two, as places were available, the Ameri-

cans flew us out, lodging us hospitably, meanwhile, in the transient pilots' dormitory hut. Remembering that there were still three bottles of Scotch buried in the company's car, we dug them out and brought them into the hut to hand over to our hosts. And a disgusting-looking sight they were, those bottles. The whisky—which might have left Scotland in good shape, but which had been liberally adulterated en route by Mr. Mackenzie King with water from the Ottawa River—was frozen into mush ice and its temperature was that of the outside air: sixty below. A good shot of that stuff, taken neat, would have killed a man. We set the bottles on the floor, and immediately they began to attract to themselves any moisture that there might be in the warm air of the hut. White whiskers began to grow densely upon them, and soon they were covered with hoar-frost to a depth of one and a half inches. They stood there all day like that, a very nasty sight, slowly thawing.

By late evening they were drinkable—they loosened tongues, and weary pilots who had been ready for sleep woke up and fought the American Civil War again. The hut seemed to be about evenly divided between Damn Yankees and Bloody Rebels. I had made friends with a lieutenant on the Watson Lake staff, J. B. Pate from South Carolina. When the argument was at its hottest Pate called out to me, "You're English, Pat. They were on our side. Where do you stand?" I had been keeping out of this domestic quarrel, though listening with tremendous interest, my sympathy being with the South. Rather hesitantly I replied that I was naturally a rebel, anyway; and that, furthermore, one of my wife's great-uncles had run guns to the South—guns in and cotton out—till his crew had gone down with yellow fever and his ship had been confiscated. This statement met with a frozen disapproving silence from half the hut and a delighted yell from the rest. "Then you're a Bloody Rebel," Pate said. "No question about it."

So it was probably as a Bloody Rebel that I was given a place on a freight and mail plane that came in from Whitehorse, headed for Edmonton, a thousand miles non-stop. The vast, cavernous interior of the thing was unheated and unlit. It was sixty below outside and an unclouded moon sent pale shafts of light through the portholes. Bodies in sleeping bags littered the floor—bodies and mail bags, a carefully lashed-down Jap aero-engine, and a propeller with bullet holes in it—somebody's souvenir? I chose a more or less free bit of floor, unrolled my warm eiderdown and got quickly into it, Eskimo mucklucks and all complete. I pulled down my fur ear-flaps and tied the ribbons, drew on moosehide mitts over the woollen ones. My head, though—it was against the metal side of the plane, and something ought to be done about that, something that would break the cold. On my left there lay what I took to be a mail-bag—a long sausage of a thing. I reached out and gave it a pull, but it was heavier than I had expected, so I put some real beef into it and tugged again, hard. This second effort must have penetrated the consciousness of the creature within so that it was moved to pull a draw-string. The neck of the supposed mail-bag opened, framing for my astonished eyes a horrid, whiskery countenance, more like the face of a walrus than that of a man. It looked annoyed and savage. "What the hell . . ." it began viciously—but then the dead weight of ninety degrees of frost smote it between the eyes, the aperture closed as suddenly as it had opened and I never saw the Thing again. Thank God for a lucky escape!

CHAPTER XV

Return to the Nahanni

That trip brought the Liard back into my life again—
and the water of the Liard flowed down through its canyons to Nahanni Butte, to the Mackenzie, to Aklavik in
the Delta whence Gordon Matthews was trading out into
the Arctic Sea. Gordon's letters had always kept me pretty
well in touch, but now I began to open again maps and
books that had lain untouched for years. Then, urged to
it by a Rhodes Scholar friend of Oxford days, the late
J. B. Brebner, then a professor of history at Columbia
University, I wrote an article about the South Nahanni
River for *The Beaver*. This, after a year or two had passed,
fell into the hands of a gentleman from Vermont, Mr.
Curtis R. Smith. He wrote to me asking for all kinds of
information, which I gladly gave—and soon nothing
would do for Curtis but that he and his friend, Frank
Wood, would put in a summer on the Nahanni and that
I should make a third. The only point which Curtis did
not make clear was that, for him, it was to be largely a
geologising, prospecting trip, whereas what I thought he
was after was the joy of a trip in magnificent scenery,
with some good fishing thrown in. This led, understandably, to some puzzlement on my part on several
occasions. . .

"Never go back," people will tell you. "Never return to
any place that has meant anything in your life—where
you have once been happy. It can never be the same

234

again." True enough—and in the case of the South
Nahanni River I knew that no machine-powered trip in
the safe company of men could ever give again the wonder
of those early years, almost a quarter of a century past,
when I had first come poling and tracking my canoe
through the canyons, all eyes for what might lie round the
next bend, heading into a blank on the map, as did
"untutored men of early ages, to whom everything unknown was marvellous."* You can only do that once.
Never again will there be the same thrill, the same sense
of achievement, of single-handed victory over obstacles.

But the South Nahanni country is big enough to provide always something new, and there was a queer sort
of Rip van Winkle pleasure in returning to it after twenty-
four years to find that one had become an old-timer, a
part of the history of that empty land. Nor had things
changed too much: the Nahanni watershed, at a guess,
measures some 45000 square miles, and still in all that
lonely country there was, as usual, only one man in that
summer of 1951—my old friend, Albert Faille, the man
who had taught me the ways of a canoe. And equally as
usual, nobody knew where he was, and no man, white or
Indian, had set eyes on him for a year. Situation absolutely
normal.

We had ten whole weeks to play with and things seemed
to be lined up for a good trip: the water was about right
and the weather seemed to be set fair. We had come up
the Alaska Road to Fort Nelson in July, and from there
we started north, leaving the road to pursue its westward
course to Watson Lake and the Yukon. We dropped down
the Fort Nelson River and down the Liard to Nahanni
Butte, the three of us in two canoes. There we fell in with
Fred Sibbeston, up from Fort Simpson with his power
boat, and with him we made a quick trip up to the Falls
of the Nahanni, caching our light canoe in Deadmen's
Valley en route, and our eighteen-foot freight canoe at
the mouth of the Flat River, a hundred miles up from the

* "Siren Land," by Norman Douglas.

Butte. From the Falls we ran down to the mouth of the Flat, said good-bye to Fred, and then, with pole, line and paddle, struggled our freight canoe some seventy-five miles up the Flat to the mouth of Irvine Creek. There we cached our outfit and made a sashay on foot westward, through a notch in a mountain barrier and on towards the jagged peaks of the Granite Range that thrust up into the sunset out of the blue immensity of the caribou uplands. Late in August, when the first golden leaves were coming on the little poplars, we came again to the cache and loaded up and turned the canoe's nose downstream—down many a riffle, through the Gate of the Nahanni and through the upper canyons, down to Deadmen's Valley, camping and climbing where and when we pleased.

There still remained Deadmen's Valley and its queer side canyons to explore, and the swift rush down the Cache Rapid into the Lower Canyon—and so on down by the Hot Springs and the Twisted Mountain, through the fast channels of the Splits, until in the end we came to a landing in the quiet water by Nahanni Butte. That gives you the bare outline of the trip . . . . . Yes—decidedly that was a good summer.

Memories come crowding in as I write here, under the trees on the shore of Shuswap Lake: the wild rush of white water in the riffles, the bobbing heads of swimming caribou near the mouth of Mary River, the swirl and struggle of the arctic grayling and the gigantic Dolly Vardens of the Flat River. I can feel again the steel-blue chill of evening in the canyons, see the golden glow of the morning sun breaking through mists, and lighting pinnacle after glowing pinnacle on three thousand feet of canyon wall. I can remember returning to camp at dusk from the heights and seeing the fire twinkling down below there on the beaches, with its trail of blue wood-smoke drifting out on to the river—blessed sight when a man is tired and hungry . . . . .

There was that July day at the Falls. We roared up

the last reaches of the Falls Canyon in the early morning
sunshine, passing within a few yards of a wolverine which
had just killed a rabbit by the water's edge. He started
to pack it up the mountainside; then he turned and snarled
at us, and in so doing dropped his prey. Hastily he retrieved it and scrambled away into a stony coulee, out
of sight among the rocks and the scrub. We swept on
round the last bend and there, at the far end of the reach
was the creaming curtain of the Falls. We had the sun
behind us and it was still early in the day: a rainbow was
tautly stretched across the face of the waterfall, and the
whole reach glittered with the flying spray. One could
come to this place twenty times and never see it so perfectly.
I had been there twice before, but not at this time of day
nor at this stage of water—and never before had I seen
the rainbow.

The Falls reach is about half a mile long and the water
is fast. Slowly, with both outboards running full blast,
we made our way up to the portage landing—a rocky,
inhospitable beach close to the waterfall. Above us the
crest foamed white and sparkling against the summer
sky; down below, in the darkly boiling waters of the pool,
one could discern the hump of heaving water caused by
the upsurge from the depths—a sort of vertical eddy. It
had vivid memories for me—of a hot August afternoon in
1927 when, drifting carelessly in my small canoe, I had
passed over the centre of the hump and found myself
being drawn down the forward slope and into the Falls.
Only sheer terror and the energy of youth got me out of
that one . . . . .

We landed and walked up over the portage trail on the
south-west bank to the calm water of the Upper Nahanni,
climbing at least five hundred feet before dropping down
again to the river. Upstream from the head of the portage
the Nahanni is like a lake, calm and placid. But level
with the upper landing there is a small rock island, and
below it the river rushes down a cataract, perhaps five

hundred feet in length and with a drop of about forty
feet, to the lip of the first plunge. The fall itself, the
largest in the North-West Territories, with a drop of
over three hundred feet, comes down in two steps with a
rocky pyramid on the lower step that splits the final fall
in two.

There you have the statistics. But add to them the
deepest of blue skies, with snow-white thunderheads climbing into it over the barren-looking sheep mountains to
the north-east. Add, too, all the varied greens of the
northern forest—and this wild water, blue and white, lash-
ing and roaring down the cataract like some savage beast,
to vanish over the lip of the fall, clouding the dripping
pyramid with spray, thundering into the pool below. And
there still remained the rainbow . . . . . Hanging with
my left hand on to a dwarf fir, my feet insecurely planted
in the moss, I reached out over the edge of the precipice
with my camera strapped to my right hand. It was worth
a little effort—not everybody has taken a picture of a
rainbow from above. It was impossible to sight, so I pressed
the trigger blind and hoped for the best. The result proved
to be well worth the risk . . . . .

And there was Faille, the last of the old-timers on the
Nahanni. He and I had said good-bye twenty-four years
ago at the Twisted Mountain, and now, in this July of
1951, Faille was somewhere up here, the only man besides
ourselves in all the wilderness of the Nahanni. We had
thought that he might be above the Falls, but we were
mistaken and it was not till we were forty miles or so up
the Flat River that we came on his sign. As we were eating
our midday meal by the water's edge a grizzly shuffled
into view, working his way along the base of a cliff on
the far bank. The bear seemed interested in something
in an eddy over there, but Frank shouted at him and he
scuffled away, with an annoyed "Woof!", up the mountainside. Later on we crossed over to investigate, and

found a huge dead wolf, with a bullet hole in him, bobbing up and down in the clear water.

We found Faille camped by the big pool at the mouth of Irvine Creek. "So you've come back," he said to me as we shook hands, "after all these years!" The rest of that day went by and the whole of another one, as we talked, ate, and drank up the rest of Curtis' rum for him. Frank was fishing in the pool and setting nightlines as well: several outsize fish came ashore to grace the table; one whale of a Dolly Varden had seven mice in him, all lying the same way, head to tail, and another contained six mice, one lizard and one small fish. What with Faille introducing Frank to new and wilder ways of cooking trout, the place soon began to hum gently of baked fish and timber wolf.

For Faille had been in the wolf business. He had been up the Nahanni since the fall of 1950 and, for the first time in his life, had had scurvy. Not recognising the malady for what it was until his teeth began to get loose, he was still pretty weak in the spring and early summer; and at that season the timber wolf, bringing the young out of the den to teach them to hunt, is interested in anything, including a weakened man. Unfortunately, from the wolves' point of view, they had picked the wrong man to demonstrate on. Four great wolves lay dead, one on our side of the river, two on Faille's side on the bar at the mouth of Irvine Creek, and one in the bush—and not one was over two hundred yards from Faille's mosquito net: the closest fifty yards. Then there was that one in the eddy down the river, and two more that had dragged themselves away to die—seven in all, good shooting. We cremated one and dragged the rest into the river— brutes the size of Shetland ponies.

Faille was camped over the river from us in the big spruce. In 1928, when I had last camped there, the old carved tree was still standing. *Irvine Creek,*" it said. " *July 1 1921. A. F. E. Brown. Frank Rae.*" And below

that: *"July 1 Rain. July 2 Rain. July 3 Rain. July 4 Rain."*
These two men, still well known in the Yukon in the
early Fifties, had made their way to this remote spot on
foot through the mountains. How one would like to know
which way they came, what they shot and ate, what diffi-
culties they met and overcame! How many tales of how
many northern Odysseys must for ever remain untold!

And now the old tree had fallen, and Faille had rolled
it over and cut the blaze out to take it down to Fort
Simpson—that fall, or perhaps next year, in 1952, it mattered little to him. Twice at least he had spent over two
years on the Nahanni without seeing a living soul. We
stood by the old blazed tree talking, Faille and I. He had
been down on the Mackenzie for six years, and during
that time a fire had swept the Irvine Creek flat and burnt
his old cabin. "I had some idea of coming back here,"
he said, "but not now; not after this. It was a perfect
country, all a man could wish for—and now look at it!
It was so beautiful here, before."

The next morning all of Faille's stuff and all of ours
was in his cache, and he disappeared northwards with
his pack on his back, up the long trough of Irvine Creek
that runs through to the Upper Nahanni. For another
eleven months he was not seen by men . . . . . We crossed
the river, cached the canoe and started westwards, through
the burnt muskeg towards the first of the granite ranges.

A couple of days later I left camp in the evening and
followed the stream up a stony coulee that came down
from the mountain to the south. The coulee lay deep in
the shadow, and I turned and climbed up to the western
rim, up a fresh slide of broken granite, over small grassy
ledges where the gentians grew. On the ridge the sudden
blaze of the sunset light was dazzling for a moment, and
I sat down on a slab of granite and took out and wiped
the old Zeiss monocular that has seen so much in its time.
Below and to the west lay a gently undulating plateau,
cut by streams into small valleys with low, easy divides.

The plateau seemed to be treeless, and beyond it, many miles away, lay a range of weirdly shaped mountains; fantastic and unreal they seemed, outlined against the setting sun. That could be the Granite Range, the south-east end of which I had touched so many years ago at the Flat River Canyon—touched and thought of ever since! There was a slight weather haze that split the evening rays into a thousand particles, and in that golden glory of light I saw a strange thing—a great bay in the wall of the Granite Range, and in that bay a tower of rock, isolated in the vast cirque of the mountains and so shaped that it looked like a black column of smoke, evil and menacing. Against the low sun it was an amazing sight and for a moment I thought it *was* the smoke of a huge fire. It was like something out of Rider Haggard's fertile imagination—like his Ethiopian's Head.

Behind the Granite Range, and set back perhaps another ten miles, a second range of serrated peaks showed faintly. The Yukon boundary, that had to be; for the map was of little use to us here. "Mountainous country—unmapped" was all it had to say, and the Flat River ran through it as a dotted line. To the south-west the plateau sloped up to a skyline, perhaps three miles away; and, crossing that skyline, the glass showed me two caribou alternately grazing and breaking into short, fast runs. They seemed to be worried about something. Wolves? Away down below lay the sleeping camp, set by its blue alpine lake among the last dwarf firs of timberline. Mountains lay to the east and to the north—but the light was fading now and it was time to be getting down to the shelter of that little clump of firs. The sun had set, the great moment had gone and the glory had departed, leaving a memory that could never fade.

Frank went back to his fishing by Irvine Creek. Curtis and I went on westwards over the plateau. It was a fine country to travel over. Great stretches of it were open moorland. There were small valleys and meadows of good grazing for the string of packhorses we wished we had. Here and there were groups of small firs or willows, and over much of the country the dwarf "black birch" grew thinly; where it was thick we called it by other and more vivid names. The streams flowed, crystal clear, over sparkling granite gravel—and through all this ran the caribou trails, wide, easy to follow and beautifully engineered. There was a limit to what we could carry so I shot a caribou and we lived on that.

There comes, unfortunately, a point of no return beyond which it is foolish to press. On that last day we lunched well by a stream at the head of a sheltered pocket in the hills, toasting caribou steaks over the fire on willow forks. Then we left the tea-pail and the outfit there, all ready for supper, and pushed on. At a small lake, set amongst gentian and grass of Parnassus, I stopped to change a film. Curtis passed on over a ridge and out of sight, and when I followed over that ridge there was only the great grey-green upland and no Curtis. Time went by—it was late afternoon now—and I perched on a huge outcropping of granite and waited; to shout would have been a waste of time in that big, empty country. It would have been as a sparrow twittering on a pebble . . . . .

A deep, closely forested valley, hitherto unseen and cutting far back into the plateau, now lay between us and the Granite Range—which was close. Out of this Curtis finally re-appeared, and we made our last move forward—we knew now that we had reached the turning point. A lone caribou was walking over the stony slopes on the far side of the new valley, and not too far away lay the big coulee and the black tower. Judging from the rocks on our side, the coulee was cut across by a geological fault—and now that it was unattainable, Curtis knew for a certainty that it held the lost Nahanni gold. Gold? Why, that was nothing! Rubies, roc's eggs and the onyx stone—anything the heart might desire. Sadly we turned

our backs on all these riches and headed back on the long
trail to supper and on to our last camp . . . . .

A couple of days were spent at the Irvine Creek camp
before we headed down the Flat. On one of these I went
to the top of a cone-shaped mountain that lay to the
north-east, to get a panorama of pictures. A thunderstorm
blacked the country out for me so I dropped down a
thousand feet to the nearest trees, cut myself a shelter
beneath an old fir, and made tea and ate some bannock
and cheese. When the rain stopped I climbed up to the
ridge again, but thunderstorms were still stalking over
the surrounding country and it was not till eight p.m.
that I could get the pictures I wanted. I passed the time
in watching, with the glass, a grizzly away up on the far
slope of the little valley of the fir trees. He was digging
out a marmot: the clods and rocks flew right and left,
and presumably he got his marmot in the end, for he
ambled off most contentedly up the mountainside, over
a ridge and out of sight. It was a longish way back to
camp, so in the end I got benighted for my pains, and
put in a few hours of nightmarish slumber under a thickly
spreading spruce on the flats of Irvine Creek, huddled in
an old shooting jacket and with a small fire at my feet.

Meanwhile the others had taken the canoe up the Flat
River, fishing and geologising. At Faille's old cabin site
they came on a wonderful stand of raspberries, and they
were well stuck into this when Curtis heard a noise like
a sneeze and Frank distinctly heard what he thought was
the hiss of a snake. They turned and looked towards each
other and were surprised to see, right in line between
them, a grizzly standing on his hind legs, equally surprised and looking from one to the other. By this time
they were a pretty tough-looking sight, and the grizzly
was the first to crack. He gave one more sneeze and then
dropped on all fours and beat it out of the raspberry
thicket. As he ran he bashed into a tall, slender, fire-killed
spruce with his shoulder. The dry top whipped back and

snapped and came down on his rump, and with a startled roar the bear bounded forward and disappeared. Taking it all round, things may be said to have gone off very smoothly on this occasion. The grizzly must have been asleep in the berry patch when Curtis and Frank got there, and it was just a piece of luck that neither of them walked right on to him . . . . .

Down the jade-green water of the Flat River, down many a riffle slid the canoe; and we came, in a short two days, to the mouth of the Flat and to Faille's original cabin of 1927, where I had been the solitary guest at the house-warming supper in that far-off September. There we picked up stuff that we had left cached, and then we hit the grey-green, driving flood of the Nahanni, preceded magnificently by an outrider in the shape of a swimming caribou.

For three days we camped at the Gate, that strange place of deep shadows and silent, eddying water. You can lie there on the moss and the blueberry bush, on the rim of the pillar of the Gate, and stretch out an arm and drop a stone sheer, almost a thousand feet into the river.

An easy day's run brought us down through the Second Canyon and into Deadmen's Valley, and there we camped on the site of the cabin that Gordon Matthews and I had built for the winter of 1928-9. The same tall spruce looked down on the clearing—taller now, so that the midday sun barely reached that spot at all—but cabin and cache were gone. They had been burnt, perhaps by the Indians, and they had vanished so completely that it was hard even for me to say where they had been. The young spruce, the wild roses and the cranberries had taken over; and the creek, in some bygone flood, had swept away the dog-house. Not one thing remained to mark the site except the stout top of our 4-ring, collapsible cook-stove which lay there in the moss—mute and rusty souvenir of many a good feed.

But if the buildings had vanished, our hunting trails,

we found, were still plain and easy to travel, kept open
by the game. They were open, that is, in the green timber;
but above timberline an astonishing change had taken
place: the scrub had crept out into what, in our time, was
open country, advancing up the mountainside in a jungle
so dense that a man with a pack and rifle could hardly
shove his way through it. Reports of the same sort of thing
have come from different northern countries, and it seems
to be part and parcel of the general rise in average temperature that has taken place in the northern parts of the
world since about 1840—a rise which is marked by the re-
cession of glaciers, the climbing of barren mountains by the
trees, the northward migration of the cod from Newfound-
land to Greenland. A poor lookout for the mountain sheep
if the trees continue on their victorious march . . . . .

One evening I left camp late and followed the river
trail up into the snyes where some old, old cabins are
hidden away, the work of Klondikers, perhaps. They are
built of upright logs, and have fireplaces of stone and
clay set in the centre of their floors. They stand among
tall, black spruce from which hang long, venerable beards
of grey-green moss. A sense of eld and of decay and of
tragedy pervades that haunted spot. Nothing would induce
me to camp there, and I have often wondered what fate
overtook the builders of those cabins, and left behind
that chill feeling of horror that comes over one there,
even in the glittering sunlight of a winter's day.

We travelled up the Dry Canyon, into a barren, shut-in
world of water-worn stone where no bird sang and no
stream flowed to break the silence. We climbed the Little
Butte at the outlet of Deadmen's Valley. From its crest
we could size up the Cache Rapid which we had to run
to pass from the Valley into the Lower Canyon; and we
could turn and look back upstream to Second Canyon
Mountain and the line of spruce where the bodies of the
Macleod brothers were found in 1908 by Charlie Macleod's
search party. The Valley was given its name that very day.

The Cache Rapid found us at the parting of the ways. Curtis and Frank, with the big canoe, had decided to run it on the left. I was always one for tradition, and since I had been told that my old route down the right bank of the riffle was now impossible owing to a recent rockfall from the canyon wall, I had decided to prove that it could still be done. Both parties planned to land half-way down, they on the island and I in the eddy behind the rockfall, and to walk ahead and look the lower end of the rapid over.

We passed Ram Creek and the Little Butte, and shot past Starke's Rock and down the upper riffles in famous style. I was in the lead with our sixteen-foot canoe, and I swung into the eddy behind the rockslide, turned upstream and looked around for the others. There they went, past the island and going at race-horse speed. Curtis was shouting something, but the uproar of the Nahanni made hearing difficult. It sounded like "To hell with looking!" I saw the big canoe rise on a wave, and Frank, paddling bow, made a complete air stroke. Then they vanished down the hill of water into a turmoil of white . . . . . an exhilarating sight and I wouldn't have missed it for anything.

All right then—to hell with looking! and I headed the little canoe downstream, close in to shore. The pace quickened and all went well till a rock about the size of a trapping cabin loomed up with the whole force of the Nahanni pouring over it. The channel between it and the shore was full of sharp rocks, so I swung out about forty-five degrees and avoided the rock but caught the wash from it on the side. This had the effect of turning my little canoe broadside on to the Nahanni—a novel experience for me and one that I can do without in future. This state of affairs lasted for three waves and three desperate heaves of the paddle. I got things straightened out in time for the big waves at the foot of the rapid, and I climbed into view of the others over a wave so big that, according to Curtis, I was hidden and only the bottom of the canoe was visible. "We were just coming up," he called out, "to pick up any stray limbs and any useful junk that might come floating down to us!"

Our next camp was half-way through the Lower Canyon at the mouth of Patterson Creek—which somebody had named after me, knowing that I had used its rocky stream bed to climb out of the canyon into the sheep country. From that camp we took a day and climbed up the creek gulch to the plateau that lies four thousand feet above the Nahanni. As we all three had different ideas as to the proper time to set out from camp, we decided to travel independently. I set out around six a.m. and climbed in the cool, in the morning shadow. I found the high prairies unchanged: the south-west wind was singing over them and, as of old, quartz crystals lay in the gravel beds, glittering against the sun. But autumn had turned the green, flower-starred upland of my July, 1928 trips to its September browns and reds—and where were the sheep of those earlier days? Fifty-five head, I had counted once, of the wild sheep resting on these upland pastures, shining-white against the green. And today—two wolves and not another living thing, not even Curtis or Frank. Could that be the answer? Wolves? There was a tremendous upsurge in their numbers in the early Fifties.

Another forty miles saw us down past the Hot Springs and the Twisted Mountain to the trading post at Nahanni Butte—and the Nahanni summer was over. All that now remained was to work the two canoes the three hundred miles south to Fort Nelson and the Alaska Road—upstream, up the Liard and Fort Nelson Rivers. It was a tough prospect, and we were bracing ourselves to tackle it when into the Nahanni mouth came the requisite god in the machine.

The god was Ed Cooper, up from the Mackenzie, in a hurry to get to Fort Nelson, driving his boat and scow night and day in the full of the moon. Just a piece of wonderful luck, and not the first we had had by a long sight. Curtis always claimed our good fortune as his own private contribution to the outfit. "The Lord looks after Curtis," he would say when a thunderstorm had just missed us, or when, in descending some steep scree, we had incautiously loosed off a ton or two of rock into the valley below. "The Lord always takes care of Curtis, and you two are with me—so why worry?"

In short order Curtis made a deal with Ed Cooper. Soon we were slinging our outfit on board; soon we found ourselves headed south, surging up the Liard. Evening was coming on—a calm, perfect evening and the surface of the great river was like glass. Searching for a place to lay my eiderdown, I chose the foredeck of the scow and then went aft in search of supper.

It was late when I left the pilot house. Ed Cooper had long since bunked down in the little cabin-galley, and somewhere or other Frank and Curtis were safely in the Land of Nod. Ernie Villeneuve was at the wheel; the engine was running sweetly, all out, as smooth as silk; the night was a riverman's dream. Overhead a great September moon fought a losing battle with a magnificent aurora that streamed and spilled across the sky, putting the stars to shame. Every colour of the rainbow was in it, and they in turn were reflected in the calm waters of the river. The moon was down below there, too, and so were the golden poplars that lined the banks and crowded on the islands. And behind us, all this glory was split by our wake into a million pieces of gold and silver.

I made my way forward, and soon I lay wrapped in my eiderdown on the foredeck, listening to the rush of the Liard current beneath me, far removed from the thrum of the engine.

To the north the rocky spurs of the Mackenzie Mountains marched by, white and cold-looking in the moonlight. The Mountains of Youth they would always be for me; and when, I wondered sleepily, would I be seeing them again? Soon I decided; and the sooner the better—

there was not time for another twenty-four years to go
by . . . . . But it had been a long day and the rush of the
river under the nose of Cooper's scow was certainly very
soothing—it seemed hardly worth while making definite
plans, at least not till the morning . . . . .

Inadvertently I closed one eye—and then the other.

CHAPTER XVI

A Cook's Tour

Four years later, on July 12th, 1955, I breakfasted in Gordon Matthews' house in Vancouver, and then was driven by him to the airport. From there a C.P.A. plane flew me across central British Columbia and over the Rockies to Fort St John. Then northwards, over the old trail—which by now I had travelled with a dogteam, on foot, with packhorses, in a U.S. Army carry-all, in a British Yukon Navigation Co. bus, and three times by plane—to Fort Nelson, and so to Watson Lake. There George Dalziel, the famous "Flying Trapper" of the Thirties, now owner of B.C.-Yukon Air Service met me and carried me off to his house.

Two hours later a B.C.-Yukon Air Service "Beaver", piloted by Vic Maguire, rose over the lake, circled and climbed into the north-east. The evening was perfect: west wind, summer clouds, blue sky and small, wandering showers, far apart. Visibility also was perfect, and the one passenger was all eyes . . . This was a country that I had studied on the few available maps, read about in Warburton Pike's *Through the Sub-Arctic Forests*, and always wanted to see. And now here it was, flowing towards us out of the north-east, a vast carpet of small undulating, northern forest with, here and there, an isolated mountain rising above timberline. We crossed the Coal River and then the Hyland, and I was able to pick out Warburton Pike's mountain west of that river. Then we crossed the head of the Beaver River where my cousin

Christopher and I had been, the year before, with a twenty-foot fishing canoe. We crossed the gentle, ill-defined Yukon—North-West Territories divide, and Maguire pointed and shouted to me above the noise of the engine. I looked north and saw the headwaters of Caribou Creek—magic waters for me, for they flowed down and into the Flat River by Starke's old winter cabin of 1928. And all the time, beneath us, the shadow of the plane flitted across the endless small forest, with its patchwork of meadows and an infinity of beaver dams. You could spot them unfailingly: a creek would be winding along in its normal, absent-minded way; and then, without warning, it would expand into a small lake, a blue, shining eye in this carpet of many greens. The lake might have beaver houses in it, or there might be high, well-drained banks and a colony of bank beaver inhabiting it—but always there would be the dam, straight or slightly curved but obviously a constructed thing and plain to see. And then another and another on that same stream, and still more to right and left on other creeks and springs, as far as the eye could reach—never have I seen so many. But they did nothing to lessen the incredible loneliness of this empty land. There was no single thing here to show that men had ever passed this way: no trail, no ruined, mouldering cabin, no mark of fire or clearing. Yet I knew that until recently the Nahanni Indians came through this country every winter, every Easter time. Somewhere through here ran their trail from Deadmen's Valley to their spring hunting grounds on the Beaver River in the Yukon. Past the rock-walled Gate of the Winds they came, and up the Meilleur River—I knew that, because I had followed their trail for many miles on snowshoes. But they were on snowshoes, too, driving dogs, and there remained on the ground no sign to mark their passing. And in spring they did not return this way: they built skinboats out of moose-hide and departed down the Beaver, down the Liard, and so again to Nahanni Butte—furs, families, dogs and all.

And somewhere in this country of small trees and lonely isolated mountains towards the head of Caribou Creek, the first white men, travelling light and living by their guns, had made their first contact with the Nahannis. But that was John M. McLeod's party in 1823 and 1824, and that was a hundred and thirty years ago—time enough for all trace of their camp fires and their signal beacons and their mighty feasts of sheep and caribou to have vanished long since beneath the healing moss.

Mountains upheaved themselves ahead of us, mountains with bare tablelands and rolling, open slopes of grass. Those were the south-west slopes of the Tlogotsho Range that lay back of the Bald Mountain in Deadmen's Valley. They were John McLeod's great hunting ground; and I had named them, after questioning the Indians, just a hundred years after McLeod's time. Now, below us, racing creeks were gathering themselves into a small river. That was the Meilleur, Maguire said, and down it we flew, leaving the Tlogotsho on our right, heading straight for Second Canyon Mountain, passing through the Meilleur Gap and coming into Deadmen's Valley in the sunlit calm of a cloudless midsummer evening . . . From Gordon Matthews' house in Vancouver to Deadmen's Valley—not, as of old, in four months of arduous travel, fighting ice, floodwaters, rapids and mosquitoes, but in one wonderful, lazy day, and it not over yet! No fitness was required, nor strength nor skill. Travelling thus, one travelled as might a sack of potatoes, relying—as a potato would have to rely—on a pilot's judgment and cunning. Any fool could reach any remote and well-defended valley in this way, and many have. Yet there remains one comforting thought, and that is this: You may alight in your chosen spot as from a magic carpet, all clean and glorious, but you won't stay that way for long. You come down, in the end, to your own feet and your own strength and sweat—and by that unescapable reality is the wilderness still protected.

The reason for my presence in Deadmen's Valley was

Curtis. That trip we had made four years ago, together
with Frank, had opened for him a new and wider horizon.
The Nahanni country had cast its spell over him and the
green hills of Vermont were no longer quite enough. Nor
was the life of a business man in the little town on the
shores of Lake Champlain. What Curtis wanted to do,
above all things, was to find and establish a new mine.
Down at Nahanni Butte in 1951 he had been told of a
splendid deposit of galena and copper away back in the
canyon ranges, north from Deadmen's Valley. On winter
evenings, in the book-lined library of his home, by the
flickering light of the fire—so like that of a camp fire in
the wilds—this dream, like all our dreams, like mine of
the Granite Range, had become a certainty. And now, in
1955, he was off, taking in a well-known geologist, and
with Gus Kraus from Nahanni Butte to freight the party
in his riverboat and guide them to the prospect. And
nothing would do but I would come along.

I said, no. I couldn't see that I could do anything except
act as a sort of mascot to Curtis and be an added expense.
In any case I couldn't get away till July and they planned
to leave the Butte in June. I was all against that: I pointed
out that the mosquitoes were frightful in June and that
the Nahanni would be in flood—both major obstacles.
Events, I heard later, proved that I was right. It took them
ten days, with the expenditure of fifty-five gallons of
precious gas, to struggle up against the flood to a little
above the Twisted Mountain. There they were forced to
camp and wait for a lower stage of water. In camp the
June crop of mosquitoes almost murdered them; and Curtis
watched with awe the Nahanni driving into an old-
established island, thickly wooded with old, tall spruce.
Day by day the island grew smaller and smaller; and by
the time the river had dropped enough for them to continue on their way there was nothing where that forested
island had been, only an insignificant shingle-bar.

Maguire flew in while they were in that camp, and

somehow contrived to land his Beaver on the racing flood. He brought out one more letter to me, arranging for me to fly in and meet the party in Deadmen's Valley near the foot of Second Canyon Mountain, where the valley of what Gordon and I had christened the Nameless Creek (simply because we couldn't agree on a name) provided a way in to the galena vein. I gave up the struggle and said, yes—hence my arrival in the Valley with Maguire that summer evening. It now only remained to find the prospecting party and join them.

We crossed the Nahanni at the mouth of the Meilleur and flew up the far bank, over the long line of spruce that marked the McLeods' last, fatal camp,* until we could see into the first reach of the Second Canyon. We were looking for a riverboat beached on a sand-bar or moored in some safe eddy—a boat that would have, we expected, something white conspicuously displayed upon it to catch our attention. And above all, we were looking for the smoke of a fire, the one unfailing, plainly visible sign. But we could see nothing.

Meanwhile, down below, Curtis was hurrying madly, on battered feet, down the last stretches of the Nameless Creek. He was paying the penalty for insisting on travelling in light, rubber-soled shoes through that country of steep screes and broken rock, instead of in stout-soled, leather mountain boots that steady and protect the ankles. He had been forced to abandon the party, which was on its way in to the prospect, and an Indian had been sent back with him. Courage alone will not suffice to speed a man with damaged feet; something more was needed, so Curtis told the Indian to get ahead and do something about the incoming plane which they both could hear.

* Two of the McLeod brothers of Fort Liard, Frank and Willie, together with a third man, made a second expedition into the Nahanni country in search of gold in 1905. They did not come out, and eventually a search was made. The bones of the two brothers were found in 1908, in the valley between the Lower and Second Canyons of the Nahanni. From that day onwards, this valley has been known as Deadmen's Valley. "Headless Valley" is meaningless—a newspaper expression only.

Maguire and I passed over the boat, which was drab-coloured and inconspicuous, and was tied up, Curtis told me later, in the deep shadow of the canyon wall, in an eddy and protected from driftwood by an improvised boom. The shadow was made still deeper by the glare of the evening sun in which we were flying, and the boat remained hidden from us. So we swung over to the far side of the Nahanni. Downstream we went, to the centre of the Valley and the site of the cabin that Gordon and I had built twenty-seven years ago, and on down to the mouths of Prairie Creek—where Maguire seemed to think the outfit might be, since he had a rendezvous there with Curtis' geologist, Dirom, around July 18th. But nowhere was there any sign of life. So we turned up river and tried Second Canyon Mountain again. Still keeping our eyes skinned for a boat, we failed to observe the Indian who was now dancing a war-dance on the beach—though far too close to the trees for good visibility, and not even attempting to light the necessary fire. Curtis was still in the bush, ramming his way through it with the persistence of a tank, cursing canvas shoes, idiotic Indians and, thirdly and lastly, the fading note of a plane that was obviously once again turning and winging its way down river.

"You know this river better than I do," Maguire said. "Where else would they be likely to be?"

"Well," I said, "we could take a look at the Little Butte at the lower end of the Valley—there's a good place there. Or they might be stuck in the eddy at the foot of the Cache Rapid, waiting for the water to drop before they tackle that. Then there's the first island in the canyon below the rapid; I know that's a stopping place of Gus Kraus'. And then the Hot Springs."

"We'll take a look at the lot. And I'll fly her right through the canyon. They may be in trouble some place in there. We'll each watch our own side."

I nodded agreement, hoping that the nod was casual and easy, as from one to whom flying the wildest canyon in

Canada was nothing but pure routine. Inwardly I thought "God's truth!" and I took a firm hold of my seat with my left hand and braced my right against the window—though quite what that would have achieved as a safety device I now wonder.

The Little Butte, glowing in the yellow evening light, sped towards us and passed by—and no fire smoke drifted from the gravelly flat at the foot of it. The angry white streaks of the Cache Rapid swept round their shingle island, as they always did—and no boat lay in the eddy below. And on the island where Kraus sometimes camped there was nobody. The deep shadows of the canyon had closed in upon us now and the sun was low. Here and there splashes of light still fell upon the canyon walls, and across one of them I saw the plane's shadow pass, wingless and distorted like that of some ungainly bird. I have climbed in several places to the topmost cliffs of that canyon, each time with an aneroid in my pocket, and they tower four thousand feet above the river. Those high cliffs form the extreme width of the canyon, set back a step or two from the grey limestone precipices that rise directly from the river. These last vary, in the heart of the canyon, from two thousand to two thousand five hundred feet, and Maguire was flying far below their tops. Promontories jutted out from these tremendous cliffs. These had been heated all day on one side by the sun while their opposite sides lay cool and in the shade. The plane, approaching them on their heated side, was wafted gently over them—you could feel the uplift of the rising air. But on the far side, the cool side, it invariably fell into an air-pocket; and then the nearby canyon walls on either hand, the spur ahead, the vast high cliffs that towered above us—all the unbelievable scenery—would fly upwards, and the traveller could see himself falling visibly into the dusky, violet-shadowed pit at the bottom of which raced the driving, foam-streaked ribbon of the Nahanni in semi-flood. Through all this, for thirteen miles, flew the Beaver, a

metal insect, dwarfed almost to nothingness by this gigantic cleft in the plateau. I could recognise old camps of mine
on the beaches and the scenes of old struggles with the
river, but naturally, never a sign of Curtis' party—and
then the cliffs tapered off and we flew out over the Hot
Springs reach, into the open and into the friendly light of
the sun. With a feeling of relief I let go of my seat which
I had held tightly all the way through. I came out of that
hole a better man than I went in, for I somehow felt that
I had seen, in their true proportions, the vast smallness of
man and the infinite majesty of God. And once again let
me take off my hat to Maguire.

His voice came to me above the roar of the engine. "And
now what?" he was saying. "We can't hunt for them all
over the Splits. Too many channels. I'm going to have a
look at the North Pass Creek camp where they were
denned up for the flood. Something may have gone wrong
and held them there."

"And if they're not there we might look in the eddy
below the point of rock at the Twisted Mountain."

"Yes. And then we'll go, following the river, to South
Nahanni and we'll put in for the night at Kraus' place.
Mary may know what's happened, or they may even be
there."

So we did all that, but of course with no results, and
Mary Kraus had nothing to tell us. For her, Curtis and
Co. had vanished into the blue a month ago and that was
that. What we did get from Mary was her charming
Indian smile, coffee and a much-needed supper, and her
large living-room floor to throw our beds down on, safe
from the ferocious mosquitoes of South Nahanni. Outside,
the sun was skating low along the northern horizon. Soon
it would set for a little while, but there would be no
darkness. Vancouver was a thousand miles to the south-
ward and it had been quite a day.

We rose from the floor next morning at the ungodly
hour of two-forty, loaded up and took off. This time we did

not fly through the Lower Canyon, but we came down low in Deadmen's Valley. Again we missed spotting the well-camouflaged boat, and Curtis and the Indian were sleeping. Again they had no smudge going, and they woke only to hear the sound of the Beaver as it vanished into the Second Canyon. By this time Maguire and I had decided that the missing party might well be up the Flat River, for Maguire had heard of a plan to meet with Faille who was known to be somewhere in his one-man kingdom, up around the Granite Range. Nevertheless, we carefully flew the whole hundred miles of the Nahanni to the mouth of the Flat, pausing once to circle back through the Gate where I thought I could see a boat drawn up on the beach. But it proved to be only a slab of rock with a white patch on it and throwing a shadow just like that of a riverboat. We followed up the Flat River for about eighty miles, passing over Faille's camp of the seven wolves at Irvine Creek, and the pool of the monster Dolly Vardens. Then we turned south, up a high valley, and landed on the upper Skinboat Lake.

The arrangements for our reception in these alpine solitudes were of the best. Strung out along the shore was the orderly encampment of a prospecting company, North-West Explorations Ltd. We could see the office tent, the tent of the two Okanagan Helicopters men, pilot and mechanic—a tent which served also as their machine and repair shop—a smaller tent, and a large and well-appointed cook-tent. There was also, we saw with pleasure, a convenient, log-built float jutting out into the lake. A cold wind was sending the sparkling wavelets slap against it in tiny bursts of spray—and now, instead of jumping and floundering ashore, probably with our boots full of water, we found ourselves stepping out on to the float with dignity and ease—much in the manner of a fact-finding delegation from the U.N., or any other group of work-shy V.I.P.'s who neither toil nor spin. The camp boss, Dave Barr, was there to greet the two distinguished strangers, whose insides by now were rumbling plaintively. Then Dave turned and led the way to the cook-tent, and he never did a kinder thing. Breakfast with this outfit was at five a.m. and we had arrived just in nice time for it.

As far as B.C.-Yukon Air Service was concerned, my job was over for the time being. We had failed to find Curtis on the day appointed; and now Maguire had to move, with the Beaver, the plane-of-all-work of the North, this head-quarters camp of NWX from the Skinboat Lakes to Landing Lake on the upper Flat River, at the foot of the Granite Range. Al Smiley, the helicopter pilot (English) and his mechanic, Jack Rich (Australian) came in and sat down. Oscar Schmidt, the cook, loaded all our plates with hot-cakes and bacon. The maple syrup went round, the coffee was poured, and the move was discussed by all concerned. I took no part. I was just a piece of undelivered baggage, on its way back to Watson Lake in the evening with Maguire. But I listened with enormous interest.

All the prospecting crews were scattered around in the mountains, and now it seemed that, to shift this cumber-some camp, they were short-handed. They were going to move to Faille's Island in Landing Lake—and they were going to be all the more short-handed from the fact that one man would have to go with Maguire, and then stop on the island to help unload. And who was that going to be? Because there was the lumber floor of the cook-tent to take up, and the tables and benches, to say nothing of the machine outfit, the office files and photograph boxes, and Lord knows what besides. And nobody was going to let any other man pack the stuff for which he personally was responsible—that was one thing certain.

This was my chance. I knew exactly where Landing Lake was, but I had never seen it. And Faille might be there—for nobody in this outfit had as yet set eyes on him.

"How would it be," I said, "if I help to load the first lot of stuff into the plane, and then go with Maguire?

Then I'll stay on the island and help him off with the loads as he brings them in."

Dave Barr looked pleased. "If you would, that would be great," he said. "All right—now let's get at it."

An hour or so later the eager tourist was once more on his way. The suffering Beaver was crammed with a miscellaneous jag of everything imaginable, piled on top of a basic load of cook-tent stuff which Oscar wanted out of his way so that he could get at his floor. Northward we flew, down to the Flat River and across it. Soon, on a bench above the river, an odd-shaped lake appeared with an island or two in it—a lake of the most gorgeous colours, every shade of vivid blue and green. The largest of the islets was connected to the mainland on its south side by a shallow ford. That was Faille's Island and Maguire circled it, came down on the lake and taxied up to the grassy northern shore of the island, as close as possible to the cabin.

We fixed up a hasty, makeshift causeway of logs and boulders and then got at the unloading. Maguire handed me the stuff out of the Beaver, case after case, and I teetered off with it over the slippery logs and stones on to the island—and then across the coarse grass of the flood level and on to the dry bank. The sun blazed down. I sweated. Maguire sweated. At first he hadn't much to do and I had the long carry. But, as time went on, Maguire had to grub stuff from deeper in the innards of the plane and that evened things up a bit. Finally I staggered ashore with the last two cases of Oscar's stuff and the Beaver roared down the lake and disappeared.

Thunderheads were piling up beyond the Granite Range and I started in to carry the more perishable things up to Faille's cabin. It was empty and dank but, knowing his habit of leaving a message behind whenever he set out on a journey, I looked on the inside of the door. And sure enough, there it was; and as usual Faille, not belonging, properly speaking, to this card-indexed century of ours,

had spelt it as might a man of two hundred years ago—
exactly as it suited him:

Albert Faille. Yun. 3. 1955. Gone up Flat.
Bike here Yulay. 1. 1955. Stay till 10th.

But something had gone wrong with that plan; he had
probably failed to run on to any game up the Flat,
because he had come and gone again before the end of
June:

Here on Yun. 25. 1955. on the way to
Ervine Crike no grub cant stay.
Albert Faille.
PS stay at ervine til 10 Yulay 1955.

If only he had been able to stay here till this day of
grace, 13 Yulay, it would suddenly have rained grub from
the skies.

But why all the detail? Had he been expecting Curtis?
He could not have known about NWX. Suddenly furious,
I said aloud once again, in the empty cabin, my piece
about optimistic starts in June of the floods and the
mosquitoes. For now, with the breakdown of all the
streamlined planning, Albert Faille was out of grub and
heading down river. And what had he been thinking of
all the come and go in the skies above this mountain
kingdom that had been so long his very own? He must
have seen the Beaver reconnoitering his island, and the
helicopter fluttering around the passes of the Yukon
Boundary Range. For the method of NWX involved a
good deal of flying. Headquarters would be established on
some lake, such as Landing Lake, on which the Beaver
could land, and where the helicopter could find a level
landing on the shore. The camp would be in touch with
Watson Lake by two-way radio, and the Beaver would
bring in all the party needed in the way of mail, supplies
and repairs—as requested by Dave in his evening report.
Out in the mountains four separate prospecting parties
would be maintained: three two-men teams of competent,
run-of-the-mill prospectors, skilled in the ways of the bush,

well able to recognise the ores of the commoner metals
and intelligent enough to spot anything unusual that
might lead to a discovery, even though they might never
have set eyes on it before. The remaining field party, the
fourth, consisted of a trained geologist with two third-year
university geology students as his assistants. These men
also worked on their own, but in the event of anything
interesting being turned up by one of the other parties,
they could be moved in to concentrate on it.

The helicopter was the connecting link between the
outlying parties and the main camp. It flew the prospectors
to their locations, kept them supplied while there, and
eventually moved them. What it needed, apart from
weather that was neither too hot nor too windy, was a
level place to land on. That straight away eliminated
mountain sides; and consequently the out-camps were
limited to either the river bars or the open flats, or to
the timberline country—by some alpine lake, perhaps, or,
for shorter periods, on the open tops. But definitely either
right up or right down, and usually up. It took several
trips to move one of these camps. First of all Al Smiley
might take Dave up to the camp to discuss the results
obtained there and plan the move. Then Al and Dave
would flap off along the range and reconnoiter the next
camp-site for that party. Al would then return Dave to the
main camp and set off once more, alone, to move the out-
camp to the new location—which he would do in two
flights, taking one man and half the outfit on each trip. A
helicopter is a weird-looking object at best, and it looked
doubly odd when watched from Faille's Island, diving
into some impossible cleft in that western range—to
emerge in a few minutes and crawl along the face of a
tremendous precipice, only to disappear again between
the peaks into a new and hidden alpine basin. It looked
like some queer machine straight out of the pages of
H. G. Wells, poking about up there.

As the out-camps were moved further and further into

the north-west over the area assigned to NWX for the summer, headquarters camp would have to be moved also, in a number of flights by the Beaver, to some new and more convenient location; and it was with one of these moving days that we were now coping . . .

Load after load came in, and I carried and sweated, piled and sorted, carried stuff up to the cabin and sweated some more. Then Maguire brought a message from Dave: instead of going off to Watson Lake, to return with the Beaver to Deadmen's Valley on July 18th, the day Dirom was due to be picked up, would I care to stay here on the island until then as the guest of NWX? Maguire would be calling here on his way to Prairie Creek.

I sent back an enthusiastic Yes. One couldn't be bothering George Dalziel the whole time; and five days in the hotel at Watson Lake, jammed in with dusty tourists wending their weary way to Alaska and back, would have sent me raving mad. But here there was lots to do and see. Between plane-loads I had already got around the island and had a good look at the ford. I could see that one could easily get off the island on foot—easily, that is, if you carried your trousers in your pack and tucked your shirt well up. Oh, decidedly yes—there were possibilities here.

The next flight of the Beaver brought some oranges and chocolate bars and a whacking great sandwich "for the stevedore", who received them gratefully. He needed them by that time—and, to make lunch perfect, he rummaged in his own pack and fished out a teapail, carefully packed with tea and sugar, cup and spoon. Up went a little curl of wood-smoke and soon the water was boiling. Down fluttered Al Smiley, alone and with a hefty jag of tools and personal stuff in the passenger seat. He set the helicopter gently down on the grass of the foreshore and was graciously pleased to accept a cup of tea. It was just as well that we had that refreshing brew, because the Beaver returned just as we had finished it. In it, amongst other things, were Oscar and his cookstove—a genuine, old-fashioned, wood-and-coal, farm cookstove, a period piece and not a small one. NWX must have combed the prairies for that thing; it weighed about a ton by the feel of it. Using the cook-tent lumber as skids, we slid it out of the Beaver and on to the beach. Maguire then prudently beat it for the Skinboat Lakes, leaving the three of us laying a trackway of lumber across the grass. Up this, with heaves and grunts, we slid the cookstove, through the bush and over the threshold into Faille's cabin. By the grace of God it just went through the door. Now, at last, Oscar was installed—more or less, anyway. All was well.

The Beaver returned with Dave and Jack Rich and the sweepings of the Skinboat camp. The helicopter outfit's tent went up. Dave fought single-handed with the office tent. The Beaver vanished beyond the mountains. I set up my little bug-tent between two trees. Dry wood was cut with a power saw and split, and Dave and I carried a good jag of it in to Oscar who produced supper out of chaos— a veritable rabbit out of a most unlikely hat. If only Faille, tired and hungry, could have walked in now! After supper we got the rest of the stuff sorted and under cover. A wolf-like howl from Oscar betokened evening coffee. We sat around, relaxed and easy; the day's work had gone without a hitch. The sight of a frying-pan prompted me to tell some story or other, and Oscar capped it with one about a certain George Davidson, a character of his youth, and a coffee-pot.

Davidson and his much younger partner, Miner, were living, at the time of this incident, in their cabin on their mineral claims out from Alice Arm, on the northern B.C. coast. They were doing the requisite amount of development work to hold the claims. The cabin was very small, so Miner always lay in the upper bunk while Davidson got up and made breakfast. One morning Davidson upset the coffee-pot. In a fit of rage he kicked it round the cabin, and it bounced back at him and jagged him on the shin with its sharp spout. Miner, who was young, a good shot and full of the devil, watched this performance with interest, not saying a word. Quietly he reached for his six-shooter which was hanging above his head, and with it, from his bunk, he shot a hole through the coffee-pot.

Davidson: "What the hell did you do that for, you god-damn fool?"

Miner: "Because I ain't goin' to see no hell-fired coffee-pot get the best of no partner of mine!"

That was a reasonable enough explanation, and peace and amity, Oscar assured us, were promptly restored . . .

By now it was late and we departed to bed. There was no darkness.

Owing to weather it was a week, not just five days, that I was to spend on this island. The time never dragged. To start with, our helicopter was grounded—something ailing in the tail rotor assembly, the experts said. There followed a striking demonstration of the speed of modern communications. The gang immediately got busy and climbed up to the highest point of Faille's Island. There they got their aerial strung out between a couple of tall old spruce; and there I left them completing their arrangements and connecting up the two-way radio, which would remain up there in its weatherproof box. I waded off the island and followed the game trail to the outlet of the lake and down the creek channel to the Flat River. Then up the Flat for an hour or two till I came to a canoe camp of Faille's of that spring. His camps never varied and this one looked just like those we had once made together on the Nahanni: a good sandy bay in an eddy, lots of dry wood about, a stake driven in the river, and a shelter and fixings for a mosquito net on the bank. That was my turning point, and from there I went back to the lake and off in the opposite direction from the ford, following the down-valley trail. I came on a moose standing in the shallows at the head of the lake, unperturbed, evidently, by the come and go of planes. Now, if only Faille had run on to that moose here, a couple of weeks ago, his grub problem would have been

settled and we might have found him on his island. I came
back to camp in a spit of rain, absolutely ravenous and
only saved by Oscar who rose to the occasion with coffee
and biscuits. This five a.m. breakfast was apt to make a
man hungry by four in the afternoon. There were two
reasons for it. Firstly, the altitude at which the helicopter
was flying. To reach these alpine camps it needed the
cool, heavy air of the early morning or late afternoon and
evening; the thin, hot air of midday had not the same
sustaining power. Equally, a wind could ground it, and the
strongest winds often came with the heat of the day.
Secondly, the North-West Territories summer is short, and
this was an expensive outfit to maintain. Nobody was up
here for the good of his health, and the long days had to
be used to the full.

After supper I went up to the radio position with Dave
and listened to him getting through, at his appointed time,
to Watson Lake. Communication was good and Dave
reported the move and put in for the necessary tail rotor
parts for the helicopter—every spare part number being
checked back by Watson Lake and finally agreed by Dave
. . . To finish with the helicopter's troubles—Dave's message would reach Okanagan Helicopters in Vancouver
that same evening, a Thursday. With that company's system, the parts would be on a C.P.A. plane leaving Vancouver for Watson Lake at eight a.m. the following
morning, Friday. They could have been here on the Flat
River that same evening, but the Beaver was busy on
another assignment, and Maguire actually flew them in on
Saturday. Thinking again of the months that it once took
to reach this place from Vancouver, the whole thing
seemed like magic to me. One thing, of course, was needed
to make the magic work—and that thing was essential:
money, and lots of it.

As Dave and I came down the little hill Oscar's wolf-
howl sounded through the trees and we all gathered for
the evening coffee and conference. Jack Rich had a few

observations to make on Australian beer, and on William Younger's "Revolver" ale as supplied in New Guinea. I told a story about an octopus which made the bunch laugh, and Oscar banged his head on a knot on a roof-pole in a corner of Faille's cabin. "That reminds me," he said after he calmed down, "of a story I once heard about an old trapper. The door of his main cabin was too low for him and there was one knot in the lintel that he banged his head on, regular, for eighteen years. The day came when he was through and leaving the cabin for the last time. He put his pack on and picked up his axe and rifle, and he took one last look around. Then he went out, banging his head according to custom. He didn't say a damn thing. He set down his pack very carefully, and he laid his rifle gently down on top of it—all very quiet and methodical. Then he took the cover off his axe and cut off the knot and trimmed the log nice and smooth—made a real job of it. *Then* he let himself go: "You god-damn bastard," he shouted, "that's fixed you! I've been meaning to cut you off all these eighteen years!"

Searching for the moral of this story, we went thoughtfully to bed.

I took a day and went down the Flat River. I took a great big hot-cake and bacon sandwich from Oscar this time, and the teapail and an iron ration of chocolate and raisins from my own pack. Once across the ford—I had that ford down to a system by now—I went up the lake and then through an old abandoned channel to the present river. I got down as far as the head of the canyon, finding two river camps of Faille's on the way. The Flat River was medium high, but there were tracks of moose, wolverine and wolves on the small beaches that were showing. And all the time, beyond the river, I could see where I had come walking alone into this country nearly thirty years ago. I had carried only a teapail then; if I shot a partridge I broiled it on the end of a forked and pointed willow, and if I caught a fish I baked it on a slab of rock. And now,

here I was again, just about as near and just about as
far as ever from the Granite Range. And I couldn't leave
camp and set out for it because I was tied to the arrival
of the Beaver.

I was away twelve hours on that trip and it was nearly
nine when I got in. Oscar produced a late supper, which
not every camp cook will do, by a long sight, and Dave was
visibly relieved to see me. He was so obviously relieved
that I realised for the first time that, to these young men,
I was old—too old, apparently, to be loose in the bush
alone. Brings it home to a man, that sort of thing does.
But Oscar, who was as old as I was, and older, hadn't
been worrying at all.

I spent most of the next morning with Dave in the
office tent. I had brought chunks of the rock back for
him from the canyon head, where the strata stand on
end, limestones and argillites; and I had noted down for
him the angles of dip and various other bits of information on the river outcroppings. I browsed over the air-
photos of the area: they made clear many things that had
once puzzled me. I could follow the trip that Curtis and
I had made four years ago across the granite plateau, and
I could look down on the big coulee and the black tower.
They weren't many miles from this camp as the crow flies,
but they were quite a way as he hops. In between lay
the Granite Range, the barrier, mirrored to perfection in
the quiet waters of Landing Lake.

"Can you confidently say," I asked Dave, "when you
have searched an area in this way and found nothing,
that there's nothing to be found?"

"No," he said, "we can't. We can cover a lot more
territory in a season than the old-time prospector could,
but we're just as capable as he was of missing something
valuable by a few yards."

Later on, that same year, I asked the same question of
a well-known mining engineer and got the same reply,
only with more detail. "Certainly not," he answered. "No,

you can't bank on thoroughly covering a country that way. For one very good reason—you find yourself fighting against human nature, which, in spite of all the gadgets, does not change."

"How's that, Emil?"

"Well—put yourself in the place of the camp boss. You've been given a plane and a helicopter, so you're going to use them. So four times out of five your field parties are going to be up high, timberline and above. Now, some things are best tackled from below, looking for traces in the loose float and following them up. Supposing these guys that are camped at timberline find they have to work *down* to check a thing—just how much further down a mountain is a man going to go when it's getting on in the afternoon and he's tired, and every step he takes downhill is making it harder for him to get back uphill to camp again when he's still more tired? There's going to come a point when he's going to quit and climb up to camp and supper and bed—maybe just when he should go on down. Whereas the man from down below— all he's got to do is to scramble down hill when his day's work's done. Much easier, and he'll stay with it longer. No—there's no fool-proof, watertight way of going at it, and whichever end you tackle it from, up or down, you come in the end to a man's feet, and a man's strength and will. And that's that."

The days continued fine. I went off with Al Smiley in the helicopter on one of his trips; went on foot a long way up a trail that seemed to head for a gap in the Granite Range; sat on the bank of the island in odd spare moments and wrote a page or two of a book that I was busy on. Then the weather went to pieces on us: rain poured down and the mountains wrapped their heads in cloud. Dave and Al took to their tents; Jack Rich and I spent most of the time yarning with Oscar in the cabin. Oscar came up with more stories about Davidson, the man the coffee-pot attacked, and produced one gem of a tale about a bear in a canoe which I wrote down soon after this trip was over, and which forms the next and last chapter of this book.

The rain stopped, but still the clouds hung around the Yukon range and the Beaver could not come. Owing to the tail rotor trouble and then the day's rain, the helicopter routine had been upset. Al now flew off to bring in one of the out-camps. He found only one man there. The other, Axel Bergman, becoming fed up with waiting, and deciding something had gone wrong, had started out on his own down the mountain and there was no sign of him to be seen. His luckier partner now sat in Faille's cabin; and from the way he was eating one could be dead certain that Oscar's cooking was far ahead of his or Axel's.

After supper I produced a bottle of rum and some genuine, authentic lemons that I had been hoarding for Curtis. This outfit, I felt, deserved it. They had taken me in, a homeless waif, and been kind to me. I don't remember so much of that evening except that somebody came out with a horrific tale about a chance encounter of this mountain wilderness: one of the NWX prospectors had happened on a thing that few men have ever seen—the mating of grizzly bears.

"Good Lord!" I said. "That was no place for a man to be. What did he do?"

"Do? He was up on a nice, high, sheer cliff and he stayed there. He felt it was a clear case of 'Let no man put asunder.' "

The next day, July 20th, was cloudy with a dry, warm wind. The Beaver came in as we were eating lunch, and it had on board Coveney, the manager of the American Smelting and Refining Co. (Asarco) outfit at Quartz Lake in the Yukon. Choking down my pie and coffee, I rushed out and broke up my camp. Good-byes were said, and we took off.

A little distance down the Flat and on the far side something moving caught my eye—a blue wisp of smoke

drifting inland from a shingle bar and a tiny figure waving. Without the smoke I should never have seen the
man. That was Axel, and we turned again for Landing
Lake to alert Al and the helicopter. Then we left the
friendly camp again for Deadmen's Valley ...

Diron's smoke rose plain to see from a grove of spruce
just above the stony delta of Prairie Creek, but there was
no sign of a boat or of Curtis. Maguire put the plane
down on the Nahanni heading upstream, and eased it in
towards the bank. It was taking, he told me afterwards,
1000 r.p.m. just to stay in one spot on that fast water.
This wasn't the best place on earth to bring a plane in
to shore—one wing, we could see, would have to slide
over the bank and in between the standing trees. "Do you
think you could get a line to him?" Maguire said to me.
"There's one in back here. If you could get the loop over
the forward cleat on the float and throw him the line?"

Coveney had already fished out a coil of line and was
handing it to me. I took it and climbed out on to the float
and crawled gingerly forward. It wasn't much of a thing
to crawl on, I was thinking: seven inches or so of grey
metal with the river rushing past beneath. I got the
braided loop in my right hand and there, ahead, was the
cleat—in fact there was nothing in my mind except the
job in hand; nothing, that is, until I woke up and
realised that the empty space in front of my head had
death in it. Storm clouds had climbed over the sun and
the afternoon was darkening. There was not even a blur
or a flash to show me where the propeller was making
its 1000 r.p.m.—just plain air with a tangle of trees and
the bank beyond. Cautiously I reached forward, keeping
low, and caught the cleat in the loop. I flung the line to
Dirom and he began to pull in on it and to steer the
wing by hand between the trees. Gradually the Beaver
was eased in to the shore eddies and Maguire cut the
engine. I looked in at the door, to see him very pale and
mopping at his forehead. "Oh, God!" he was saying "Oh,

God! I should have warned you. And then it was too late.
I couldn't leave the controls, I couldn't stop the engine,
and it was no use shouting to you. Were you aware of
the propeller?"

"Yes," I said brazenly.

"Thank God for that! I was looking to see your head
fly out into the river. Right in sight of your old trapping
cabin, too. What an ad. that would have been for your
book: Author Loses Head in Headless Valley!"

The book to which Maguire was referring, *The
Dangerous River,* was about the Nahanni and had been
published the year before. Very likely my decapitation in
the centre of this legendary valley *would* have boosted
the sales considerably. It would have done even more for
the legend. A great idea, from every point of view.

Let some one else try it . . .

Coveney and Dirom threw themselves on the latter's
camp. I doused the fire. Maguire took an axe and cut away
a sweeper—a big spruce that had collapsed into the river
ahead of the Beaver, but which still adhered by its roots
to the bank and would hinder our departure. The tree fell
into the water at the last stroke of the axe, a mass of green
branches all pointing downstream. The Nahanni took it
and drove it in between the floats, and there it jammed,
its branches all tangled up with the struts and cross-
braces—a devilish mess. Maguire and I took our axes and
gingerly trimmed the spruce; but we did not dare to cut
too close for fear of holing the floats. So we did what we
could with axes, and then tried to shove the sweeper deep
down and away with the plane's canoe paddles. Useless—
it wouldn't go. "All right," Maguire said. "Leave it. I think
I can shake it off when we get going."

I jumped ashore again and sought Dirom. "Where's
Curtis?" I asked him. "Gone on up the river? Surely he
was to have been here?"

"He's gone down to Kraus' place at South Nahanni,"
Dirom replied. "He wanted you to follow in the plane."

I stared at him in amazement. Down? What in heaven's name for? It seemed incredible that they should go back down again.

Maguire had overheard us. "I suppose you'll want to go there now?" he said, and I nodded assent. "I suppose I should," I added.

"All right, then. I think I can make it. But we'd better hurry." And he pointed down-river where the thunder-heads were now piled high behind the Canyon Range, towering mountains of snow-white cumulus with ominous purple shadows in their folded valleys—blue-black clouds racing, dragon-shaped, out of the north-east across their sunlit headlands. And here, in Deadmen's Valley the gloom was deepening.

We threw Dirom's stuff into the Beaver, and Maguire and Coveney climbed in. Maguire started the engine and I repeated my act with the forward cleat and then climbed aboard. Dirom coiled the line and threw it to me. He shoved the wing out from between the trees and then, as the Beaver was easing out into the river, he made a wild leap for the cabin door. This was no place to fool around in: the water was deep and fast under that cutbank, and for an anxious moment I saw an athletic khaki-clad figure in breeches and logger's half-boots flying through the air. Then he made contact, one leg slipping into the water, and hung on. I grabbed him by the jacket and half hauled him in, and we slammed the door. The passenger list was complete . . . The ceremony just described corresponds, in bush-flying terms, to walking out from the airport building to the waiting Caravelle or Britannia, handing one's boarding pass to a smiling air-hostess and choosing a seat.

By this time Maguire had us out in the river and starting to surge upstream. The roar of the engine increased and we moved forward. Our spruce tree came too, and the Beaver vibrated with the added strain. Nobody spoke or made a sign. I knew that bit of river between Prairie Creek and Gordon Matthews' and my old cabin as well as I know any bit of river on earth, and I knew we had just so much space to take off in. If the spruce stayed with us as far as the cabin, then we had had it, because just above the canoe landing there was a riffle that was too fast and strong even for the hard-working, go-everywhere Beaver. I just sat and watched the old, familiar trees march by and wondered—what next? Down-river again and get rid of the spruce in a turn?

Earthquake tremors came from below: the Beaver was trying to fly. This was too much for our tree; some branch must have given way, for we suddenly shot upwards as if some giant had kicked the long-suffering Beaver in the behind. Everybody smiled and nodded approval and Maguire swung inland, to the south, towards the spurs of the ram-haunted Tlogotsho. Then he turned east, gaining height and heading for Jackfish Mountain in the queer half-light of the wandering storms. A gloomy shadow had settled on the Nahanni country; and to complete the picture I had, as usual when thunder is about, a splitting head. But beyond the shapeless bulk of the mountain, now softened by the falling rain, would come Nahanni Butte, and Curtis and a welcome, and, thank God, tea—tea, the unfailing mender of fat heads. And journey's end. Or at least, a new beginning.

We cleared Jackfish Mountain and looked for the Butte. But all we could see was a swirling mass of storm cloud with forked lightning stabbing from it, and the piled masses of cumulus towering beyond. Still the long, dark clouds raced in front of them—now like war canoes in shape, now turning by some black magic into Chinese dragons or queer, heraldic leopards. But for ever on the move, writhing and twisting like serpents.

Rain was falling on the Beaver, which was beginning to rock and plunge. Clouds were driving past beneath us. Maguire spoke. "I can't go down into that," he said. "We might be grounded and my radio wouldn't reach Watson

Lake. We'd be overdue, and with this weather they'd think
we were down somewhere and in trouble. We'll have to
turn and head for Quartz Lake." Even as he spoke the
plane was swinging. Soon we were passing over the open
slopes of the Tlogotsho and heading up the Meilleur; soon
the green, unbroken forest with its patchwork of beaver
dams was flowing once more beneath us. In the west the
sky was cloudy but calm, and the Beaver settled down
again to even flight. Rivers began to flow south to the
Liard: we were in the Yukon now and once again I was
just a piece of futile, undelivered freight.

Curtis told me afterwards about that storm at Nahanni
Butte. That lonely mountain, with the flat lands stretching
away on three sides of it, brews its own weather and can
create appalling winds. Curtis said that great big willows,
almost of tree size, were bent level with the ground by that
wind, straining and quivering like storm-laid grass. The
wind took the roof off Kraus' storehouse and churned up
huge waves in the big sweep of river. The waves took out
Kraus' landing, just where the Beaver would have been
tied, and fetched down into the river at that spot several
yards depth of the twenty-foot bank. The lightning blazed
down in liquid streams of fire, the thunder crashed, the
wind rose to a scream, and everything that was loose took
wing and flew. Maguire's retreat had probably saved a
plane.

Quartz Lake was like a sheet of glass, and the place was
still and silent except for the friendly jangling of horse
bells. Asarco used horses: they could reach this camp by
pack train, coming north from the Alaska Road somewhere near the Hyland River. Three horses were grazing
in the meadow between the lake and the camp, and as we
walked along the float to shore a notice greeted us:

Asarcoville-by-the-Lake. (it said)
Rest Home for Tired Geologists.
Hunting.

Riding.
Fishing.
Swimming.

Coveney and Dirom looked at each other and grinned.
We walked up to a cook-tent that was even more magnificent than Oscar's at the Skinboat Lakes, and a cup of
coffee settled the hammering in my head—that, and the
fact that the storm was now far away in the North-West
Territories. I went out to walk by the small, quiet lake,
leaving Coveney and Dirom and Honeysett, who was in
charge of this diamond-drilling project, to their business.
The sound of the bells came softly on the evening air.

Quartz Lake drains to Coal River which flows south to
the Alaska Road. A creek nearby drains to the Hyland
River through a small canyon in the plateau. The odd
thing about that canyon was that a band of mountain
goats had made it their home, though there were no true
mountains anywhere near. How did they come to be there?
How did the first pioneering billy-goat and his family
come to find that canyon in the Yukon Plateau? Or, if
they were not hunted by men, would goats still be found
in many places such as this, far from the rugged mountains with which they are now associated? As for the
mineral prospect, which was now being drilled by Asarco,
it was the only showing of interest, they said, in a
thousand-square-mile block, fifty miles by twenty, that
had been carefully prospected—and even on to that they
had landed, it seemed, almost by a fluke.

Maguire appeared, walking along the float from the
plane where he had been busy. The other men emerged
from the cook-tent. Coveney very kindly asked me if I
would care to stay a week with Asarco here at Quartz
Lake as I had done with NWX on the Flat River. I
thanked him and said, no—and many times since then
have I kicked myself for that. I should have enjoyed it.
But all these people were here with a purpose; and, by

contrast, this Wandering Jew existence was getting me down. I had seen a lot of country, which is good for a man, and I had met with much kindness and hospitality, which is even better. Yet all I had really achieved so far was to pile up a large bill for Curtis and fail to find him. Whether, now, to pile up still more, or to cut the losses?

"What will you do, then?" Maguire asked. "Stay at Watson Lake and come in with me next week?"

"If I did, we'd be right back where we started—looking for a boat somewhere on the Nahanni."

"That's true enough. If they're going up the Flat they won't stay at the Butte for ever. And summer's getting on."

To decide, with no facts to decide upon, is hard. But suddenly I knew what I would be doing: I would be going south from Watson Lake on the same plane as Dirom, the following day. . .

*　*　*　*　*

A handful of gravel rattling on his bedroom window awakened Gordon Matthews in the small hours of July 22nd. Three a.m. is not the normal visiting hour in Vancouver, and he put his head out of the window, peered into the darkness of his garden, and said in an annoyed tone of voice, "Who the devil's that?"

"It's me, Gordon. Don't talk so much, and let me in. I've had a Cook's tour of the Nahanni country, and the grand finale was engine trouble at Fort Nelson—hours and hours of it. Give me a bed and I'll tell you all about it in the morning."

CHAPTER XVII

The Bear Voyageur

Up to this point this book has recorded, in a series of sketches, the education of a new Canadian as he makes his way through the Canadian scene—first by saddle-horse and canoe, finally by plane and helicopter. That education is not completed yet: I, being the new Canadian in question, know that only too well. Still, one must make an end of a book somewhere, and in what better place than in the house of a friend? Besides, five more years were to pass before I came again to the South Nahanni River, and that, as Kipling says, is Another Story.

So I plan to round off the book with the tale of Oscar's to which I referred in the last chapter—the story of the bear in the canoe. I have a purpose in doing this. Being, as I have already said, not yet completely educated in these things, I need my readers' help: I want to know if this story can be true. A black bear is such an unpredictable animal that I, personally, would not put anything beyond him. It is only five days ago, from the time of writing, that I saw one dive into a corrugated iron culvert pipe, and so pass beneath a main motor highway in the Rockies, only to emerge and caper joyously right in front of my car, apparently just full of the pure zest of living. There is nothing a black bear won't do, and I think Oscar's tale is a true one. After all, a wild animal that can conceive the idea of getting into a canoe with me and a pile of trout and a rifle, is not going to be done out of his

278

accustomed seat by any Swede and his packsack, however
noisy the Swede. But this is a matter for judgment rather
than for argument—and it is for judgment that I submit
to you, exactly as it was written down nearly eight years
ago, the Tale of the Bear Voyageur . . . . .

The rain was getting heavier and the first muddy drops
were starting to soak through the sod-and-pole roof and
fall on the table of the old trapping cabin. Oscar had
been holding forth to me on the subject of bears and the
horrible jackpots they got people into, but he cut himself
short and rose hastily. "Give me a hand to stack this
grub on my bed," he said. "There's rocks and spruce-bark
over the sod in that corner and maybe it'll stay dry. We
can tarp up the rest of the stuff on the floor."

Oscar's life had been a varied one. He had been cow-
puncher, packer and prospector in his time, and now, this
summer, he was cooking for NWX in the Mackenzie Mountains of the North-West Territories. On this dismal afternoon Oscar and I were sitting in Faille's cabin, feeding
wood into the stove and trying to keep things dry. Outside
the rain lashed down on the sod roof and on the hissing
surface of the lake. The helicopter was grounded; and out
in the mountains, in four lonely, scattered camps, above
timberline and by the shores of alpine lakes, the field
parties would be cowering in their shelters or beneath
overhanging rocks, cursing this storm—which might well
be snow for some of them. Streamlined modern prospecting
had skidded wetly to a standstill.

Oscar put two fresh-made pies into the oven of the
cookstove and shut the door on them. "There's supper," he
said. "That is, if we can keep the oven from floodin'. And
there goes that bear with the twin cubs again—she must
have a regular round that way." And he pointed through
the open door and across the lake to the distant shore. He
had eyes like twin telescopes: all I could see was a dim
movement through the blueness of the storm.

"I figure there's two reasons why Faille built his cabin

on this island," Oscar went on. "One—there's hardly any
mosquitoes on it; and that's a queer thing for July in
this Flat River country. And, two—maybe it's kind of off
the trail a bit for bears and wolverines. Though that's
only my guess. The way a bear'll swim if he ever winds
anything, a bit of water's no protection."

"Not much," I said. "I remember one time I was fishing in a big eddy below the Long Canyon on the Finlay.
There was a bunch of fresh-caught fish in the canoe. I
was sitting quite still and just drifting round and round
—and paying no attention to what I thought was a bit
of old burnt log floating round with me. And, believe it
or not, it was a black bear, and I just woke up in time
or he'd have been into the canoe with me. I grabbed a
paddle and flicked that canoe down the rapid below the
eddy—a grayling couldn't have moved quicker. A seven-
teen-foot prospector canoe is just not big enough for a
man and a bear."

"No," Oscar said. "But a twenty-foot freight* is—and
for *two* men and a bear. I'll tell you a tale—"

"A bear in a canoe? Do I *have* to believe that?"

"Now just hold your horses a minute. Give me a chance.
This is a true tale and I had it from Big Paul himself:
the first time I heard it was when we was workin' a
prospect together in the Coast Range. Big Paul was no
liar and I've heard him tell about that bear a good half
dozen times, and he never varied a word. Put a couple
of sticks in the stove and I'll take a look at my pies. And
then I'll tell you about Big Paul and Axel and the bear."

So we fixed the stove and the pies, and then I sat myself down to listen . . . . .

The time, Oscar said, was around 1900. Late for the
main Klondike rush, Big Paul and his partner had found
a streak of rich pay gravel on a bench a little way up a
creek that was tributary to the Stewart River. They
brought a grubstake up from Dawson by canoe, enough
to last them over a year with any luck—and that meant,

---

* A canoe twenty foot long, fifty-two inches wide, and twenty inches
deep.

with a moose or two added. They worked their claims
through that first summer, and then all through the winter
—burning and thawing and bringing the gravel to the surface. Now and then they took a panful of dirt over to
the cabin they had built on the larger flat beyond the
creek where the building timber grew. They panned it out
there, in the warmth where they could keep water un-
frozen, just to see how they were getting on; and what
they saw encouraged them.

Spring came to the Yukon; the Stewart River ice went
out and Big Paul's creek ran free. To cross it, in order
to get to the claims, he and his partner fixed up the same
rigging that they had used the previous summer—a line
across the creek, stretched between two trees, and a block
of wood with a well-rounded and polished hole in it
through which the line was passed. The block slipped
easily to and fro on the line; to it the canoe was attached
by a short length of trackline that could be adjusted to
suit the height of water. The whole thing made a sort of
a cable ferry and a stroke or two of the paddle was enough
to get the canoe across.

The pay-streak seemed to be easing off a bit, and the
dump was thawing. The two partners started in to clean
up, and they shovelled and sluiced and sluiced and shovelled, and all went well. Occasionally they took a day off
and did some more prospecting across the creek—sinking
one more shaft—and it was on these occasions that a she-
bear with a good-sized yearling cub in tow began to do
some prospecting around the main camp on her own
account. The men were running low in grub and they
couldn't afford to take chances—so they shot the mother
bear and added her to the larder. They shot at, and missed,
the yearling.

But the yearling didn't go clear away. He would come
back from time to time, and then he would hang around
looking lonely and forlorn and pretty sorry for himself.
Sometimes he would disappear for a day or two, prob-

ably on a log-bashing expedition in search of grubs, but he always returned. Big Paul felt a bit remorseful about knocking off the yearling's mother, and the yearling didn't seem to want to do any harm or bother anybody. Finally, to cut a long story short, they tamed him and he became a part of the outfit. He even learnt to cross the creek in the canoe with them, sitting gently down amidships on his behind like a civilised Christian . . . . .

Summer dipped towards autumn and the wild berries ripened on the hills beyond the creek. The bear rarely crossed over on his own account but he always thoroughly enjoyed the days when the men worked down the shaft on the bench. He would cross with them in the canoe and then wander off on his own—and he became bigger and fatter, and his coat was getting a most wonderful shine to it.

Finally it became time to break camp and get going, down the Stewart to the Yukon and down the Yukon to Dawson. The clean-up had been good but the pay-streak seemed to have petered out. There was no reason to stay longer.

The partners were worried about the bear. He was a personal friend by now and they felt responsible for him. To take him down to Dawson was out of the question— they might as well shoot him here and now and have done with it. Then they got an idea. "We'll break camp," they said, "and have everything packed, ready to load up and go. Then we'll take a pick and shovel and cross the creek as if we were going to put in a day on the bench. We'll start work as usual and he'll mosey off up the creek. When he's well out of sight we'll beat it back to the canoe, load the outfit and hit for the Stewart . . . . ."

They couldn't think of anything better, so they did that and all went smoothly. The bear headed happily for his favourite berry patch, upstream and out of sight, and the two men went quietly down the hill and crossed the creek feeling rather shamefaced at deserting a friend.

They needn't have worried. Before they could load more than a piece or two into the big canoe they heard frantic shouts from across the creek. They looked up and, by God, it was Axel and he had come this way after all!

Axel and his partners were working some claims over the divide to Indian River. Axel had been over on a visit in the wintertime and it had been arranged then that, if he didn't go in to Dawson with some Indian River outfit when the fall came, he would come over and go down the Stewart with Big Paul. He was a couple of days overdue but they had waited . . . . . And now, there he was—making wonderful time over the deadfall and round the rocks with a nice, slick, shiny bear close on his heels! You had to hand it to that bear—his routine had been upset, there was no canoe available, and a complete stranger was loping along just ahead of him, raising hell about God knows what—and still he behaved like a Christian and a gentleman.

"Damn it," said the bear's foster-fathers, "here this silly something goes and turns up at the last something minute and now we got the whole something job to do again!" And Big Paul got into the canoe and flipped it across the creek with the paddle.

Axel wasted no time getting into that canoe. He got into the fore end of it, knelt down, eased his heavy pack off his shoulders and swung it round in front of him. And all the time he was talking hard—or rather, shouting, after the manner of the Swedes when something has excited them. But Big Paul wasn't paying much attention; he just sat on his bedroll in the stern and laughed like a loon at the quiet, assured way in which the bear got into the canoe and sat down close behind Axel. And at intervals he thanked God Axel hadn't got a rifle.

"Ja, by golly," Axel was shouting as he bent over his pack, "dot vos yust a piece of luck for me you fellows vos not gone." They were in midstream now and Axel was feeling happier. "Ay tank dot damn bear has beat it," he went on, casting a glance at the deserted bank; then he turned his head round, the more easily to bellow at Big Paul. He found himself looking practically down the bear's throat and, with a wild yell of "Yesus!", he hurled himself straight over the nose of the canoe and was swept away down the stream.

The canoe fetched up against the bank. Sobbing with laughter Paul and his partner tore across the point to try to intercept Axel who, they knew, was in grave danger of drowning. They found him in deep water, under a cut-bank and held down by the spiky branches of a big spruce that had fallen into the creek. They had a devil of a time getting him out of there, and every time they thought of Axel's face in the canoe when he saw the bear they laughed till they cried.

First they got Axel free of the branches and then they got a line down to him—a line with a loop in the end of it. The Swede had been a longish time in the water, and the cold and his first panic fear seemed to have numbed his wits; however, he managed to get the loop under his armpits and Big Paul drew the line tight. Then they hauled him up, Paul on the brink heaving and lifting, and his partner behind taking up the slack and snubbing round a tree. It was just as well they played it that way because, when Big Paul heaved Axel's head and shoulders over the lip of the bank, the bear, who had taken a keen interest in all these wild doings, was right there to give the distinguished stranger a friendly welcome—and the first thing Axel saw was the bear's face grinning at him from about the same range as before. His English vocabulary was not very extensive and he was evidently a man who could quite easily get into a rut: he let a scream of "Yesus!" out of him and did his best to fling himself backwards into the creek.

That finished Big Paul—he just sat down and rolled on the ground. His partner had strength enough to take one extra turn of the line round the tree, "just so as to keep

Axel from spoiling the show," and then he sat down and rolled, too. They wept and shouted together, and now and then they hit each other—and their insides ached and ached. Most of Axel was still dangling over the water but his frantic, yellow-whiskered face stuck up over the bank at ground level, roaring out prayers and the most dreadful threats in his mother tongue. Every time the two men felt like sobering down a bit, one sight of that bellowing, rampageous gargoyle was more than enough to set them off again . . . . . But it worried the bear. All *he* wanted to do was to *understand*, Big Paul said—but they couldn't tell him. They were past telling anybody anything by now.

In the end they managed to stop laughing long enough to drag Axel up and over the edge of the cutbank—with him fighting them every inch of the way. They had one hell of a job calming Axel down and introducing him to the bear—but, as Big Paul saw it, a man couldn't rightly blame the bear for that. Out of the four of them he alone had minded his manners and behaved like a gentleman . . . . .

Silence fell on Faille's cabin. Oscar got up, turned his pies in the oven and took a sight through the open door. The rain was easing off a bit, and blue sky showed in the west behind the Yukon peaks, which were cloud-free now and covered with fresh fallen snow.

"And *now* maybe you'll believe in canoe-ridin' bears," Oscar said.

Something in the way he spoke told me that there was more to this story of Big Paul. "Well—and how did they get out of there in the end?" I asked. "I mean, without the bear?"

"Oh, they worked the same kind of trick again," Oscar replied. "And Big Paul said the way Axel loaded that canoe a man would 'a thought he was headin' in to record a claim on Eldorado! Just crazy to get a-goin', he was, before the bear could get things figured out. He said by Yumping Yiminy *he* wasn't goin' again with no bear in

no canoe—no, by Yupiter, not even if he had to hump
his pack all the way across the divide again to Indian
River!"

"And you think that's a true tale?"

"Well, I do. And I'll tell you, for one thing, why. Big
Paul always had trouble finishin' that story. When he
came to that bit about where they had Axel snubbed to
a tree and his face just showin' above the cutbank, he would
bust out laffin' fit to kill himself. He wasn't a young man
when I first knew him—and the older he got, the worse
he got. Screamin' like a jackass till he was clean out of
wind and purple in the face. That was evidence enough
for me: you just *knew* that it was Axel he was seein', away
north in the Yukon, prayin' to God and cursin' him and
his partner and that bear.

"And I'll tell you another thing. Big Paul was in his
seventies when he died—not so many years ago, somewhere
down Kamloops way. He died sudden, one evening in a
friend's house; they figured it was his heart. All I heard
was that he died happy—he was laffin' and enjoyin' himself right to the end. It wasn't till some years afterwards
that I heard he'd been tellin' a bear story. Then I knew.
In his mind he'd gone back in time to 1900 and north a
thousand miles. And after all those years it was that yellow-
whiskered, roarin' face of Axel's that killed him."

ENVOI

A reviewer (he must have been a man of vision,
though I cannot remember his name or paper) when commenting on my book, *THE BUFFALO HEAD*, wrote:
". . . once again we accompany the author in his flight
from the twentieth century." Or words to that effect.

I suppose he was right. Certainly the things that I have
most enjoyed in this western country can be no different
now from what they must have been one, or even two,
hundred years ago. A river is still a river, and a canoe can
still go where no other craft can follow. A horse is still as
he always was—fast or slow, sure-footed or clumsy, intelligent or a fool. A moose in a shallow lake, standing
among the lily-pads, is still the eternal picture of Canada,
and a moose-steak grilled on a forked willow tastes now
exactly as it must have done in 1763.

As for this marvellous twentieth century in which we
live—after what we have already seen of it, why should
we look there for miracles? I can see no reason there for
optimism, nor do I think we are likely to see much improvement in what remains of this wonderful age of war
and destruction. On the contrary, the human race being
what it is, we shall be lucky if things do not become a
great deal worse. That being so, an old-timer may, I hope,
be pardoned for sometimes looking back.

In my forty years in the mountain West I have seen
many changes. I have watched, over thirty years ago,

Indians paddling their canoes across the wide sweep of
the Mackenzie, from Harris River to Fort Simpson Island.
Today those same Indians, supposing that they were out
of gas for their outboards, would consider it impossible
to make the trip at all. And I think sometimes of a rancher
friend of mine—a man who used always to be on the back
of a horse, slim, active and quick-moving. There came
the four-wheel drive and the light truck, and the bull-
dozer making jeep trails where only horse and game
trails had been before. That man climbed off his horse
and into the driver's seat—and the last time I heard of him
was from a mutual friend, a cattle-buyer.

"Jim?" came the answer to my inquiry. "Oh, Jim's
doin' fine. You wouldn't hardly know him now. If I had
Jim in a feed lot, in the shape he's in today, I'd say he was
just right for shippin'!"

There you have two instances out of millions where,
in each case, the machine has destroyed a skill; devaluing,
as well, endurance, hardihood and physical fitness, and
leaving behind a man who is of less use both to himself
and to his country.

Would that be progress? Or could it be only change?

The generation before mine was raised on Kipling,
the poet of action and of Empire. They were saturated in
Kipling, and, since from them came the people who taught
and drilled my generation, we absorbed the same ideals.
The simple virtues that Kipling preached became almost
ends in themselves. In the States Jack London was singing
the same song, glorifying the pioneer virtues of courage,
endurance, loyalty and fitness—and many were listening.
Kipling had the good fortune to die before his dream-
castles came tumbling about his ears; but his teaching,
sneered at even before his death, was simply that a strong
man armed keepeth his house. That was what it boiled
down to; and the institution to which Kipling looked for
strength and continuity was the Empire, out into which
he urged the young men to go.

So, like Kipling, many of us believed in the simple virtues and in the Empire—and not only those who were raised on Kipling. There were also men like old John Petersen, a Swede and one of my friends from Little Prairie. What was it that he said to me? "I am a citizen not only of Canada, but of the whole Empire now." The same ideal was before his eyes, and he was proud of it—not angry or ashamed. No weight of sovereignty was felt: only pride in the membership of a good club. St. Paul had that same pride of membership. "Civis Romanus sum."

And now that Empire of ours is shot to pieces because he who should have been the strong man armed was not armed at all, and his strength had been undermined by little men, working from within. Well—that was not the first Empire to go rotten at the core, by any means. None the less, it was a pity, seeing that it has not been replaced by anything better—only a rag-tag and bobtail of dictatorships and republics and self-seeking men who remain in the Commonwealth for what they can get out of it, using secession as a blackmail threat when short of silver spoons.

Those ideals which we once held—they, too, have gone, for it is only fools who hold to ideals today. Lip-service to some far-off cause, far enough away to be quite safe—yes. Not, of course, the full citizenship of the Canadian Indian and the return of his lands, or a fair proportion of them: that would be coming unreasonably near to home. But the handing over of any white farm-lands anywhere in Africa to the tender mercies of black or brown—that is safe enough. No consequences arising out of that could hurt us here. And, above all, no ideals. They went out with the last war.

But if the old times and the old ways are not worth keeping, they still may be worth recording for the benefit of a mechanised, enlightened posterity to whom a horse will have become a snob "status-symbol", a plaything in a show—or have we reached that point already?—

and a canoe nothing but an unsafe craft that Indians use in races, on days of festival, for the entertainment of the alien race that has taken away their lands, their fish and game, and their way of living.

And so, in my character of unrepentant old-timer, I have arranged these word-pictures of the West, from horse to helicopter, much as one might arrange a collection of old photographs in a family album, in the hope that—while not overlooking their inestimable value as source material to the historian of the glorious future—some other old reprobate, reading them and remembering his own youth, may get himself a smile.